Theatre and Performance Practices

General Editors: Graham Ley and Jane Milling

Published

Christopher Baugh   *Theatre, Performance and Technology*
Deirdre Heddon and Jane Milling   *Devising Performance*
Helen Nicholson   *Applied Drama*
Cathy Turner and Synne K. Behrndt   *Dramaturgy and Performance*
Michael Wilson   *Storytelling and Theatre*

Forthcoming

Greg Giesekam   *Staging the Screen*
Deirdre Heddon   *Autobiography in Performance*
Philip B. Zarrilli, Jerri Daboo and Rebecca Loukes   *From Stanislavski
    to Physical Theatre*

Dramaturgy and Performance

CATHY TURNER
AND
SYNNE K. BEHRNDT

palgrave
macmillan

First published in 2008 by
PALGRAVE MACMILLAN
Houndmills, Basingstoke, Hampshire RG21 6XS and
175 Fifth Avenue, New York, N.Y. 10010
Companies and representatives throughout the world.

PALGRAVE MACMILLAN is the global academic imprint of the Palgrave
Macmillan division of St. Martin's Press, LLC and of Palgrave Macmillan Ltd.
Macmillan® is a registered trademark in the United States, United Kingdom
and other countries. Palgrave is a registered trademark in the European
Union and other countries.

ISBN-13: 978–1–4039–9655–8 hardback
ISBN-10: 1–4039–9655–5 hardback
ISBN-13: 978–1–4039–9656–5 paperback
ISBN-10: 1–4039–9656–3 paperback

This book is printed on paper suitable for recycling and made from fully
managed and sustained forest sources. Logging, pulping and manufacturing
processes are expected to conform to the environmental regulations of
the country of orgin.

A catalogue record for this book is available from the British Library.

A catalog record for this book is available from the Library of Congress.

10 9 8 7 6 5 4 3 2 1
17 16 15 14 13 12 11 10 09 08

Printed and bound in China

To M, with thanks

Contents

PART III

Acknowledgements

First of all, we would like to thank the dramaturgs, directors, scholars, performers and critics who have assisted us, many of whom have given very generously of their time. They include: Henrik Adler, Ruth Ben-Tovim, Karen-Maria Bille, Janicke Branth, Steven Canny, Anne Cattaneo, Cath Church, Anthony Dean, Liz Engelman, Christine Fentz, Petra Fischer, Thomas Frank, Frauke Franz, Penny Gold, Noel Greig, Pil Hansen, David Lane, Olaf Kröck, Niels Lehmann, André Lepecki, James Leverett, Nell Leyshon, Ruth Little, Claire MacDonald, Louise Mari, Bettina Masuch, Emily Morse, Christian Parker, Ben Payne, Brian Quirt, Duska Radosavljevic, Esther Richardson, Kjetil Sandvik, Anke Mo Schäfer, Hanna Slättne, Lloyd Trott, Janek Szatkowski, Lynn M. Thomson, Heather Uprichard, Kitte Wagner, David Williams, Sarah Woods and Maja Zade.

Thanks also to those at the Brecht Archive who assisted with our research into Brecht's dramaturgs.

We are grateful to Jo Dereza, former Marketing Officer at Exeter Phoenix, for talking through 'Audience Builder' with us and directing us to relevant resources.

Thanks to the University of Winchester for funding our research in the US, Germany and Denmark. Special thanks to those of our colleagues who have been supportive, reassuring and lively sounding boards throughout this research.

Thanks to our editors: Graham Ley for his invaluable, sound and tactful advice in commenting on drafts and to Jane Milling for her support and help throughout the project.

Thanks to Kate Wallis and all those at Palgrave who have worked on this volume and have been patient with us.

Thanks also to those closer to home, to Stephen, Margaret, Martin, Marc and Anne for everything and to baby Alice, who deserves a mention, even though she didn't help much.

General Editors' Preface

This series sets out to explore key performance practices encountered in modern and contemporary theatre. Talking to students and scholars in seminar rooms and studios, and to practitioners in rehearsal, it became clear that there were widely used modes of practice that had received very little critical and analytical attention. In response, we offer these critical, research-based studies that draw on international fieldwork to produce fresh insight into a range of performance processes. Authors, who are specialists in their fields, have set each mode of practice in its social, political and aesthetic context. The series charts both a history of the development of modes of performance process and an assessment of their significance in contemporary culture.

Each volume is accessibly written and gives a clear and pithy analysis of the historical and cultural development of a mode of practice. As well as offering readers a sense of the breadth of the field, the authors have also given key examples and performance illustrations. In different ways each book in the series asks readers to look again at processes and practices of theatre-making that seem obvious and self-evident, and to examine why and how they have developed as they have, and what their ideological content is. Ultimately the series aims to ask questions about what are the choices and responsibilities facing performance-makers today?

Graham Ley and Jane Milling

Introduction

In many respects, this is an impossible book to write. The terms 'dramaturgy' and 'performance' both cover such vast areas, demand such a comprehensive grasp of art practice, past and present, as well as a broad and diverse understanding of contemporary cultures that it could seem an act of *hubris* to even begin, knowing that we are unlikely to do justice to both, or to either term.

On the other hand, begin we must. While we are bound to offer a somewhat pragmatic and inevitably limited perspective, it is important to break some ground, to provide an introduction to the diversity of thought and practices surrounding dramaturgy and the dramaturg. Both of us are involved in teaching 'dramaturgy' and when we are asked what the word means, and what a 'dramaturg' might be, it is not helpful to state that these questions are unanswerable. A provisional or partial answer, acknowledged as such, may be the beginning of a new enquiry. We aim to provide an overview of contemporary possibilities, suitable for those who are encountering the subject for the first time, as well as for those who have encountered it only in particular areas of its application.

We are writing during a time of exciting expansion and uncertain direction for the UK dramaturg. There has been a recent surge of interest in the role within UK theatre, together with a corresponding examination of the related term, 'dramaturgy'. A number of symposia have been established in order to discuss the emerging functions and roles of the dramaturg: at these, it is still necessary to spend time discussing definitions and general concepts, while also examining 'case studies', simply in order to clarify terms and practices. This was notable, for instance, at 'What is Dramaturgy?', Birmingham Repertory Theatre, 3 June 2005 and at 'Dramatrix 05', London Oval Theatre, 12 December

2005. The word is also creeping in to other contexts, to live art, to dance and beyond. German dramaturg Thomas Frank's visit to the UK in 2006 helped to demonstrate that dramaturgs need not be the dusty, literary theatre historians that many working in experimental and live art practice had rather believed them to be. Frank had by then worked with UK artists such as Robin Deacon, Mem Morrison and Lone Twin at his theatre, the Sophiensaele, in Berlin (he is now director of DieTheater, Vienna). One could scarcely imagine a figure less reminiscent of G. E. Lessing.

Though the concept of dramaturgy and the practice of the dramaturg are widely accepted and established across mainland Europe, this is still not the case in the UK. Until very recently, most literature on the subject in English was to be found in articles written by international academics or books published by Canadian or American scholars (for instance, Jonas, Proehl and Lupu 1997; Rudakoff and Thomson 2002). These books deal specifically with those countries' dramaturgical practices and traditions and are usually edited volumes of essays and interviews. Bert Cardullo's *What is Dramaturgy?* (1995) is also a volume of essays by different authors, offering perspectives on various countries' dramaturgical practices. A rare glimpse of a British perspective is offered in *Dramaturgy: A User's Guide*, a booklet which was published following 'Dramaturgy: An International Symposium', organized by Central School of Speech and Drama and Total Theatre and held at Central School, 17–19 September 1999. This gathers together contributions from invited speakers. However, Mary Luckhurst's *Dramaturgy: A Revolution in Theatre* (Luckhurst 2006a) was the first book to be written from a UK perspective, discussing the role of the dramaturg within Britain. Luckhurst's book gives a largely historical account, and is most helpful in outlining the field. As she rightly claims, the framework she offers enables further work to take place, and she acknowledges the need for expansion on this groundbreaking research (Luckhurst 2006a: 263).

We believe it is now necessary to broaden the picture to include a wider range of practices. While we do provide some historical context, our focus is on articulating contemporary approaches to dramaturgy and the practice of the twenty-first-century dramaturg. Rather than documenting the 'mainstream' of UK practice (if one can speak of such a thing in relation to such new developments), our intention is to discuss a spectrum of possibilities and to place these in relation to ongoing international debates.

In discussing both historical and contemporary practices, Luckhurst is primarily concerned with the dramaturg's work with new writers, which is indeed the dominant emphasis within the UK. Britain has a strong tradition of playwriting and the development of new writing has been and continues to be a growing area and focus. It is therefore, perhaps, natural that UK discussions of the role of the 'dramaturg' have a tendency to focus on the relationship between the dramaturg and the playwright, between dramaturgy and the play. However, the dramaturg's role has always extended beyond new writing in mainland Europe and increasingly does so in Britain. It is also the case that across mainland Europe and North America, dramaturgs are exploring new approaches to devised theatre, dance and performance art – developments that are reflected in UK practice, to some extent. It is important that these roles are also considered in order to open up new opportunities and, potentially, new ways of working. We therefore give space to discussing this work, which seems significant to the changing environment and to the wider context.

We also discuss the related term 'dramaturgy', which cannot simply be understood as the activity of the dramaturg and may, indeed, be considered without reference to the dramaturg at all. The word 'dramaturgy' can be very widely applied and though our focus is on theatre practice, we are interested in extending our discussion of dramaturgy in relation to dance, cross art-form work and new media.

The origins and nuances of the terms 'dramaturgy' and 'the dramaturg' are discussed in more detail in Chapter 1, but it may be helpful to give an initial summary here. Though the words are linked, 'dramaturgy' can be separated from the 'dramaturg': while the term 'dramaturgy' applies to the general composition of a work, the 'dramaturg' is a specific professional role.

The 'dramaturgy' of a play or performance could also be described as its 'composition', 'structure' or 'fabric'. Where the term 'dramaturgy' is used to describe an activity – 'doing dramaturgy' or even, in Lynn Thomson's North American variation, 'dramaturging' (Thomson 2006: 4) – this activity concerns an engagement with the work's composition. 'Doing dramaturgy' usually implies a discussion of compositional strategies and effects; for instance, those students undertaking non-vocational courses in 'dramaturgy' are likely to be engaged in some form of performance analysis. The word, 'Dramaturging', 'shaping the dramaturgy' or 'dramaturgical work' may all imply an engagement with the actual practical process of structuring the work, combined with the reflective analysis that accompanies such a process.

It is clear that there can be composition, performance analysis and even performance making, without the necessary involvement of the dramaturg. We can therefore discuss the term 'dramaturgy' in isolation from the professional role of the dramaturg. If we do not make this distinction, we seem to be saying that works without dramaturgs have inadequate or even non-existent dramaturgies: this would clearly be a ludicrous claim. Indeed, it is impossible for a play to be entirely *without* a dramaturgy, any more than it can be without structure or compositional strategy.

On the other hand, the professional dramaturg specialises in an understanding of dramaturgy and is able to bring analytical and compositional skills to assist in all aspects of the theatre-making process. The role has its traditions, histories and established practices, as well as its ongoing debates and developments. Given the dramaturg's expertise, an interest in the term 'dramaturgy' runs parallel with an interest in the profession and it is logical to address both terms within the same volume, while avoiding the confusion that arises if we assume that dramaturgy relies, or should rely, on the presence of the dramaturg.

Dramaturgy

If we are to discuss the role of the dramaturg in Part II, we will need to bring to it a sense of what is meant by the word 'dramaturgy', which is the dramaturg's field of expertise.

Essentially, we are using the word to describe the composition of a work, whether read as a script or viewed in performance. While it is a term for the composition itself, it is also a word applied to the *discussion* of that composition. In other words, when we are engaged in (doing) dramaturgy, we are looking at the composition or dramaturgy of a work.

Perhaps it is important, however, to clarify the need for a dynamic and fluid conception of what 'composition' means in the context of performance: rather than attempting to pin down the meaning of a work, once and for all, dramaturgy tends to imply an observation of the play in production, the entire context of the performance event, the structuring of the artwork in all its elements (words, images, sound and so on). It also requires an awareness that theatre is live and therefore always in process, open to disruption through both rehearsal and performance. If the dramaturg attempts to sketch a 'map', perhaps this will always be in pragmatic and tentative relation to the territory of the performance event. Thus there is a dynamic, contextual and, indeed, political dimension to dramaturgical practice.

This tension between the fixity of concept and the fluidity of performance is illuminated by referring to the ways in which the word 'dramaturgy' has been used in other contexts. For example, Erving Goffman (Goffman 1959) has used it to discuss social behaviours, the roles we play in communicating with others and in presenting ourselves to the 'audience' that surrounds us. Goffman suggests that our encounters may be considered as scripts, including not only our words, but also our gestures and actions. Like all scripts, our social interactions include an element of structure, rehearsal and repetition, enabling recognition and referencing a social order. Yet we also own them and experience them as unique moments of encounter. Goffman's theories have been applied to diverse social contexts, from his own application of them to asylums and prisons, to more recent discussions of Internet chat rooms (for example, Sannicolas 1997).

'Dramaturgy' need not only apply to dialogue. Architects have related it to the ways in which buildings suggest the possibility of a range of uses, and are 'completed by events' (Fretton 1999: 15). As architect Bernard Tschumi puts it, architecture is 'seen as the combination of spaces, events and movements ... our experience becomes the experience of events organized and strategized through architecture' (Tschumi 2000: 176). So, for Tschumi, conceptual, 'ideal' space exists in dynamic relation to lived space. While Tschumi does not use the term 'dramaturgy' (though he does use other performance-related terms), he is clearly describing architecture as a dramaturgical practice, one in which there is a deliberate deployment of structure in order to provoke or enable live events. Nick Kaye comments, 'Tschumi provides for an architecture ... always *in performance*' (Kaye 2000: 52, italics in original). One might suggest that if Tschumi looks at the performance of architecture, the theatre dramaturg looks at the architectures of performance.

Though we can use the terms 'performance analysis' and 'dramaturgy' more or less interchangeably, perhaps the former, with the roots of 'analysis' in the Greek word 'to unloose', implies a sense of unravelling the different strands of a work, while the latter, closely linked to the idea of 'composition', the bringing together of parts, implies an attempt to view them in relation to each other.

Elinor Fuchs' useful article, 'EF's Visit to a Small Planet: Some Questions to Ask a Play' (Fuchs 2004), encourages us to view the performance work as a whole, as an organic world with its own rules, systems and coherence. It provides an evocative model for a dramaturgical approach. The dramaturg's 'toolkit' for discussing dramaturgy often produces suggestions for ways of summarizing and encapsulating overall structures. Fuchs' image of the theatre work as an independent planet is one of the most poetic examples. Dramaturg Kitte Wagner, at the Betty Nansen Theatre in Copenhagen, suggests that she asks general questions of a developing production, such as, 'What is the attraction? What are the dynamics? What are the elements? ... How many "postcards" are there? I call them postcards ... I mean, just strong, visual images' (Wagner, 2005: 14). There are numerous other examples of ways in which, as Anne Cattaneo puts it, the dramaturg is 'someone who keeps the whole in mind' (Cattaneo 1997: 6).

As theatre and performance have changed through history, dramaturgies have also changed. For much of the history of theatre and drama, theatre has been defined by the play and dramaturgy has often been defined according to play structures. As Peter Szondi demonstrates in his *Theory of the Modern Drama* (Szondi 1987), shifts in thinking about theatre have occurred when shifts in playwriting have occurred. And, indeed, play texts are often our most complete records of performances. However, we must remain aware of the limitations of the discussion of literary texts, since we cannot rely on words alone to describe or to predict the dramaturgy of a theatre event. Patrice Pavis, for example (Pavis 2003: 21–3), warns that in analyzing performance, we cannot assume that the script exists in causal relationship to the event: the performance must be considered as an independent occurrence, which cannot be explained as a realization of authorial (or directorial) intention. The dramaturgy of the play text is therefore something rather different from the dramaturgy of the play in performance, which is always situated in space and time. Nor are playwrights the only theatre-makers who influence dramaturgy, since all theatre and performance makers whose work provokes or suggests new compositional strategies are involved in changing dramaturgies.

Why do dramaturgies change? A short answer might be to say that the ways in which we see and read the world change, challenging or augmenting the perceptions that we have previously held. If each performance work can be viewed as its own 'planet', it is true that, as Fuchs suggests, we might want to be careful about considering it as a portrait of the actual planet that we inhabit; however, it does give us a vision of another possible world, another way of re-visioning experience. When we return to our own 'planet', we may become more aware of aspects we had not previously noticed, or simply aware of the differences between the world we inhabit and that of the performance. We therefore suggest that the development of new dramaturgies is invariably political, in that they provoke us to look at reality through new eyes.

The Dramaturg

The role of the dramaturg, as opposed to the concept of dramaturgy, has its roots in the practice of mainland European theatre and, specifically, that of Germany. By the time the term arrived in Britain, it already had a long history behind it, including its transformation in Germany from a largely critical, literary role, as occupied by G. E. Lessing, to the more practical engagement of the 'production dramaturg' instigated by Brecht and others. Dramaturgs across Europe continue to debate their function and possible functions within the theatre, while being employed across a range of performance forms and theatre development activities.

Therefore, although the concept of the 'dramaturg' is not unfamiliar to those involved in making theatre in mainland Europe, this is not to imply that the role of the mainland European dramaturg has some monolithic unity. On the contrary, the very fact that the role is well established gives scope for a wide variety of dramaturgs to work in diverse ways in different theatre and performance contexts.

The conventional role for the German dramaturg is within the management structure of a state-funded theatre. Here, the *Chefdramaturg* works with the artistic director to plan the repertoire, a job that includes research into new plays (that is, identifying suitable works for production rather than writer development) and selecting established works. The dramaturgical department (the number of dramaturgs varies, depending on the size and funding of the theatre) may also have responsibility for aspects of casting, for writing programme material and liaising with marketing departments. A 'production dramaturg' may be allocated to specific productions, working with the director in rehearsal, probably offering advice on textual changes, researching contextual information, offering comment on the evolving work and so on. This practical involvement is a more recent development, evolving through the work of Piscator and Brecht, to become well established during the 1970s.

However, this description does not exhaust the dramaturg's practice within the German theatre, nor practice across other European countries. Dramaturgs are working as curators and creative collaborators within experimental work and dance, while the development of new writing, not always the German dramaturg's principal concern, is the subject of debate and diverse projects and programmes in both mainland European theatre and higher education.

The dramaturg's role in developing new writing is best established in North America, though it is also, perhaps, most widely debated in the US, for that very reason. In North America, as in the UK, dramaturgs began to appear when regional subsidized theatres began to be established in the 1960s. The dramaturg was initially seen as part of a European model of state theatres, with no well-established tradition of the American dramaturg. However, the first literary manager in America, modelled on British lines, appeared well before this and Zelenak argues that, earlier in the twentieth century, playwrights like those of the Provincetown Players in effect acted as dramaturgs – a tradition that was then replaced by the Yale model of the dramaturg as 'in-house critic' (Zelenak 2003: 105). Yale-trained Ben Cameron, of the Theatre Communications Group, admits that the early rhetoric was 'problematic', encouraging a rather self-important view of the dramaturg as 'critic' or 'conscience of the theatre', a tone he now regrets (Friedman 2002: 4).

Because of this importation of the dramaturg's role from the European theatre, the 'German' model of the dramaturg is better established in the American theatre than in the UK, and the US dramaturg sometimes works across the whole repertoire, rather than focusing solely on new writing. However, the American dramaturg continues, in many contexts, to be closely associated with new writing, partly because of the previous legacy of literary management and partly because significant early employment of dramaturgs took place at the Eugene O' Neill Theater Center, with an emphasis on developing new North American work.

Dramaturgy has also become a recognized and widely taught subject within higher education in the US, since the Yale School of Dramaturgy was established in 1977. In the UK, now that Leeds University's Bretton Hall is closing, only Queen Margaret University College, Edinburgh allows third year undergraduates to specialize in dramaturgy, while the University of Kent offers Dramaturgy as a fourth year Masters specialism. Masters level programmes are now offered at a few universities, including Kent, Glasgow, Nottingham, Birmingham, Central School, Goldsmith's College, London and Queen's College, Belfast. None of these pre-dates the 1990s. It continues to be more common for British universities to include dramaturgy modules within broader undergraduate and postgraduate programmes, and a few universities allow the choice of dramaturgy as a focus in a final project, or include the study of dramaturgy as one aspect of MA programmes that focus on 'Text' or 'Playwriting'.

While the role of the dramaturg within the UK appeared around the same time as the American dramaturg, with the establishment of state-subsidized theatres, it has taken about forty years for the UK dramaturg to appear in significant numbers and as the subject of sustained debate. Though Kenneth Tynan's role at the National Theatre offered an example during the 1960s and there have been gradually increasing numbers of significant dramaturgs or, more usually, 'literary managers' in theatres since then, it is only in the last decade that we have seen the rapid professionalization of the role, with the number of literary managers doubling in the first 5 years of the new millennium (Luckhurst 2006a: 200). Discussion of its breadth and diversity is still more recent. While aspects of UK theatre structures and funding may have inhibited the development of the dramaturg in earlier years, what has changed in the last decade? Why the current interest?

Why Now?

At the beginning of the 1990s, new writing in the UK seemed to be at low ebb. The production of new work dropped to 7 per cent in the latter half of the 1980s, with audiences preferring productions of classics, adaptations and musicals, partly due to the funding cuts instigated by the Thatcher government. However, from 1992 onwards, new writing seemed once again to be on the rise, in both quality and popularity. David Edgar gives a number of reasons for this: the opening of two works by American writers, Tony Kushner's *Angels in America* and David Mamet's *Oleanna* in 1992; the continuing successes of writers such as David Hare and Caryl Churchill in the UK; the growing self-help movement among writers, including the establishment of writers' organizations; the trend set by Stephen Daldry (at the Royal Court) in directing new writing; television's 'virtual abandonment of the single play' and writers' discovery of 'a subject', in the crisis of masculinity (Edgar 1999: 26–8).

Though Edgar does discuss government funding of the arts in the late 1990s (with mixed feelings), he does not accord state funding much direct credit in either instigating or sustaining this resurgence. The relationship of both funding and development to the actual quality of new work is, of course a questionable and chequered one. Jeff Teare, then director of Made in Wales, writes lugubriously in 1999 that the profession of the dramaturg might well begin to appear 'if the American model of plays being developed without actual production takes further hold in the UK due to decreasing funding and increasing embourgeoisification of our "New Labour" theatre … ' (Teare 1999: 5). Teare has had good reason to be bitter with Arts Council Wales, whose 'New

Writing Initiative' effectively forced the closure of Made In Wales in 2000. However, while the mode and extent of government-funded development of new writing can be criticized, new writing development did increasingly appear as a funding priority for Arts Council England as the 1990s progressed, with a corresponding growth in funding opportunities, particularly with the introduction of the National Lottery in the mid-1990s. This impetus continued into the new millennium, though the emphasis has shifted from 'new writing' to 'new work'. In 2000, the Arts Council of England commissioned the 'Boyden Report', which prescribed an investment in new work as a way to revive the English theatre. The Arts Council responded with another document, 'The Next Stage', which confirmed that: 'The production of new work will not only support the development of a generation of new voices but also benefit the industry as a whole, creating more jobs and reaching wider audiences' (Arts Council England 2000: 8), promising, among other things, new writing, new work, workshops and new literary departments.

The Lottery 'cash bonanza' may now be at an end. In March 2007, it was announced that the Arts Council would receive a 35 per cent cut in the coming year, partly because of the Olympics but also because sales of lottery tickets were in decline (see Gardner 2007a). However the 1990s boom in new British playwriting and the professionalization of literary management that grew alongside it, or perhaps, followed it have clearly played a significant role in the rise of interest in the dramaturg. Indeed, Luckhurst writes that, 'There can be no doubt that the growth of officially appointed literary managers and dramaturgs since the 1960s results principally from market demand for new plays' (Luckhurst 2006a: 202). Here, Luckhurst yokes the two terms, 'literary manager' and 'dramaturg'. However, we suggest that the interest in the role of the *dramaturg* – a role potentially distinct from 'literary manager' – is influenced by a number of other factors besides the emphasis on new writing. These factors, while possibly less dominant, have a tendency both to enrich and to confuse the current discussions of the term.

In recent years, a significant number of Britain's live artists and experimental devising companies have been working, or are beginning to work, with dramaturgs: for example, Lone Twin, Robin Deacon, Mem Morrison (all with Thomas Frank, Lone Twin also with David Williams), Vincent Dance Theatre (with Ruth Ben-Tovim), Complicite (with Steven Canny), Northern Stage (with Duska Radosavljevic), Primitive Science/Fake Productions (with Frauke Franz). Still others work with someone in an analogous position, sometimes as an integral part of the creative team (for instance, Louise Mari, with Shunt), sometimes as an 'outside eye' (for instance, Dorinda Hulton, with Theatre Alibi), sometimes combining the role of producer and creative collaborator (for instance, Nick Sweeting, with Improbable Theatre).

There are a number of possible reasons for this. On the one hand, companies have become increasingly pan-European, gaining a significant proportion of their funding and recognition from European theatres and festivals. This engagement with European practice has brought them into contact with dramaturgs-as-curators, such as Thomas Frank, Bettina Masuch, Matthias Lilienthal and others. At the same time, we have seen a growing interest in the role of the creative producer within the UK, which has some clear overlaps with that of certain mainland European dramaturgs (this is discussed in more detail in Chapter 4). In some instances, the person working as 'creative producer' might otherwise be defined as the dramaturg.

These developments have little to do with an interest in new plays and instead highlight the dramaturg's role as producer, as creative collaborator and/or as someone who brings textual, compositional skills, but does not 'author', or necessarily even write any part of the performance work. If it is common in UK practice to elide the meaning of the terms 'dramaturg' and 'literary manager', it is small wonder that confusion arises when this alternative understanding of the dramaturg's role is brought into play. However, it is significant, broadening the potential and actual spectrum of work undertaken by the UK dramaturg and, indeed, suggesting ways in which UK practice might become part of a growing interest in 'new dramaturgies' across Europe and North America.

It is our hope that this book will help to distinguish between different approaches to the role of the dramaturg, without suggesting that any particular approach should be adopted at the expense of the others. Some dramaturgs may continue to serve the playwright, and no doubt debates will continue as to how this may best be achieved. Other dramaturgs will work in different performance-making traditions and in different roles. Despite the confusion, there is no reason why a number of alternatives cannot coexist, so that the dramaturg's role becomes one of invigorating diversity.

The Structure of the Book

As outlined earlier, the two main sections of the book focus on 'dramaturgy' and 'the dramaturg' respectively. We begin by discussing the concept of 'dramaturgy', since an understanding of this is essential for a grasp of the dramaturg's role and area of expertise.

The first chapter begins by exploring the various ways in which theorists have conceived of the term 'dramaturgy'. While Aristotle's *The Poetics* must be considered as perhaps offering European culture's earliest example of dramaturgical writing, G. E. Lessing, in the mid-eighteenth century, is responsible for attaching the term to a particular critical practice (identifying a play's dramaturgy). Since Lessing, others have attempted to redefine and clarify the word. We reference, for example, Eugenio Barba's articulation of dramaturgy as the 'weaving of the performance's different elements' (Barba 1985) and Patrice Pavis's definition of it as an articulation of the performance's compositional, 'ideological and aesthetic mechanisms' (Pavis 2003: 7–8). We also discuss what is meant by a 'dramaturgical' reading or analysis.

An awareness of dramaturgy as a contextual, and therefore a political, practice informs the book throughout and is the main focus of the next two chapters. Chapter 2 examines Brechtian dramaturgy, considering the ways in which Brecht emphasizes dramaturgy as an engagement with the context of a work. This can be seen most clearly in his strategy of adapting or responding to existing literary works. This emphasis on context also produces the need for a practical, engaged and industrious dramaturg, developing the role in important ways.

We give more space to Brecht than to any other individual dramaturg or theorist because his practice is absolutely central to the modern ideas of dramaturgy that we are exploring in this book. While it is possible to examine UK dramaturgy in relation to a history of writer development, in our view, this tends to narrow the field. Brecht's work has been key to the development of contemporary dramaturgy and the dramaturg.

Chapter 3 looks at politicized dramaturgies in the UK during the last fifty years, including a discussion of agitprop and socialism, feminist dramaturgies and cultural hybridity. We aim to demonstrate that, as for Brecht, changing political objectives produce new dramaturgical strategies. Our examination of recent work leads us to the recognition that postmodernist performance might necessitate a reconsideration of our desire to categorize and group political dramaturgies and, indeed, such work challenges our modes of political analysis.

The second part of the book focuses on the professional role of the dramaturg. Much of this section is based on interviews with contemporary dramaturgs. The majority of these interviews took place in the UK, Germany or the US, reflecting the focus of this book and the main areas of influence on UK practice. We have also interviewed a number of dramaturgs from other European countries, including Denmark and Switzerland, in order to obtain a wider perspective. In selecting dramaturgs to interview and discuss, we have attempted to represent a wide *range* of approaches, both in the UK and in other contexts. Our aim is to give a sense of how the role works in practice, and we give a description of the dramaturg's activities, drawing on our interviews, as well as published accounts. It is our hope that this may prove more useful than an abstract theorization of the role, which could still leave its application uncertain.

In the UK, we have particularly been looking at those with the job title of 'dramaturg', in order to gain a sense of how the idea of the *dramaturg* (as distinct from 'literary manager', 'artistic associate' and so on) is influencing the practice of theatre. In Germany, the US and in other European contexts, we have interviewed dramaturgs working across dance, new writing, experimental theatre/live art performance and higher education, in venues ranging from large state-subsidized theatres to small studio venues, festivals and colleges, in order to get a sense of the variety of ways in which the role of the dramaturg is developing.

Part II begins by discussing the relationship of the dramaturg to the arts institution, examining the political tensions surrounding this position and referring to the history of the dramaturg, particularly in the German theatre. In the following chapters, we examine the role of the dramaturg within specific working relationships. Chapter 5 discusses the dramaturg's work with relation to the playwright. This is the best-known use of the dramaturg within the UK, yet there are many different ways of working with writers and as many different views on the actual and ideal roles of the dramaturg. We discuss the dramaturg's approach in terms of mentoring, the developing new writing industry and the influence of the 'German' dramaturg. Chapter 6 looks at the role of the 'production dramaturg', discussing the various ways in which the dramaturg works with the director to develop a specific production and drawing examples from scripted theatre, devised theatre and dance. Chapter 7 examines the dramaturg in the devising process, with reference to dramaturgs working in the UK theatre, discussing the different challenges that face the dramaturg working in this context.

As these last two chapters suggest, dramaturgy is now being considered in relation to devising and other arts practices, such as multi-disciplinary work, dance and choreography. This is why we make a range of 'millennial dramaturgies' the focus of Part III. This final section attempts to identify some recent dramaturgical developments, including the current interest in different 'levels of reality', the interest in narrative, work taking place in non-theatre spaces, interactive per-formances and the use of modern technologies (the interactive com-puter game). We suggest that all these developments pose new challenges and new lines of enquiry for the dramaturg. It is our hope that this section might be a prelude to further investigation, both by the interested reader and ourselves.

Throughout the book, we have avoided notes preferring to keep ref-erences within the text, provided they do not disrupt the flow of the discussion.

Dramaturgical thinking and practice are developing very quickly, overtaking research and publication. As we write, we are aware of emerging discussions in relation to 'new', 'expanded' or 'postdramatic' dramaturgies. For example, the Hessische Theaterakademie in Frankfurt is hosting a conference on 'European Dramaturgies in the Twenty-First Century' 26–30 September 2007. This is an exciting time to be investi-gating the field and we aim to share a sense of that excitement with the reader. We hope to have provided a way in to discussions concerning dramaturgy, its theorization and practical applications. We also hope to have provided a book that can be used as a tool to help new dramaturgs clarify their own roles, processes and ways of thinking about the dram-aturgy of performance. While the UK Dramaturg's Network provides a forum for dramaturgs to share ideas of common interest, it also seems useful to have invited some of these practitioners to describe their work for a wider audience. Above all, perhaps, we hope to encourage a sense of the diversity of the field. Dramaturgy is as diverse as performance-making itself; therefore, like performance, it is forever open to being rethought and reinvented.

Part I

1 What is Dramaturgy?

A Slippery Term

As Marianne Van Kerkhoven suggests, when attempting to sum up the different contributions to Theaterschrift's 'On Dramaturgy', the term 'dramaturgy' is not easily defined. She writes:

> It appeared ... that dramaturgy involves everything, is to be found in everything, and is hard to pin down. Is it only possible to think of dramaturgy in terms of spoken theatre, or is there a dramaturgy for movement, sound, light and so on, as well? Is dramaturgy the thing that connects all the various elements of a play together? Or is it, rather, the ceaseless dialogue between people who are working on a play together? Or is it about the soul, the internal structure, of a production? Or does dramaturgy determine the way space and time are handled in a performance, and so the context and the audience too? We can probably answer all these questions with 'Yes, but ... '. (Kerkhoven 1994a: 8–10)

Indeed, the more precise and concise one tries to be, the more one invites the response: 'Yes, but ... '. Although dictionaries and encyclopedias offer apparently clear explanations, these are insufficient to address the multiple and complex uses of the word, which has, in contemporary theory and practice, become an altogether flexible, fluid, encompassing and expanded term. As Van Kerkhoven's questions imply, 'dramaturgy' is an overarching term for the composition of a work, 'the internal structure of a production', as well as, it would seem, a word for the collaborative process of putting the work together. This sounds succinct: however, the different positions encapsulated within this explanation, combined with elusive notions of 'composition' or 'internal structure' mean that 'dramaturgy' remains a somewhat slippery, elastic and inclusive term.

Moreover, Van Kerkhoven's questions also imply that dramaturgy is something to be *sought out*: therefore we see its necessary relationship to *processes of analysis*. Indeed, the term 'dramaturgy' is often used as shorthand for 'dramaturgical analysis'. 'Analysis' itself covers a multitude of possibilities, and contemporary discourses have offered a wide range of suggestions as to what a 'process of analysis' might be. As Van Kerkhoven's enquiry suggests, we need to go beyond the idea that the drama contains a simple set of signifiers for us to decode, since 'dramaturgy' also involves and implicates the spectator's responses: the work must therefore be considered as a dynamic event.

Hence, Adam Versényi proposes that 'dramaturgy' be defined as 'the architecture of the theatrical event, involved in the confluence of components in a work and how they are constructed to generate meaning for the audience' (Versényi 2003: 386). Dramaturgical analysis implies a process of interpretation, of looking at the ways in which levels of meaning are orchestrated. Yet by describing the work as a 'theatrical event', Versényi also makes it clear that the object of analysis extends beyond the performance itself, to include the context, the audience and the various ways in which the work is framed. R. Kerry White, for example, comments that since text or performance is,

> an expression of and influence on the culture of which it is part, social function becomes an integral part of dramaturgical analysis. This involves consideration of the ideological assumptions of the time, the power structures of the society, the purpose art is intended to serve for those who patronize it, fluctuations in taste and in value given to art, and the changing relation of the artist to society.(White 1995: 49)

Where then, does dramaturgy end? How do we define the parameters of the 'work'? In his discussion of authorship, Foucault writes:

> It is a very familiar thesis that the task of criticism is ... to analyse the work through its structure, its architecture, its intrinsic form, and the play of its internal relationships. At this point, however, a problem arises: 'What is a work? What is this curious unity which we designate as a work? Of what elements is it composed?' (Foucault 1988: 198)

While dramaturgical analysis does not offer an answer to these questions, it does seek to identify the particular ways in which this 'curious unity' is created, in specific instances. Thus, the practice of dramaturgy, in the sense of analytical process, offers an ongoing, implicit exploration of what a 'work' can be.

In this chapter, we do not propose to offer a final definition of the term 'dramaturgy', since this would inevitably be reductive. While we aim to be as specific as possible, the very attempt to be so leads one to recognize the many complexities and multiple possibilities inherent in the concept and practice of dramaturgy. However, we do aim to provide some clarification of some possible uses of the word, and to exemplify what it means to look at the dramaturgy of a play or performance, or to provide a dramaturgical analysis.

There is a broad consensus that the formalization of 'dramaturgy' as a term describing a specific practice emerges with the German play-wright, poet and critic Gotthold Ephraim Lessing in the eighteenth century. It therefore seems appropriate to begin with an historical per-spective on the ways in which the notion of 'dramaturgy' has emerged into the professional theatre. More comprehensive historical accounts of Lessing's project can be found in Jonas, Proehl and Lupu (1997), Cardullo (1995), Luckhurst (2006a), Carlson (1993).

An Historical Perspective: Shaping a Dramaturgical Practice

Although the word 'dramaturgy' derives from the Greek *dramaturgia* (composition of a play), it was G.E. Lessing who first established the modern understanding of 'dramaturgy' as a theatrical concept and prac-tice, with the publication of his *Hamburgische Dramaturgie* (1767–9). Written during the brief period of his appointment as the Hamburger Nationaltheater's resident playwright, critic and artistic consultant, the *Hamburgische Dramaturgie* is essentially a collection of critical essays in which Lessing reflects not only on play composition, structure, acting and audience, but also on the state and future of German theatre and criticism. Lessing's project was ambitious, inspired by its time, and it is important to understand it in the context of the Enlightenment project.

Daniel Brewer describes the Enlightenment as a 'movement of intel-lectual and social reform' (Brewer 1993: 13). The emphasis was on edu-cation, critical questioning and empirical objectivity as an alternative to thought and behaviour based on religion, habit and tradition. Enlightenment thinkers of the eighteenth century were attempting to explain the world, not in religious and metaphysical terms, but in objective, empirical, scientific terms. For example, Hans Reiss observes, in relation to developments within literary criticism, that there was some urgency in finding models or canons of criticism that were not justified by 'reference either to established authorities or to theology, ethics and politics' (Reiss 1997: 678). The drive towards finding more objective criteria for explaining phenomena in the world also resulted in a preoccupation with systematization, categorization and (inter)connectivity. For example, Denis Diderot's *Encyclopédie*, published in various stages between 1751 and 1777, sets out to provide an overview of world knowledge and is described by Brewer as an attempt to 'compile and condense knowledge, to systematise it and display interconnection of all its branches' (Brewer 1993: 17). While there is not space to discuss Diderot's *oeuvre* at length, he also played an important role in dramaturgical thinking in the theatre (for Diderot's significance to the theatre, see also Ley 1995). His writings on theatre, and spectatorship in particular, came to influence many thinkers and practitioners, not least Bertolt Brecht.

With his *Hamburgische Dramaturgie*, Lessing attempts to develop a more rigorous, objective and analytical theatre discourse and practice, identifying some principles for theatrical renewal. He had little respect for the contemporary theatre. Victor Lange comments:

> No theatre of serious pretensions existed in Germany before the end of the century ... the picture of an irresponsible and aimless theatrical life which Goethe draws in *Wilhelm Meister* is in Germany eminently true for most of the eighteenth century. (Quoted in Lessing 1962: xviii)

Lessing set out to change this state of affairs.

In creating a theatre of 'serious pretensions', to use Lange's phrase, the theatre culture had to be addressed in its entirety, including writing, staging, acting style, management and repertoire. But importantly, Lessing also sought to reform theatre discourse, to revitalize both critical writing and theatre audiences. Lessing's ambitious project aimed to inspire, identify and champion a serious and significant theatrical art, distinct to German culture.

Lessing, as we have already noted, was also a playwright and wrote for the theatre, as well as writing about it. Prudhoe suggests that Lessing's *Minna von Barnhelm* (1767) was the 'first play of international importance with truly German characters' (Prudhoe 1973: 1). While Lessing's project, both as a dramaturg and as a dramatist, concerned the establishment of an essentially 'German' theatre, his principal desire was to make theatre relevant to a particular society, and to its educational needs, rather than to exclude foreign influences (in fact, Lessing frequently cites English theatre as a model).

Indeed, Lessing is highly critical of German audiences and their tastes in theatre. It is entertaining to read his tireless tirades against the 'superficial chatter' that, in his view, was the contemporary substitute for serious theatre criticism. In order to create a theatre of 'serious pretensions', he was aware that audiences, too, would have to be re-educated. Many of Lessing's deliberations concern the audience and the need for a critical discourse that goes beyond superficial convention and inherited assumptions. As Joel Schechter writes, Lessing 'assumed the role of public educator' (Schechter 1997: 18).

It has to be admitted that Lessing was not entirely successful in his endeavours, finding actors in revolt at his criticism, while managers were disinclined to act on his recommendations and the Hamburger Nationaltheater closed only two years after its opening. On the other hand, in the context of the Enlightenment project, it is possible to read Lessing's essays as didactic models for beginning to talk about theatre in critical, constructive, analytical terms. While we might argue that no theatre criticism is purely 'objective', his discussions aim towards objectivity. And while analysis of the art and technique of dramatic composition was certainly not a new discovery or invention, Lessing's *Hamburgische Dramaturgie* was instrumental in giving this process a name: 'dramaturgy'.

Lessing's project was itself indebted to Aristotle's *Poetics* (circa 350 BC). Indeed, as he develops his *Hamburgische Dramaturgie*, Lessing makes specific references to Aristotle's observations on dramatic composition, in his attempt to establish some sound criteria for criticism. Aristotle's outline of compositional principles places particular emphasis on the ways in which dramatic structure can shape audience experience. For example, Aristotle advises that the structure of a drama should revolve around one principal action, since the audience must not lose a sense of unity and wholeness. The play, like the most 'beautiful' of animals, should be of a 'magnitude which may be easily embraced in one view' (Aristotle 1987: Part VII, 36). Integral to Aristotle's discussion of structure and composition is a consideration of the spectator's perspective and the effect that the composition might have on its audience.

While Aristotle describes the drama as an organic whole, comparing it to a 'beautiful animal', it might be appropriate to use a more technological metaphor when trying to describe Lessing's approach, rooted in the scientific revolution. One could suggest, perhaps, that Lessing lays bare the mechanics of dramatic composition and demonstrates its modes of operation. He views it as something that is constructed and has an overall design. However, Lessing's project went further than structural analysis: he also sought to engage the public in rigorous debate about the role of the theatre in general. This contextual aspect to dramaturgical thinking later became a driving force behind much of German theatre discourse.

Lessing initiated a debate about what *dramaturgical models* could help shape a distinct German theatre. Although Voltaire was the most performed playwright at the Hamburger Nationaltheater between 1767 and 1769 (Fischer-Lichte 1999: 96), Lessing argues strongly that German theatre (and playwrights) should take Shakespeare's dramaturgy as a model. Shakespeare, he believes, is the most recent exponent of Aristotelian dramaturgy, exemplifying the principles of Greek tragedy, which is Lessing's point of reference for good theatre. Lessing argues in favour of Shakespeare over Voltaire, suggesting that the French, neo-classical playwright has a flawed understanding of tragedy.

In Lessing's analysis of the structural and interpretative differences between Shakespeare and Voltaire, we begin to appreciate his dramaturgical sensibility. One example is his discussion of the playwrights' different modes of representing a ghost on stage. Lessing argues that Voltaire uses the ghost as a mechanical plot device whereas Shakespeare's ghost feels like a 'real active personage' (Lessing 1962: 35). In clarifying what he means by this distinction, Lessing explores the implications of the two different approaches:

> This difference arose beyond question out of the different points of view from which the two poets regarded ghosts. Voltaire looked upon the reappearance of a dead man as a miracle; Shakespeare as quite a natural occurrence. Which of the two thought the more philosophically cannot be questioned, but Shakespeare thought the more poetically. (Lessing 1962: 35)

In constructing his argument in favour of Shakespeare, Lessing weaves in references to philosophy, literary studies, structural principles, dramatic composition and theatre history. Thus he approaches the argument as a scientist who reaches his conclusions through a process of careful consideration, cross-referencing and deduction.

Despite Lessing's criticism of Voltaire, his own plays were, as Prudhoe describes them, rather too 'symmetrically designed'; one critic even unkindly called them 'dramatic algebra' (Prudhoe 1973: 18). Reiss writes that, 'The German Enlightenment ... had acquired a strong moral tendency, which also permeated its literature', admitting that, 'even Lessing still expected tragedy to have a moral function' (Reiss 1997: 678). It is important to remember that although he played a significant role in developing the idea of dramaturgy, Lessing's reference to compositional rules and moral purpose is problematic if it leads us to assume that this is a corollary of dramaturgical practice. But in spite of this, his *Hamburgische Dramaturgie* remains an inspiration, making him the first exemplar of the dramaturg as someone who develops ideas and concepts from a position within the theatre institution – though Lessing was himself largely outside the theatre-making process. Indeed, one can argue that Lessing was much less insistent on rules than Aristotle (Berghahn 1997: 532). Berghahn suggests that, 'Between the dogmatism of Aristotelian rules on the one hand and the aesthetics of reader response on the other, he developed a new form of criticism' (Berghahn 1997: 527), going on to argue that in Lessing's dramaturgy, 'the critic is neither the legislator nor the disciplinarian of the poet ... he judges whether poetry achieves the effects specific to its genre, and in so doing he acts as an advocate as well as an educator' (Berghahn 1997: 527).

Lessing's writings on the art of theatre and its composition impacted strongly on subsequent theatre artists and thinkers. As Prudhoe comments, Lessing's suggestion that dramatic composition is a kind of 'transitory painting', containing both literary and visual elements, came to influence the German theatre artists Johann Wolfgang von Goethe and Friedrich von Schiller and the emphasis they put on 'grouping, lighting, scenery and movement' (Prudhoe 1973:19).

In 1783, Schiller was appointed dramaturg in Mannheim and, like others in the German theatre at that time, drew up his own proposals for a *dramaturgie*, modelled on Lessing's famous work. It was never written, but the proposal demonstrates the influence that Lessing had upon him. Like Lessing in Hamburg, Schiller's experiences as a dramaturg in Mannheim were not entirely happy ones. However, the influence of Lessing's dramaturgical project paved the way for Schiller's dramaturgical dialogues at Weimarer Hoftheater, with Johann von Goethe.

While Lessing worked alone, wrestling with defining the parameters for a new theatre, Goethe and Schiller, working in creative partnership, were instrumental in creating such a theatre at the Weimarer Hoftheater, under Goethe's direction from 1781.

It is also with Schiller and Goethe that we begin to see the possibilities of the critical and creative dialogue between director and dramaturg.

Although a playwright in his own right, Schiller essentially became a dramaturgical dialogue partner for Goethe and together they explored staging techniques; systems of actor training; systems of directing and rehearsing; ensemble practice and textual analysis facilitated by reading through playscripts with the actors. As Erika Fischer-Lichte observes, the Weimarer Hoftheater was essentially run as an experimental stage (Fischer-Lichte 1999: 148) where Goethe and Schiller developed a new theatre aesthetic in a dialectical exchange between theoretical reflection and practical exploration. Together, they began to develop comprehensive staging ideas, with the explicit intention of orchestrating all theatrical elements into a unified whole. As Prudhoe observes, it is therefore with Goethe that we see the emergence of a directorial practice in which the performance is viewed as a whole (Prudhoe 1973: 95).

While both Goethe and Schiller were writers, they were eager to value and examine all the elements of production, sonic, visual and verbal, working together to create an overall production concept: their concern was with combining elements to construct a coherent totality. This is evident in their very elaborate stage directions, where one senses that Goethe and Schiller's plays are developed with a clear vision for the text's practical realization.

Marianne Kesting comments that Schiller and Goethe's practice demonstrates their interest in the relationship between form and content (Kesting 1959: 17). For instance, they are concerned with the ways in which new content might also necessitate new forms. This, among other things, led to a heightened awareness of what Tom Sutcliffe, in relation to Schiller, calls the 'relationship between the narrative and its frame' (Sutcliffe 1998: 61). As Sutcliffe points out (Sutcliffe 1998: 62), some of Schiller's narrative and structural devices, such as his use of the Chorus, paved the way for Brecht's concept of *Verfremdung*, discussed in Chapter 2.

There was a strong impetus for Goethe and Schiller to develop new stage strategies to present their plays, since their writing broke with the conventions of the time. Goethe's writing, for instance, showed a disregard for the neo-classical unities of time, space and action, and defied theatrical conventions by placing violent action and language on stage. His plays were structurally adventurous and epically meandering: as Lamport writes, Goethe's *Faust* was structured in a manner of 'leaps and bounds; leaving the audience to fill in the details' (Lamport 1971:28).

Hence, Goethe and Schiller's theatre practice was deeply informed by their dramaturgical thinking about theatre, its possibilities and challenges. They not only wrote and directed plays, they also wrote *about* theatre and through their theoretical writing sought to develop new questions and new dramaturgies.

Luckhurst summarizes the influence of the eighteenth-century pioneers in 'dramaturgy':

> From the late eighteenth century onwards theatre in Germany, Austria and Scandinavia became far more than a matter of entertainment: it became part of an Enlightenment mission to acculturate audiences, and part of a nationalist agenda to foster a people's identity and their collective values. In Germany, in particular, theatre came to occupy a central role in the country's cultural life, and Lessing is just the beginning of a line of trial and error which can be traced to Brecht and the very many dramaturgs working in Germany today. (Luckhurst 2006a: 40)

We will be discussing Brecht in detail in Chapter 2. However, these early examples from German theatre history provide us with an important foundation for understanding what might be involved in dramaturgical thinking and practice.

Dramaturgical Analysis: Form and Content

Dramaturgical analysis necessitates an articulation of a work's architecture. Dramaturg and curator Norman Frisch draws parallels between dramaturgy and curation, which he describes as the process of finding an 'appropriate presentational format for the subject under investigation' (Frisch 2002: 273). Frisch points to the dialogic relationship between *what* is being presented and *how* it is presented. In other words, dramaturgy concerns the relationship between subject matter and its framing. According to Frisch, dramaturgy is about 'joining form and content in a work. Or at least bringing them toward one another into the same magnetic field' (Frisch 1994: 154). So the question here is: 'How and with what consequences do form and content relate?' Further dramaturgical questions might then be: 'How does structure shape audience perception? Is content to be found in a given structure?'

This is best considered with reference to specific works and their dramaturgies. Let us look at the compositional arc of the 'well-made play', as exemplified by Eugène Scribe's *Le Verre D'Eau* (1842). The play is methodically crafted and based on a set structure (as outlined in 1863 by Gustav Freytag in *Die Technik des Dramas* [Freytag 1922: 93]), leading from 'exposition', through conflict, crisis and reversal to *denouement*. It fundamentally relies on plot and the humour arising from a sequence of cause and effect. There is little room here for examination of character or evocation of inner dreams and longings.

Primarily concerned with lust and wealth, each character is in pursuit of tangible, material goals. Nor is there any sense that there is an intrinsic conflict between the demands of the public and personal spheres: it is simply a matter of bringing them into convenient alignment. Although the plot hinges on the revelation of secrets, none of these threaten the fabric of society, the logic of its events or the shared perception of reality. As Gilman writes:

> The well-made play was one of almost entire visibility, which is to say it possessed no dimension beyond what was literally placed before the audience's eyes and ears ... its characters moved through dramas whose values were wholly corporeal ... the very notions of ego – selfhood – and soul were what were missing from the French *pièces à bien faites*. (Gilman 1999: 69)

One can see that the play's structure tends towards a particular view of the world, one in which individuality and philosophical enquiry are of little concern, while political manoeuvring, the intricacies of social functioning and the humour in conflicting desires are of endless fascination. The play structure implies a social structure. Scribe's play presents a highly controlled, patterned, courtly social *milieu*, plotted with an almost mathematical precision. Its heroes (if it has any) are those who can outwit their opponents, turning the twists in the plot to their own advantage. The play's conflicts or tangles are of a kind that can be resolved quickly, in an 'unknotting' or *denouement* in the final scenes.

In Scribe's play, there is a congruence between form and content, but it is possible for a play to be shaped by collisions between the way it is structured and elements of the world it seeks to examine. Henrik Ibsen's *Vildanden* (*The Wild Duck*) (1884) is an interesting example of this. In his early apprenticeship at the Norske Theater, Bergen, Ibsen directed no less than twenty-one of Scribe's plays (Gilman 1999: 53). Though critical of the form, Ibsen makes use of the basic structure of the well-made play, rather as if it were the respectable house, within which the characters of *The Wild Duck* struggle to live. However, this structural similarity does not imply a fundamentally similar dramaturgy. Other factors must be taken into consideration.

As one of the proponents of naturalism, Ibsen seeks to give us an impression of his characters as real people, with memories and desires, past injuries and present secrets. He therefore needs to make us aware of the unseen factors that determine their lives. However, for the very reason that these are hidden, they cannot be placed directly on the naturalist stage. Moreover, as we have seen, the structure of the 'well-made play' tends to lead away from meditative introspection, towards a chain of linked events. Ibsen's solution is to invite us to look beyond the literal meaning of his text to discover its symbolic implications. One might therefore follow Quigley in using the term 'symbolic naturalism' to describe the work (Quigley 1985: 120).

While Ibsen's plot structure appears to move along in a similar manner to Scribe's, his use of symbolic content shifts the way we see this progression. We understand that the 'wild duck' is not simply a duck, but represents deeply felt desires and injuries within the characters themselves. Though she is primarily identified with Hedwig, she is identified with other characters at other times. She presides over the mysterious attic room, which becomes a kind of 'inner stage' (glimpsed through a half curtain) suggesting scenographically that there are two levels of reality. Both literally and symbolically, this space contains all that cannot properly be accommodated within the architecture of both house and well-made play. 'A little world' is crammed in under the eaves, complete with stunted trees, rabbits, chickens and, of course, the wild duck itself. The family clings to this alternative reality, which provides a fantasy of space, freedom and power. Williams articulates this cherished symbolic realm as representative of 'the life that might have been possible and is still deeply desired', which is, 'by definition not available as action. The figure of the wild duck is [Ibsen's] solution ... ' (Williams 1973: 57–8).

The wild duck clings to the roots in the depths of the water, until the hunting dog hauls her to the surface. Gregers Werle (who identifies with the dog) forces the family members out of their dream worlds to confront reality (the realities of the past as well as those of the present). Both actions are intended as rescue but are highly ambiguous. Ibsen demonstrates – to us and to his characters – that their inward selves do not match their outer social lives. The dramaturgy of the well-made play and the social world it implies is ultimately incompatible with the longings encapsulated in the symbolic elements of the text. Yet that social structure cannot be broken: no alternative is suggested. *The Wild Duck* does not open out onto other possible realities – that is, other possible dramaturgies. Its horizons are limited, its dream spaces crammed into its attics.

In Samuel Beckett's *Waiting for Godot* (1953), we have a very different structure, implying a very different view of the world. One can consider its anti-climactic and cyclical dramaturgies as a challenge to narrative-driven theatre convention itself. Daniel Albright suggests that Vladimir and Estragon, the two tramps, are:

> Two Characters in Search of a Stage, a conventional stage that offers such conventional satisfactions as a script, a concatenation of events, a subject of conversation, an action directed toward a goal, a tragic death, a comedic marriage, anything. They would like to be part of a regular play, but they find themselves in a play by Beckett. (Albright 2003: 51)

Albright implies that Beckett's quiet dismantling of the conventions associated with a traditional play structure is a way of suggesting that its comforts – its certainties of identity, placing, journey and resolution – are false ones. On the other hand, Beckett is also referencing a different set of dramatic structures, inviting an allegorical reading as we identify cyclical patterns associated with the death and resurrection of the passion play, or hints of a spiritual journey structure.

Vladimir is painfully aware of the Christian imagery of the situation, the tree that resembles the cross, the possibility that he and Estragon resemble the two thieves, the tantalizing chance of redemption through repentance. By contrast, Estragon rejects this reading, insisting on hunger, pain, lust and other corporeal urgencies, which may be eased by the physical comfort offered by Godot. However, Estragon's uncertainty about this material world causes him discomfort and he is constantly frustrated by its limitations. At the end of the play, both readings seem uncertain. The leaves that appear in Act Two do not herald redemption and Estragon, unlikely ever to have a roof over his head, cannot even be sure whether the boots on stage are the ones he left there the night before.

However, there is a further performance tradition hinted at in the characters' dialogue, for there are times when both seem to be tragic clowns. In the final moments, the characters' wish to hang themselves turns into a piece of clowning, a tug of war between the two, one of whom has his trousers around his ankles. It is both comic and tragic, energized and despairing. 'I can't go on like this,' says Estragon; 'That's what you think,' responds Vladimir. Despite themselves, they are committed to the game, committed to the pursuit of meaning despite its inevitable failure.

In examining *Waiting for Godot* we might posit that Beckett's structure refuses the comforts of both the 'well-made' play and the 'passion'. Only a desperate clowning remains, as a kind of solace. Thus its form encapsulates an Absurdist rejection of purpose and meaning.

These examples demonstrate that a story is understood not only in terms of what happens, but in terms of the ways in which we recount it, order it, negotiate it, structure it. The 'narratives' of all these works are not merely structures of linked events, but forms that encapsulate questions, affects, emotions, stories and discourses. Dramaturgical analysis must try to outline the different questions the play provokes on a philosophical, ideological, socio-political and aesthetic level. The ability to identify and conceptualize differences and similarities between different plays and performances, to articulate what is distinct about a particular dramaturgy, is therefore central to dramaturgical thinking.

The Weave of Performance

Yet, as our opening comments suggested, a discussion about dramaturgy has wider implications than are encompassed by a consideration of eighteenth-century dramaturgical practice and goes beyond play analyses that are reliant on reference to classical forms, or indeed to the text as the principal element. If Lessing's example and practice has laid the foundations for the often-cited definition of dramaturgy as 'the technique (or poetics) of dramatic art, which seeks to establish principles of play construction' (Pavis 1998: 124), changing dramaturgies and contemporary performance practices have introduced new approaches. Certainly, within some modernist and many postmodernist works, we can identify narratives or stories that challenge the possibility of coherent story-telling, or stories that negate their own telling. In many works, the verbal text is not the only, or even the main structuring element.

Before discussing a more contemporary view of the idea of 'dramaturgy', let us briefly look at Sarah Kane's late plays, which exemplify some of the potential challenges of postmodernist writing. Kane challenges us to identify the compositional logic that binds together the way she organizes action, time, space, character and dialogue. By her last plays, *Crave* (1998) and *4:48 Psychosis* (1999), the narrative has become radically fragmented. Neither play contains act or scene breaks, instructions for staging, or character descriptions. Only letters, rather than names, indicate characters in *Crave* and there is no ascription of lines in *4:48 Psychosis*. Within this world, there can be no clear definition of identity. Rather than describe Kane's world as an imploding one, as David Greig does (Greig 2001: xvi), it might be truer to say that there are no longer any boundaries between external and internal. Instead we find a complete undecidability, while the possibility of interplay and exchange is as much the source of terror as it is of energy or solace. It is as though there can be no certainty about the delineation of character, or the moment where one character becomes another, or is identified with another. The dialogue could be viewed as fragmented monologue or as coalescing multiplicity. The space of utterance is also undecidable. Perhaps the open-endedness of this dramaturgy is also its tragedy.

It may be inappropriate for us to attempt entirely to resolve these ambiguities in our dramaturgical analysis, since to do so would be to reduce the complexity of the work. This does not mean that we cannot suggest possible readings, but our task may be to keep these readings open, fluid and plural. Open-ended dramaturgies, like Kane's, require us to consider structure and content as dynamic and continually to be kept in process, rather than as elements to be fixed and resolved.

What therefore becomes particularly interesting about Kane's open-ended work is that it invites us to consider her texts in performance, as 'compositions' in time and space, as opposed to viewing them solely in terms of literary form and content. Of course we can examine any dramatic text in terms of its performance potential, and perhaps we are obliged to do so; however, the openness of Kane's dramaturgy means that these plays – more than most – are only completed by the decisions made in the performance-making process.

In order to illustrate this, one might compare the striking differences between productions of *4:48 Psychosis*. For instance, Wanda Golonka's Frankfurt production (2002) was a form of 'installation', placing the audience on the stage, seated on swings, in the same space as the actor (Marina Galic). Alternatively, in Laurent Chétouane's Hamburg production (2002), the actor (Ursula Doll) was presented in a minimalist space, with the focus on the tensions in the voice and body (Müller-Schöll 2004: 47). To give another example, a student production directed by Phillip Zarrilli (2004), divided the lines between multiple protagonists.

The complex inter- and cross-disciplinary dramaturgies that have emerged in the twentieth century have also led to an emphasis on the live performance and the performance text, as opposed to the written play. Both the 'open' text and devised work demand that we consider the composition of the performance as a whole. This shift towards an equal consideration of every element within the theatrical event has led to new attempts to define 'dramaturgy'.

It is important to stress that this is not a fundamental break with Lessing's approach to analysis. Lessing's own analysis was not purely text-based, but related to theatre performances, the 'transitory painting' of dramatic composition. And, indeed, similar principles remain at work. Dramaturgy still implies an analysis of the orchestration of elements within an overall architecture. However, we find that contemporary theorists tend to describe dramaturgy in rather different terms from Lessing, placing greater emphasis on the non-literary elements. For instance, Eugenio Barba describes 'dramaturgy' as a synthesising process, a 'weave' or 'weaving together' (Barba 1985: 75) of elements. The endeavour to conceptualize new types of theatrical dramaturgies is also found in the development of terms like 'Visual Dramaturgy' (Arntzen 1994), 'New Dramaturgy' (Kerkhoven 1994a), 'Open Dramaturgy' (Imschoot 2003) and, possibly 'Textual Landscape dramaturgy' (Lehmann 1997). All of these describe the turn from a compositional logic based on the primacy of the verbal text, to a logic according to which this primacy is not assumed, so that other elements (visual, sonic, physical) may be equally significant, or may dominate, or may combine to create, as Lehmann puts it, 'a mutual disruption between text and stage' (Lehmann 2006: 92).

In Barba's conception, performance can be seen as a complex network of 'actions'. He clarifies that by 'actions' he means all the elements of the performance that 'work directly on the audience's attention, on their understanding, their emotiveness, their synaesthesia' (Barba 1985: 75). These 'actions' can be woven together in many ways with different consequences. The compositional logic of a work determines the structure of the weave. This is discussed further in Watson's analysis of 'Fragmented Dramaturgy' (Watson 1993:100–3).

A fabric can be woven and composed in a number of ways. The choices that one makes about colours, stitching, shapes, threads, impact on the very nature of the textile. Correspondingly, Barba offers an understanding of dramaturgy as the overall texture that is created by the relationships and interaction between elements in a performance. For example, Ian Watson cites Barba's distinction between *concatenate* and *simultaneous* plot structures: 'The simultaneous plot structure ignores linearity in favour of having several actions taking place at the same time, without regard for their causal relationship' (Watson 1993: 94).

Though Barba describes dramaturgy as a 'weave', one could refer to the image of a mechanism (Pavis 2003: 8), or 'architecture' as we have mentioned previously. The common feature of these metaphors is the way in which they each suggest the interconnection of many different parts. One could also consider 'dramaturgy' as a complex network of signifiers. Contemporary artists and theorists Mike Pearson and Michael Shanks use the term 'dramaturgy' to describe an 'assemblage', the process of 'ordering or patterning' the different elements into a performance structure: 'What begins as a series of fragments is arranged in performance: Dramaturgy is an act of assemblage' (Pearson and Shanks 2001: 55).

Returning to the metaphor of a 'weave', we might think of identifying the significant narrative threads of a work – the 'red threads' that stand out within the overall design. For example, we might trace the trajectory of a linear story through a number of plot points towards a resolution. However, we might also have a more complex structure, combining a multiplicity of significant 'threads', complicating the way we understand the terms 'plot' or 'story'. We see this, for example, in the work of Pina Bausch, Alain Platel, or the Wooster Group. Here the audience will have to connect seemingly disparate, diverse and juxtaposed elements, moments and narratives. These works are organized according to a different compositional logic from the linear story.

For example, in Forced Entertainment's *Bloody Mess* (2004), different performers had apparently unrelated trajectories; music was played without seeming reference to the scene; attempts at meaningful articulation were interrupted by a woman in a gorilla suit; clowns squabbled over chairs; a cheer-leader shouted and danced, while two naked men carrying cardboard stars talked about different kinds of silence. And yet these disparate elements were, despite the show's title, carefully woven together to create an intricately structured, if apparently chaotic, whole.

Although diverse and seemingly disparate, the many threads of such a performance are, however subtly, held together and orchestrated according to a set of structural and narrative principles. Whatever determines the connection of these threads, this interrelation might perhaps be viewed as a complex narrative in its own right. Pearson and Shanks write:

> We might regard the dramatic structure of devised performance as constituting a kind of stratigraphy of layers: of text, physical action, music and/or soundtrack, scenography and/or architecture ... Dramatic material can be conceived and manipulated in each of these strata which may carry different themes ... we might now imagine situations in which tracks are run in parallel, with and against each other, without relative mediation. Or where from time to time performance exists variously as one, two or three tracks only. Material in one track will inevitably mediate material in another; they are read and interpreted onto, into and through each other, whether they have natural affinities or not. (Pearson and Shanks 2001: 24–5)

The combination of narratives, tracks, or 'strata' produces new meanings that are not inherent in any of the elements if viewed singly. How do we articulate such a dramaturgy? Here, we do not have one

forward-moving story, but a cluster of parallel, intersecting, juxtapos-
ing, colliding stories and narratives, producing new narratives from
their very collisions. Yet if the composition seems 'fragmented' or arbi-
trary, it is only seemingly so. With this kind of composition, we have a
complex dramaturgy, where we cannot simply identify a single narrative or story that combines the elements. But we still look for the forces
that fold these many strata into a work.

David Korish uses a different metaphor, but is essentially talking
about such forces when he cites Ferdinando Taviani's interesting notion
that dramaturgy consists of ' "the links" that exist in the chain of elements of dramatic action' (Korish 2000: 288). Thus dramaturgy does
not merely concern a chosen structure, which determines a linked
sequence of events, but is found in the 'links or bridges which hold
these events together' (Korish 2000: 288). It could be suggested that we
develop the dramaturgy of the performance when we understand *how*
and *why* actions and events relate or connect. In devised performances
it is not uncommon to see a structure where different episodes or blocks
of material have been loosely linked or collaged together. It is the 'links'
or the 'bridges' between events that are, in fact, key to understanding
the 'inner logic' of the piece. Transitions are not just a question of moving from one moment to another; it is in these transitions that the
dramaturgy of the performance is discovered.

To summarize, contemporary views of dramaturgical analysis tend to
stress the consideration of the performance as a whole and emphasize
that, in looking at a work's dramaturgy, we need to consider how all elements interact. As Pavis writes, dramaturgical analysis offers: 'An initial
synthetic approach to performance; it avoids a fragmented perception
of a performance by underlining its lines of force' (Pavis 2003: 8).
Unlike forms of performance analysis that make use of a particular theoretical framework (for example, semiotics), focusing on specific elements of the work, dramaturgical analysis regards the performance as a
complex web of elements, and aims to identify the ways in which these
connect (or fail to connect). The patterns that are found reveal the
implicit ideological, compositional, philosophical and socio-political
ideas that drive the performance. To describe this as a 'synthetic
approach' does not imply that dramaturgical analysis imposes a specific
compositional logic on the work. As we suggested earlier, a work such as
Kane's *4:48 Psychosis* may need us to keep our readings open and plural.
When, for example, Aston and Savona suggest that the some types of
theatre 'subvert the notion of a hierarchy of signs by offering a collage
of signs which cannot be ordered or made sense of' (Aston and Savona

1991: 101), dramaturgical analysis need not attempt to 'make sense', but can identify this subversive strategy and its effects.

As mentioned in our introduction, Elinor Fuchs gives a useful starting point to thinking about the dramaturgy of a performance or a play, in her article, 'EF's Visit to a Small Planet: Some Questions to Ask a Play' (2004). In notes originally written for students, she encourages the reader to think of the performance as a 'world' or 'planet': 'Mold the play into a medium-sized ball, set it before you in the middle distance, and squint your eyes. Make the ball small enough that you can see the entire planet, not so small that you lose detail, and not so large that detail overwhelms the whole' (Fuchs 2004: 6). Fuchs then proposes a series of questions, 'What is space like on this planet?'; 'How does time behave on this planet?'; 'Is this a public world, or a private?'; 'What changes in this world?' and so on. Fuchs' approach pushes us to consider all the elements in their relationship to one another, rather than breaking them down into separate elements, such as 'character' or 'staging'. Fuchs concludes: 'Of course you can construct meaning in this world in many different ways. Construct it in the most inclusive way you can. There will still be more to see' (Fuchs 2004: 9). Fuchs emphasizes inclusivity, the means by which we examine the organic structures of the performance, and their phenomenological impact upon us, rather than regarding the work as a series of signs to be de-coded, or attempting to evaluate it according to the ways in which aspects of our own 'worlds' seem to be represented within it.

Dramaturgy and Context

We have argued that contemporary dramaturgical analysis tends towards a consideration of the performance as a whole. However, there might be some disagreement among dramaturgs as to whether or not dramaturgical analysis should invariably relate to a work's practical realization. Andreas Kotte argues that it should do so, and he uses the term 'dramaturgy' to indicate the process whereby something gains a practical shape or comes into a material form (Kotte 2005: 206). This might be a way of making a distinction between a *literary* analysis of a verbal text, considered as a self-contained system, and *dramaturgical* analysis, which looks towards the translation of verbal text into live performance. On the other hand, while there might be this difference in emphasis, to insist upon a clear demarcation would be a simplification, giving insufficient credit to the complexity and scope of both dramaturgy and literary criticism.

One can certainly consider the dramaturgy of a script without making specific reference to that script in a particular production. Indeed, we have done so in our earlier play analyses. A script is a composition in itself and therefore capable of dramaturgical analysis. However, even such analysis is likely to provide hints and starting points for a development of the work into performance.

We have argued that some plays are fundamentally 'open' compositions and are not complete until they are given performance. While others might be more receptive to literary analysis, one can argue that all dramatic works are, in some senses, open compositions. Since dramaturgy tends towards a consideration of the work in context, it may be that it is necessary to approach a play in performance, as a live event. A dramaturgical analysis of a written text is therefore somewhat provisional, since it must be acknowledged that any discussion that confines itself to the script on the page has certain limitations: there are aspects of text in performance (for example, its vocalization) that can only fully be explored through and in reference to live performance itself.

Gad Kaynar makes an interesting distinction between what he calls an ' "academic reading" of a dramatic text' and a 'pragmatic interpretation of it as a performative text intended for stage realization by a specific director, designer(s) and actors' (Kaynar 2006: 246). Here there seems to be a distinct difference between the 'academic', theoretical, hermeneutic reading of a play and the reading that is informed by, 'highly practical considerations, deriving from a text's intended stage realization' (Kaynar 2006: 246). This also crucially points to the contextual nature of dramaturgical thinking. If dramaturgy concerns the architecture of the theatrical event, we need to look at the ways in which a performance or play is situated within the context of a community, society and the world. Dramaturgical analysis necessitates a consideration of the question: 'Why are we performing this play or performance right now at this moment in time and for what audience?' We might also ask: 'What is the link or bridge between the work and the world and its audience?'

Kaynar argues: 'I believe that dramaturgy ... should deal concurrently with the professional performative and extra-performative, empirical and phenomenological, play of the world, wherein the work is planned to be performed' (Kaynar 2006: 247). He goes on to propose that one looks at the contextual ' "behind-the-scenes" features ... socio-political, human, institutional, organizational, administrative, structural and financial that

lend a theatre production a considerable part of its meaning and effect'
(Kaynar 2006: 249).

It would seem that dramaturgy may not be inherent in the play text,
but may be produced and shaped through the work of a particular company, reflecting the process and production conditions that impinge on
it. It will also be shaped by the audience, by its responses and what it
brings to the work. Dramaturgy is therefore produced through a dialogue between the play and a particular community of people in a particular time and place. De Marinis offers further analysis and discussion
of spectatorship and dramaturgy (1987), while Lynn and Sides (2003)
offer interesting perspectives on dramaturgy and collaborative structures.

If we return to Foucault's definition of a 'work' as a 'curious unity'
(Foucault 1988: 198), one could argue that dramaturgy extends that
unity to encompass not only the production and the producing company, but also the audience and its context. A dramaturgical analysis of
the performance is thus a contextual analysis where the performance is
considered as part of a wider network of meaning.

If 'dramaturgy' is a word we use when we discuss structural, compositional and contextual principles of a work, and the ideas and narratives
that drive these principles, it may have applications beyond drama or
indeed, the theatre. Pearson and Shanks propose that dramaturgy can, in
fact, be considered as a term for many kinds of 'cultural assemblage'.
They write:

> Dramaturgy, as cultural assemblage, works equally with settings, people,
> bodies, things, texts, histories, voices, architectures. In these connective
> networks that are the dramaturgical, it is usual to consider things and
> people as separate, their conjunction considered after their distinction.
> We propose instead the inseparability of people and things, values, etc.
> (Pearson and Shanks 2001: 89–90).

Thus, Pearson and Shanks suggest that dramaturgy concerns the
interconnectivity of things in the world. They do not confine it to the
theatre, but open it up as a term that could be applied to discuss many
different phenomena: 'settings, people, bodies, texts, histories, voices,
architectures'.

Similarly Erving Goffman (1959) has used 'dramaturgy' to describe
social behaviours and T.R. Young and Garth Massey are sociologists
who extend the idea of dramaturgy beyond the theatre, writing about a
'dramaturgical society', which they define as 'one in which the interaction between an atomised mass of people and the major institutions and

largest organizations is deliberately managed' (Young and Massey 1990). Here, they use 'dramaturgy' as something that operates coercively, to control social interaction. However, they posit the idea of a 'critical dramaturgy' that might analyse and reveal:

> the uses of dramaturgical devices that prevent reciprocal communication and the emergence of authentic self-structures and cultural forms, and which obstruct the collective establishment of societal goals which reflect the needs and interests of the entire population. (Young and Massey 1990)

Similarly Lamers implies that social events have a dramaturgy. He illustrates this through the example of political demonstrations and citizen–police confrontations in Amsterdam in the mid-1960s (Lamers 1994). Borreca also discusses dramaturgy in relation to social life and politics (1993). We have come a long way from the theatre event here, yet Eckersall suggests that within theatre, too, dramaturgy may be 'critical' and can be 'subversive' in that it, 'keeps an open view … It is a memory of possibilities, or traces of creative processes that arise and are potential.' It can offer 'a sense of refusal and resistance to closure' (Eckersall 2003). While the idea of 'dramaturgy' could imply a tendency towards systematization and 'management', at its best it implies responsiveness, an awareness of the connections between things and is able both to facilitate and critique them.

2 Brecht's Productive Dramaturgy: From Emblem to 'Golden Motor'

The 'radical transformation' of the Theatre

The dramatist, director and theorist, Bertolt Brecht, is associated with a gradual, but decisive shift in thinking about the theatre, taking place during the first half of the twentieth century. He was not alone: for example, the Russian director Vsevolod Meyerhold pre-empted many of his dramaturgical strategies, as did Brecht's friend and one-time colleague, the German director Erwin Piscator. However, until recently, Meyerhold's work was little known in Western Europe while, paradoxically, the post-war context of the Federal Republic afforded Piscator a lower profile in the west than the German Democratic Republic ensured for Brecht. Furthermore, neither Meyerhold nor Piscator produced a very extensive body of theoretical writings. Brecht did so, and as a playwright, he was also able to leave play texts that survive as an invitation to revisit his work; furthermore, he was careful to document his productions, some of which toured to Britain and the US. Brecht's work, then, presents us with the most coherent, sustained and well-documented attempt to *rethink* the contemporary theatre since G.E. Lessing's urging of a revitalized German drama in the eighteenth century. While both Brecht and Lessing combined the roles of critic and playwright, Brecht took his practical experimentation further, eventually establishing his own theatre, the Berliner Ensemble, in East Germany (the German Democratic Republic) in the 1950s.

38

In Chapter 1, we discussed the relationship between dramaturgy and composition, but we also suggested that dramaturgy requires us to look beyond the immediate structures of a play, to the play's performance in a specific social and historical context. For Brecht, this attention to context is the most crucial aspect of his dramaturgy and determines the composition itself. We previously described dramaturgy as a 'weave' of elements; however, Brechtian theatre seems to demand a more dynamic image. In *Leben des Galilei*, Brecht's Galileo suggests that the sun, now revealed to be central, need no longer be regarded as a mere stellar coat of arms, but as a 'golden motor'. We might apply this metaphor to Brecht's transformation of dramaturgy, which is no longer conceptualized as a beautiful design or emblem, or even as an architecture, but as a mechanism, generating debate and action. Marx wrote: 'The philosophers have only interpreted the world, in various ways; the point is to change it' (Marx 1845: XI). As Brecht wrote in 1952, his theatre was 'directed towards [the] transformation of society'. Rather than describe, 'it must strive to alter its surroundings. From now on it could only hope to form its images of the world if it lent a hand in forming the world itself' (Brecht 1964: 240).

Piscator described Germany in 1929 as experiencing:

> a time when there was the greatest unrest in all spheres of life … a time which was torn and split by the crassest political, social and intellectual conflicts … a time when every man who could see beyond his own personal interest had to feel committed. (Piscator 1980: v)

This was the year of the Wall Street Crash and a resulting world depression that paved the way for Adolf Hitler's rise to power. In Germany, the decline of industry, chronic unemployment and temporary bank closures, divisions within the political left and parliamentary instability all provided Hitler with the opportunity to increase his influence. In the 1929 elections the biggest losses were among moderates, with Communists gaining ground, but with the biggest gains made by the Nazis; Hitler was made Chancellor in 1933. The year 1929 was therefore a turning point. It was followed by the gradual suppression of Berlin's revolutionary cultural activities, with many artists (including Piscator and Brecht) driven into exile during the early 1930s. Despite this, many of these artists continued to be committed to opposing fascism.

Piscator's own commitment was mirrored by that of Brecht himself. By 1929, Brecht had already written his first plays and begun to formulate his dramaturgical theory. He wrote, in an essay of 1927, entitled

'The Epic Theatre and its Difficulties':

> It is understood that the *radical transformation of the theatre* can't be the result of some artistic whim. It has simply to respond to the whole radical transformation of our time. (Brecht 1964: 23, italics in original)

To some extent, Brecht's political commitment was emerging before the late 1920s, but it was during this period that he undertook a thorough study of Marxism, which subsequently underpinned his discussion of a theatre that might help to change society. John Willett writes:

> The distinctive clarity and detachment of Brecht's style enter his work with his growing interest in Marxism ... Scrupulously and systematically his methods were pared to fit a particular view of society, a particular method of analysis, reached in a particular sharp crisis in German history before the parties clamped down on art. (Willett 1984: 211)

Despite being driven into exile during the years of Nazi government and ensuing world war, Brecht continued to develop his theory and practice until his death in 1956. For him, a politically effective theatre, one that could oppose fascism and war – and capitalism, which he regarded as connected to both – would have to be a radically new theatre, employing new strategies. It would need to reach out to its audiences, and beyond them, to new audiences. It would have to respond to the urgent needs of its time. It would have to operate in dynamic relationship to its context.

Brecht was at once a critic, writer, director and dramaturg, roles that are often closely related, and certainly were for him. While his work as a writer continued throughout his life, these roles varied in significance over different periods. At the start of his playwriting career, he also worked as a theatre critic and, during the 1920s, as a dramaturg under Max Reinhardt and, subsequently, in collaboration with Piscator. When in exile from Nazi Germany he wrote the majority of his best-known plays, including *Der Gute Mensch von Sezuan* (1940), *Mutter Courage* (1939), *Der Kaukasische Kreidekreis* (1944) and *Leben des Galilei* (1939 [first version]), all of which were first produced in the 1940s. On his return to East Berlin after the war, he was artistic director of his own theatre.

For Brecht, every element of the theatre, from front of house to the details of the stage properties, was important in establishing a politically significant practice. His essay on the epic theatre (cited above) continues by suggesting that the principles of the 'epic' theatre affect not only the dramaturgy of the play text, but also acting style, staging, music and the use of film (Brecht 1964: 23). This 'working out' of the principles of his theatre was a never-ending task, one that Brecht often addressed in the-oretical writing, but was eventually able to explore through sustained practice. It is evident, even in these early essays, that Brecht wanted to revolutionize the theatre as a whole, not merely playwriting: through creating revolutionary theatre events, he hoped to contribute to a social revolution.

When we consider 'Brecht's dramaturgy' we have an enormous body of theory, plays, letters and anecdotes to consider, all of which combine to give a sense of his complex, multiple, contradictory and shifting con-ception of the ways in which theatre might change to meet the demands of the age. Yet we must also focus in on the dramaturgy of individual works, in order to analyse the ways in which his theatre operated in spe-cific instances. This chapter therefore concerns Brecht's 'dramaturgy' on both a macro and micro level, at some points discussing the 'drama-turgy' of a play, at others, the wider issue of 'Brecht's dramaturgy' as a totality. We will also find ourselves meeting the modern dramaturg for the first time, for it is with Brecht that the 'production dramaturg' begins to emerge. Indeed, one might say that Brecht's dramaturgy pro-duces the need for the new dramaturg – a dramaturg who is deeply involved in reconstructing the theatre for a new society.

In an interview with Emile Copfermann for *Théâtre Populaire*, Joachim Tenschert, a dramaturg from the Berliner Ensemble, gives a brief history of the German dramaturg's role in which he emphasizes the efforts made by politically engaged writers of the nineteenth cen-tury, such as Heinrich Heine, Karl Gutzkow and Heinrich Laube. Such writers, Tenschert suggests, wished to challenge the contemporary pen-chant for light entertainment and the tendency for directors to trivial-ize serious work. He therefore associates the rise of the German dramaturg with the writer's need to identify and watch over a directo-rial and ideological 'line' (Copfermann 1960: 41).

Luckhurst suggests that Tenschert, who joined the ensemble after Brecht's death, 'overstressed his case', giving the impression that the Brechtian dramaturg was a 'conceptual dictator rather than a facilitator' (Luckhurst 2006a:138). Though Tenschert does misleadingly imply a rather solitary, doctrinaire and humourless figure, the pursuit of clarity in presenting social contradictions, tensions and interactions, here iden-tified as central to the dramaturg's role, is also crucial to Brecht's dram-aturgy as expressed in his plays, dramatic theory and theatre practice.

Brechtian dramaturgy depends on the identification of the precise political significance of each moment, its place within the whole and the
mode in which it may be most effectively understood by its audience.

A word Brecht emphasized was *fabel* or 'story': the story itself provided the 'line' along which social tensions would be encountered, very
often with comic effect. Carl Weber, who trained under Brecht as
directing assistant, actor and dramaturg echoes other former members
of the ensemble when he confirms: 'Brecht was mainly concerned with
the play as the telling of a story to an audience, clearly, beautifully and
entertainingly' (Weber 1967: 103). A need for active, practical, involved
dramaturgs arises out of this, since his theatre presumes a whole range
of dramaturgical skills and activities.

Brecht's Dramaturgy: Re-contextualizing
the Theatre

Brecht's 'telling of a story' was, in fact, frequently a matter of '*re*-telling'
a story. The decision to work with the stories and structures of past theatre works allowed Brecht to revisit and rearrange the building blocks of
the theatre – its literature, as well as its scenography, acting styles, presentation and contexts. This re-visioning of the theatre was essentially
political, driven by a belief in the emancipation of the working classes
and the role of the revitalized theatre in provoking its audience to
thought and action. Paul Walsh suggests that there is a tendency to
reduce Brecht's dramaturgy to notions of personal 'style', overlooking
his, 'radical rethinking of the relations of the production that link
dramatic texts, producers ... audiences and society' (Walsh 1990: 104).

As Walsh goes on to discuss, one of the ways in which Brecht challenged the authority of the existing tradition was in his approach to its
repertoire:

> Brecht sought to free actors and directors, and their audiences,
> from ... hierarchies of power embedded in tradition by replacing acqui-
> escence to authority with personal commitment to exploring and eluci-
> dating in production the relationship between past culture and present
> function. (Walsh 1990: 104)

Adaptation is therefore a crucial aspect of Brecht's dramaturgical practice: a discussion of Brecht's use of adaptation helps us to take note of
key features of his dramaturgy. If adaptation is invariably dramaturgical

work, involving dramaturgical analysis, one might argue that, for Brecht, dramaturgy is frequently defined through adaptation.

Brecht's use of other writers' work is extensive and, for some, controversial. It is not possible to state authoritatively what proportion of Brecht's works are adaptations: in order to do so, at least, one would need some clear definition of what is meant by 'adaptation' and, furthermore, a clarification as to which plays can be considered as being substantially adapted by Brecht himself. Brecht's own use of the term 'adaptation' (*bearbeitung*) seems rather inconsistent, though many of his plays are based on easily identifiable texts and still others draw substantially on works by other authors. Richard Beckley argues that almost *all* Brecht's works have their roots in earlier adaptations, even when they cannot be classed as such, themselves (Beckley 1961–2: 282–3). We must also be careful in attributing work to Brecht. In his last years at the Berliner Ensemble, teams of dramaturgs adapted plays by other authors and Brecht's name is attached to most of these works. However, John Fuegi has shown that in some instances, such as *Don Juan* (1952) (based on the play by Jean-Baptiste Molière [1665]), Brecht had very little input into the text (Fuegi 1974). Some of 'Brecht's' adaptations, therefore, reflect the work of the company, rather than the individual artist; or rather, they represent his involvement in an artistic policy.

What we can say is that Brecht does not observe a sharp distinction between work that is 'adapted' and work that is 'original'. In fact, Eric Bentley recalls Brecht commenting that: 'Anyone can be creative, it's rewriting other people that's a challenge' (quoted in Peter Thomson 2006: 25). What seems clear is that Brecht consistently chose to enter into a dialogic, or indeed, dialectical relationship with other playwrights, through strategies of adaptation and assimilation. To do so was absolutely integral to his working practice. In this chapter we will use the word 'adaptation' to refer to works that are substantially based on a previous text. Unless otherwise indicated, Brecht's input into all these adaptations was significant, though others were involved as collaborators.

All writing, of course, possesses an element of intertextuality. For Brecht, however, the use of other texts amounted to a deliberate strategy. This is particularly true of the periods where he was at work in the German theatre – at the beginning and end of his career. Since Brecht's 'major' literary works are those that might be described as the most 'original', some have described his debt to other authors as a young man as an 'apprenticeship', while his adaptations during the 1950s seem to reflect an artistic decline in his latter years (for example, Richard Beckley makes the loaded, but surely tautologous suggestion that

Brecht's adaptations end 'where his most original work begins' [Beckley 1961–2: 275]). Alternatively, one might point out that after his initial assimilation of Marxism, in the late 1920s, Brecht became more hostile towards 'the classics', mellowing towards them in his latter years. However, one might also observe that during the 1920s and the 1950s Brecht was able to engage in the whole practical theatre-making process. His originality in theatrical production was arguably as striking as his literary originality; during his exile, he could only fully exercise the latter, while his years in Berlin opened up the possibility of building an 'epic' theatre as a totality. Adaptation became a key strategy in shaping this theatre.

Weber clarifies that in establishing the Berliner Ensemble, Brecht intended to pursue 'three specific traditions' of theatrical works:

Drama that presented the agenda and history of social revolution.

Plays from the classic and modern repertory which critically probed class society, to be staged in new radical readings.

Comedies from the German and international theatre to establish a tradition, which, in comparison to other cultures, German theatre was lacking.(Quoted in Weber 2006: 178)

While the second of these 'traditions', suggesting 'radical new readings', implies adaptation in itself, Brecht also chose to rework forgotten comedies, such as J.M.R. Lenz's *Der Hofmeister* (1778), in order to build up the comedic tradition, and rewrote Nordahl Grieg's 'astonishingly bad' (quoted in Hayman 1983: 334) *Nederlaget* (1937), as *Die Tage der Commune* (1948–9), to build up the revolutionary tradition (though he was to find this line of development more politically problematic). We can see from this that Brecht did not hope simply to become the representative of a new theatre, but offered a revitalized vision of German theatre as a whole. It is this breadth of vision that makes his dramaturgy comparable to Lessing's, while his artistic achievements furnish his theory with concrete (if not always consistent) examples.

As Lessing found, breaking new ground is hard work. The Berliner Ensemble's adaptations were not always met with unqualified approval. The political situation in the German Democratic Republic was delicate, with the new socialist state under construction and intolerant of 'negative' voices, which might fuel criticism and unrest. Aesthetically, formal innovation was considered with suspicion, with socialist realism remaining the favoured style. Despite his rejection of these aesthetics, Brecht was, and remained, a supporter of this new government, but not an uncritical one. While Brecht's adaptation of *Der Hofmeister* (1951) was a success with audiences, its emphasis on 'German misery' was criticized as being 'negative', while the Ensemble's adaptation of Gerhardt Hauptmann's *Der Biberpelz* (1893) and *Roter Hahn* (1901) had to close after only fourteen performances, due to the concerns of Hauptmann's heirs. Most problematic of all was the response to the adaptation of Johann Wolfgang von Goethe's *Urfaust* (1772–5), a project initiated and largely carried out by younger company members, including Egon Monk. This production met with furious criticism from the authorities, was accused of being 'anti-national' and elicited the comment from Walter Ulbricht: 'We won't permit that one of the most important works of our great German poet Goethe is formalistically disfigured' (quoted in Weber 2006: 182). Looking back on the company's previous adaptations of German classics, a critic in *Neues Deutschland* suggested that all were 'fatalistic and pessimistic pictures' (quoted in Hayman 1983: 362). *Urfaust* was given only six performances, though its closure was partly due to the illness of an actor. Weber points out that after this the company only adapted plays from the international canon, which were less well known in Germany. The response to *Urfaust* may even have contributed to the abandonment of plans for staging William Shakespeare.

While he felt impelled to react to these criticisms, Brecht must have been disappointed by them. He did not intend to 'disfigure' but to transform and revive. As mentioned earlier, his own attitude to 'the classics' had shifted. In a radio interview of 1928, he is violently antagonistic, suggesting that the theatre should 'shovel underground ... everything that we currently have of dramaturgy and the theatre', attacking Shakespeare's emphasis on 'the great individuals', and stating that Elizabethan theatre was 'a drama for cannibals' (quoted in Fuegi 1972: 293). Though his late adaptation of Shakespeare's *Coriolanus* (c.1607), *Coriolan* (1952–3) does specifically address the question of the 'great individual', emphasizing the experience of the proletariat, his attitude to Shakespeare and other past authors, as Subiotto notes, became more respectful, as he sought less to impose modern political ideas than to 'release similar political attitudes latent in the original' (Subiotto 1975: 5). In 'Kleines Organon für das Theater' (1948) he suggests that the problem lies as much in the modern theatre's inability to connect with classic works as in the works themselves:

> Our theatres no longer have either the capacity or the wish to tell [the stories of the old works], even the relatively recent ones of the great

Shakespeare, at all clearly: i.e. to make the connection of events credi-
ble. And according to Aristotle – and we agree there – narrative is the
soul of drama. We are more and more disturbed to see how crudely and
carelessly men's life together is represented, and that not only in old
works but also in contemporary ones constructed according to old
recipes. Our whole way of appreciation is starting to get out of date ... It
is the inaccurate way in which happenings between human beings are
represented that restricts our pleasure in the theatre. The reason: we
and our forebears have a different relationship to what is being shown.
(Brecht 1964: 182–3)

In other words, the context for the 'old works' has changed and necessitates a different engagement with them. His new theatre seeks to
reclaim them, to make it possible to appreciate them once more, in
ways appropriate to the twentieth century, which he goes on to identify as a scientific age. His vision is that of a revitalized theatre that uses
new 'recipes', not only in creating new works, but also in reshaping
and retrieving the living and still relevant qualities and texts of past
theatres. In building this new theatre, the old texts become 'raw material', not in a dismissive sense, but rather implying that the new theatre
will be built to include critically, yet lovingly recontextualized elements
of the old.

Brecht's *Der Messingkauf*, is a particularly significant document for
the study of Brecht's dramaturgy. Incomplete at the time of his death, it
consists of work dating back to 1937. Although it includes poems and
prose passages, it is substantially a dramatized conversation between
philosopher, dramaturg, actor, actress, worker and stagehand about a
new approach to making theatre. *Der Messingkauf* presents the dramaturg as someone who is expert in adapting and discussing play texts.
Both he and the philosopher are the most eloquent voices in articulating Brecht's vision, including his ideas about adaptation:

There's no reason why you shouldn't leave out part of [the playwright's]
interpretation, make fresh additions and generally use plays as so much
raw material ... [the writer's] words can be treated as sacred only if they
are the right answer to the people's questions. (Brecht 1977: 37–8)

As Antony Price points out (1970: 245), there are problems with this
bold statement, which presumes a coherent 'people', with a coherent set
of questions, capable of 'right' answers. However, the point is that
Brecht sees it as imperative to ensure that a play becomes a truly productive event, a catalyst to action in the modern world. A play's purpose

is not only to entertain, but also to produce a response to the urgent concerns of the day. An interest in the events of a play, rather than its artistic achievement might, he suggests, be enough to encourage one to adapt it. *Der Messingkauf* contains a discussion of the artwork as 'data', which must be effectively examined. Brecht writes, 'I'm assuming from the start that you will only pick plays whose incidents are of sufficient public interest' (Brecht 1977: 38).

Brecht's actual treatment of play texts varies considerably, from subtle shifts in interpretation, to deliberate confrontation, to strategic rewriting, to a borrowing of themes or plot elements to be reworked in a substantially new play. In another part of *Der Messingkauf*, he stresses the care and thought that must be put into adaptation, 'if you're not to spoil [the play's] beauty' (Brecht 1977: 62). The philosopher comments that: 'Too great an inclination to make changes may make for a frivolous study of the text, but on the other hand ... the possibility of alteration, and the knowledge that this may be essential, make its study deeper' (Brecht 1977: 74). In other words, a text is subjected to rigorous questioning, which may, or may not result in its alteration. Indeed, Brecht treated his own plays with a similar rigour and readiness to make changes. At the Berliner Ensemble, as we will discuss later, the period of analysis could last for months and involved serious thought and long discussions within the creative team. In *Der Messingkauf*, Brecht suggests that the actors may also be involved in interpretative activity, once they begin to rehearse the play.

While the dramaturg in *Der Messingkauf* cautions that, 'if one is going to alter one must have the courage and the competence to alter enough' (Brecht 1977: 74), Brecht's own adaptations vary considerably in the extent of textual changes made. In notes made in 1953 of a discussion concerning the first scene of his adaptation of Shakespeare's *Coriolanus* (Brecht 1964: 253–65), it is mentioned that the premise is to begin 'only by discussing changes of interpretation so as to prove the usefulness of our analytical method *even without adding new text*' (Brecht 1964: 259, my italics). Although the final version of the play does make changes to Shakespeare's text, Brecht was still wondering whether they were necessary in 1955 (Brecht 1993: 460, 18 July).

Once he had been introduced to Marx, Brecht sought a Marxist exposition of the contradictions, tensions and concerns to be found within contemporary society, while setting out the choices open to the proletarian characters in his work. This has led some to accuse him of dogmatism, but at its best Brecht's conception of Marxist 'dialectics' was, to quote Willett:

> a method of expressing 'the flow of things'; of showing that history, sci-
> ence and all human life can never be treated as static but are continually
> developing: that all causes, all effects, all relations are dynamic; that the
> time element must never be left out. It was a conception which had been
> expressed in the nineteenth century in terms of a never-ending series of
> clashes, or 'contradictions' between opposing forces … . So different
> forces will tug a man (or a family, or a society) in different directions, and
> out of this 'contradiction' some movement will come; then new forces
> will come into play, and so on and so on … such 'contradictions' become
> at once the motive-force and the social-aesthetic justification of his later
> work. They determine the plan and the means of expression. (Willett
> 1984: 193)

The complex notion of 'historicization' is important, perhaps even
representing the main strategy in creating this dialectical theatre, in
which 'the time element can never be left out'. Put simply:
'Historicizing involves judging a particular social system from another
social system's point of view' (Brecht, quoted in Tenschert 2004: 41).
Indeed, Brecht's approach to adaptation can be clarified by Subiotto's
suggestion (Subiotto 1975: 9) that Brecht views a play text not as
something remaining for all times, but as something taking place *in*
time, as an *historical event*. It is therefore open to historical analysis,
revision and reinvention, just as one might approach any other
moment in history. Indeed, Subiotto posits that Brechtian adaptation
is, in fact, a form of historical analysis. Play texts, historical figures or
historical accounts are all capable of providing the starting point for a
dialectical treatment of history. The play's 'moment' is examined,
tested, considered. Questions are raised as to what forces have created
the circumstances depicted and how these circumstances might be
changed. What alternatives were, and are, available? How might one
learn from this?

This approach is applied across Brecht's theatre. In all cases, Brecht
suggests that the events of a play should be viewed historically and subjected to an historical analysis by the director, actor, dramaturg and
audiences. He was also prepared to make changes in his own work,
according to shifts in context. For example, his *Leben des Galilei* was
altered several times, most notably in an attempt to make the scientist
less sympathetic. These alterations were partly suggested by the development of the atomic bomb and its use over Hiroshima (see Turner
2006: 143–50).

In his discussion of Brechtian adaptation, Subiotto suggests that Brecht has a triple approach to his analysis (Subiotto 1975: 5). First, he aims to bring out the latent social comment in the play; second, there is a reappraisal of the historical moment; third, and on the basis of this, the adaptation suggests that the audience should go on to reappraise the contemporary moment. For example, while Lenz's *Der Hofmeister* already operates as a social satire, Brecht clarifies its depiction of the forces that operate within eighteenth-century society and the positioning of individuals as part of a social group. He strengthens the parallels between the three young men, showing how, despite their initial differences, each finally chooses to capitulate to the emasculating forces that make them powerless in the face of a militaristic and class-ridden society. This helps to demonstrate the many different ways in which people have been persuaded into submission in the past. As the prologue suggests, the play teaches 'the ABC of German misery' (Brecht 1988:1). Yet the play ends with the suggestion that the tale is to be regarded as cautionary, that there are parallels with the present and alternatives may yet be sought.

Walsh's discussion of Brecht's analytical process clarifies its relationship to the practical work of developing a production:

> A production aims first to clarify and elucidate the socio-historical, political, and economic realities that conditioned the text's production and original reception. This brings out contradictions displaced, or silent in the text, revealed by the Ensemble through exploratory rehearsals. These contradictions are then analysed and elucidated in terms of the concrete physicality of performance and the mise-en-scène: design, gesture, characterisation, blocking. (Walsh 1990: 106)

Examples of the scene analysis undertaken for *Der Hofmeister* give us some idea of the practical slant of the discussion. As one might expect, there is an interpretation of the play: however, these comments are also geared towards the production and the methods of emphasizing elements of the play that the ensemble feels are of particular significance. The gist of a scene is explained, or key lines are identified, leading to a discussion of why certain gestures or cuts may be needed to bring out the meaning (see, for instance BA 547/09; BA 547/11; Berliner Ensemble and Weigel 1961: 88–9). Other staging elements are also considered, such as transitions, lighting and even casting. For instance, actors chosen to represent the upper classes must be full of vitality: 'Over two hundred years, Europe has come to recognize the horrible vitality of their class' (BA 547/41 our translation).

To give another example of the Ensemble's historical analysis, Brecht's adaptation of *Coriolanus* brings out the latent social commentary in Shakespeare's play, yet reappraises it by emphasizing the experiences of the proletariat. Brecht's version raises questions about the significance of the individual and the relationship between the 'great man' and the group, both of which are relevant to the modern world.

Brecht took notes on a discussion with his dramaturgs in 1953, concerning the first scene of this adaptation. The discussion starts with an interpretation of the first scene, which is agreed to be most significant in its depiction of the tensions and provisional union between the citizens and the patricians. The second part of the analysis moves on to ask what questions this interpretation raises for production: how can one show the initial tensions between the plebeians? How well armed are they? Should the hero be given more emphasis than their analysis suggests? How can Agrippa's parable be shown as both 'ineffective and having an effect'? (Brecht 1964: 257). As suggestions are explored, the conversation, like the analysis of *Der Hofmeister*, considers transitions, stage groupings, props and casting.

The discussion ends with a summary of the lessons the scene has to teach. For instance, Käthe Rülicke offers: 'That lack of a solution can unite the oppressed class and arriving at a solution can divide it, and that such a solution may be seen in a war.' Manfred Wekwerth adds: 'That the finest speeches cannot wipe away realities, but can hide them for a time.' Peter Palitzsch suggests: 'That the oppressor's class isn't wholly united either.' Brecht concludes: 'We want to have and to communicate the fun of dealing with a slice of illuminated history. And to have first-hand experience of dialectics.' When Palitzsch asks him whether this last is not a rather specialized experience, Brecht's answer is 'No' – 'simple' people also enjoy seeing how significant historical change comes about (Brecht 1964: 264–5).

The final version of the scene, following the general line of this discussion, does tend to focus on the plebeians, rather than on Coriolanus himself. Some of the changes are as directly anticipated in this dialogue, such as the entry of armed men at the end of Agrippa's parable, underlining his point with force. Others are smaller, but reflect the overall 'line' – details, such as the price and weight of olives, bread and goats milk, emphasize the material needs and down-to-earth experience of the plebeians, set against Agrippa's empty rhetoric.

One of Brecht's favourite techniques, in pinning down the analysis of a play, was the composition of short summaries, in one or two sentences, of the content of each scene. These were sometimes used as subtitles in the final scripts, or projected in production. However, they might simply serve as a tool, assisting the artistic ensemble in clarifying the 'line' taken through the work. For instance, Berlau notes the summaries for each scene of *Coriolan*. The summary for the first scene reads: 'Rome. Caius Marcius is ready to overthrow a riot of starving plebs but a threatening war with the Volscians forces the Senate to make some concession to the plebs: they receive tribunes' (BA 1769/02, our translation). This is very much in line with the interpretation made in the recorded discussion.

Bruce Gaston suggests that in the early adaptation of Christopher Marlowe's *Edward II* (1592–3), Brecht presents the play's action as being situated somehow, 'between the past and the present, incorporating elements of both' (Gaston 2003: 351). While *Leben Eduards des Zweiten von England* (1924) is an early work, and not always a representative one, this idea of being 'between the past and the present' seems a useful notion for many of Brecht's adaptations, as it also does for his many other plays that are set in a remote time and place. For instance, *Antigone* (1948) is framed by a prologue set in Berlin at the end of the Second World War. *Der Hofmeister* is framed by a new prologue and epilogue, which both emphasize the historical distance from the play, 'written two hundred years ago', and make it clear that it is intended as a lesson for the present: 'Look upon [the tutor's] servility, that you may find your liberty' (Brecht 1988: 1 and 72). *Die Mutter* (1932), though depicting a story set in Russia (adapted from Maxim Gorky's novel, *Mat* [1907]), incorporates agitprop techniques and was understood, in its first productions, to be a piece of contemporary political propaganda, teaching the tactics of revolution.

Brecht's use of historical material offers a method of setting the events at a slight distance from the audience's own experiences, to enable a more objective appraisal of the forces, the 'contradictions' at work. This is one form of '*Verfremdungseffekt*', perhaps the most famous of his dramaturgical strategies. Esslin suggests that '*Verfremdung*' is best translated as 'non-empathic distancing' (Esslin 1990: 140) though it is sometimes translated as simply 'distancing' or 'making strange' and often, somewhat misleadingly, as 'alienation'. However, Brecht sometimes used the term synonymously with 'historicization', suggesting the critical distance of the narrator, describing past events, as opposed to the involvement of the actor, expressing and embodying the action as if in the present.

This critical distance is reflected in Brecht's use of the term 'epic', as opposed to 'dramatic'. Keith Dickson clarifies Brecht's debt to Schiller and Goethe in their differentiation between narrative and dramatic works: 'All narrative forms make the present past; all dramatic forms make the past present' (Schiller, cited in Dickson, 1978: 239). Dickson summarizes the effect of 'Epic Theatre' by stating that: 'Brecht alters the basic tense of the drama, as it were, from present continuous to past historic' (Dickson 1978: 239). In the 'dramatic' theatre, the audience is invited to experience the play's events as if they are actually taking place at that moment: the theatrical illusion is constructed to suggest this immediacy. However, Brecht's 'epic' theatre requires the audience to look on the stage events as things that are being recounted, that happened in another place and time, subject to those circumstances and to the interpretation of those telling the tale. By doing this, Brecht hopes to facilitate a critical awareness that will allow the audience to identify the clashes and contradictions that shape both the tale and the telling.

Manfred Wekwerth, who trained with Brecht at the Berliner Ensemble, suggests that: 'The primary aim of epic theatre is ... to recreate the *attitude* of the narrator, who knows more about the story than the story knows' (Wekwerth 1967: 124, italics in original). Wekwerth himself defines *Verfremdung* as 'a method which searches for ways of destroying the habitual ways of looking at a thing, in order to reveal the contradictions within it, so that its reality may be perceived' (Wekwerth 1967: 119). At its heart is the idea that nothing is so close to us that it is taken for granted, nothing is seen as inevitable and therefore incapable of change. The exposure of contradictions often entails a humorous take on events, a revelation of their absurdities. This sense of wry examination of a story and its social context is essential to Brecht's concept of a political theatre that provokes a thoughtful response. One might even propose that 'recontextualization' might be another synonym for *Verfremdung*. The narrator, who 'knows more about the story than the story knows', is, like the adaptor, engaged in interpretative activity, in dialogue with his or her material. So, one can see that adaptation is, itself, potentially a form of *Verfremdungseffekt*, making a familiar text and its events unfamiliar by recontextualizing them.

Though Brecht and Piscator had rather different conceptions of 'epic', they were united in their rejection of the 'beautiful animal' of Aristotelian dramaturgy. The scope of the work must be panoramic, giving a picture of a society or culture, rather than focusing solely on key individuals. Brecht's use of interrupted, or disjointed play structures reflects his wish to give the audience a chance to step back from the action and to reflect on it. In effect, the teller pauses or shifts position in the telling of the tale and the listener is no longer immersed in it. This reduces the likelihood that the audience will identify too closely with the characters, or get so emotionally involved with their experiences that they cannot imagine any possible alternatives. Max Spalter identifies *Eduard II* as 'a kind of formal exercise' to test out an episodic structure, which minimizes suspense, reduces identification and shows the same action from a variety of different perspectives (Spalter 1967: 168–9). Beckley suggests that Brecht's fondness for interrupting the sweep of a narrative is clearly demonstrated in his subsequent adaptation, *Die Dreigroschenoper* (1928), based on John Gay's *The Beggar's Opera*: 'Unlike Gay, Brecht ends each act of the *Dreigroschenoper* on a note of dramatic tension which is then neutralized by a "Choral" built up to form an interruption, for the purposes of critical comment, in the flow of the action' (Beckley 1961–2: 280). Beckley argues that 'alternate compression and interruption' are characteristic of Brecht's early adaptations.

If the songs break up the narrative flow in *Die Dreigroschenoper*, this function could also be served with the use of projected film (as in *Die Mutter*) or simply the introduction of scene titles, projected or on placards – a technique that Brecht used more than once. The scene titles also gave some indication of what was to take place in the scene, thus, in theory at least, reducing the element of suspense.

The idea of a succession of scenes, connected yet distinct, was to remain important. In his appendices to the 'Kleines Organon', Brecht stresses that his sequences of loosely connected scenes, 'played quite simply one after another', are designed to '[unreel] in a contradictory manner ... without any cheap, all-pervading idealization ... or directing of subordinate, purely functional component parts to an ending in which everything is resolved' (Brecht 1964: 279). This, in his view, presents a more 'accurate' picture of a world fraught with contradictions and unresolved tensions.

Given this interest in an episodic structure, Brecht was drawn to Marlowe's *Edward II*, as to certain other plays for some of their formal properties, as well as to their subject matter. For instance, his interest in renaissance drama depended partly on his appreciation of Shakespeare's sprawling narrative structures, lack of concern for the classical 'unities' and undisguised theatricality – factors that were often modified in nineteenth-century German translations and productions (see Gaston 2003: 348). The Elizabethan theatre's lack of theatrical illusion is mirrored in Brecht's insistence that the mechanisms of performance should be revealed. The staging need only show what is necessary to the story, rather than trying to imitate reality. As in Elizabethan theatre, there can be direct address from actor to audience and there is no sense that the play unfolds in real time.

In some instances, Brecht seems interested in defamiliarizing an expected performance tradition, in order that an existing play's content might be better appreciated and understood. Again, this is particularly evident in his treatment of English renaissance plays. For example, Brecht explicitly states that the adaptation of Marlowe's *Edward II* was undertaken in order to challenge the conventional staging of Elizabethan drama: 'We wanted to make possible a production which would break with the Shakespearean tradition common to German theatres: that lumpy monumental style beloved of middle-class philistines' (Brecht 1994: 454).

In the production of *Eduard II*, the crowd scenes, involving the army, seem to have been particularly striking in performance. Not only were the soldiers' faces painted white, but also their movements were choreographed. Brecht seems to recall this scene in a key essay of 1937 on the *Verfremdungseffekt*, 'Alienation Effects in Chinese Acting' (Brecht 1964: 91–9), when he suggests that an actor might use white face paint to portray the 'outward signs' of terror, while remaining 'composed'. In this way, neither actor nor audience are encouraged to identify with the emotions of the character, leaving them free to respond according to their own understanding of the scene.

According to Walter Benjamin, Brecht saw the work on the battle scenes as having been crucial to his developing concept of epic theatre:

> Brecht ... quoted the moment at which the idea of epic theatre first came into his head. It happened at a rehearsal for the Münich production of *Edward II*. The battle in the play is supposed to occupy the stage for three quarters of an hour. Brecht couldn't stage manage the soldiers and neither could Asja (Lacis) his production assistant. Finally he turned in despair to Karl Valentin, at that time one of his closest friends, who was attending the rehearsal, and asked him: 'Well, what is it? What's the truth about these soldiers? What about them?' Valentin: 'They're pale, they're scared, that's what!' The remark settled the issue, Brecht adding, 'They're tired.' Whereupon the soldiers' faces were thickly made up with chalk, and that was the day the production's style was determined. (Benjamin 1973: 53–4)

The evolution of this scene suggests the way in which a range of influences and voices converged in a Brecht production. Brecht's assistant director, Lacis, had studied with the director Fyodor Komissarzhevsky *fils* (an early colleague of Meyerhold's) and it seems that she was influenced by Meyerhold's use of mechanical, choreographed movements in rehearsing the crowd scenes. In the passage above, Benjamin suggests the influence of the comedian, Valentin. Vana Greisenegger-Georgila comments that white faces and mask-like make-up were to become a common feature of Neher's design; perhaps he, too, was instrumental in finding this solution (Greisenegger-Georgila 2004: 77).

So we might conclude that one of the outstanding characteristics of Brecht's innovative dramaturgy was the way he drew on such different influences and wove them together into a coherent work. In later years, despite some unease with the adaptation as a text, Brecht highlights the importance of *Eduard II* in the development of his approach, suggesting that it saw 'the emergence of a new stage language' (Brecht 1994: 454).

Since Brecht's plays, whether adaptations or not, require at least some understanding of his approaches to staging and performance style, Brecht was anxious to create some kind of record of his performances, rather than simply publish the script alone. *Antigone* was the first of his plays to be published as part of a 'model book' (Berlau 1949) that also provided photographs of the production and extensive notes alongside them. Brecht did not expect the 'model' to be followed with too much reverence, but he did expect it to be useful in clarifying not only the verbal, but also the non-verbal aspects of his dramaturgy. In an interview of 1949, his comments on the 'model books' could also relate to adaptation (in fact, in defending the imitation of a model, he does describe himself as having 'copied' the Japanese, Greek and Elizabethan drama):

> We must work towards an increasingly precise description of reality ... this can only come about if we make use of what has already been achieved, without of course stopping there. The changes in the model ... will be the more expressive in that they represent a negation of the data: (this for connoisseurs of dialectics). (Brecht 1964: 225)

In this, as in many other ways, Brecht's practice might be said to have provided a 'model' for dramaturgy in the modern age.

Brecht and the Dramaturg

In Part II, we will be discussing the role of the contemporary dramaturg. We will find that this is quite different from the role occupied by Lessing, who was essentially a theatre critic and theorist, attached to a particular theatre. The modern dramaturg tends to be much more involved in the practical work of the theatre. While this does not always imply a direct involvement in rehearsal, the role is rarely confined to solitary desk work, though it may well include script-reading, research and critical writing. Although we will consider the dramaturg in more detail and with many examples in Part II, it is essential to take an early look at the role in relation to Brecht. In many respects, his work led to a shift in the function of the dramaturg and towards the evolution of what is now called 'the production dramaturg'.

As we have seen, his working process involved a long interrogation of the play text (the same procedure applied to his own plays as to those of others). The clarification of the *fabel* extended into rehearsal and to all aspects of production. Volker Canaris writes:

> The Dramaturg became the director's most important theoretical collaborator. Dramaturgy in Brecht's sense comprises the entire conceptual preparation of a production from its inception to its realization. Accordingly, it is the task of dramaturgy to clarify the political and historical, as well as the aesthetic and formal aspects of a play and to convey the scientifically researched material to the other participants: it must give the director, the designers and the actors the necessary 'data' to put the work on stage; it controls the scenic illusion by relating it to an empirically conceived reality – and by making this reality accessible it stimulates the imagination. This procedure enabled the Berliner Ensemble in its heyday to put on productions of quite outstanding merit. (Canaris 1975: 250)

This use of the dramaturg differed from the conventional, desk-bound role as it had become established in the German theatre. It evolved out of the needs of a new theatre, but it was also a product of Brecht's own experience as a dramaturg during the 1920s. While his first two appointments may simply have clarified the need for a more comprehensive approach to dramaturgy, his third provided him with some practical models for the use of the dramaturg.

While Brecht is sometimes derided for having wanted too much power as a dramaturg, his concern was not so much the influence of the individual dramaturg, but the notion that every aspect of play-making must be considered dramaturgically. At the Berliner Ensemble, as Russell E. Brown puts it, Brecht's approach '*both* magnified the role of the dramaturg *and* submerged it in the collective of the theatrical company' (Brown 2000: 61, my italics).

Brecht as Dramaturg: Early Dialogues

We suggested earlier that adaptation is invariably dramaturgical work. Some of Brecht's first adaptations were indeed undertaken during his early career as a dramaturg. During the 1920s, his work as a playwright and fledgling director was intertwined with and inseparable from his role as a professional dramaturg, first at the München Kammerspiele under Otto Falckenburg and Benno Bing from 1922–4; then at the Deutsches Theater under Max Reinhardt from 1924–5; and, finally, as part of Piscator's 'dramaturgical collective' in 1927–8. To some extent, these positions offered the young Brecht a training ground, although he received no formal training. The Munich theatre offered him some sympathetic advisors, such as Leon Feuchtwanger, and the opportunity to cut his teeth as a director; his second position gave him the opportunity to watch Reinhardt at work, while he learned (and borrowed) an enormous amount from Piscator, in terms of both theory and practice.

It must be acknowledged that Brecht was not a particularly successful professional dramaturg and cannot be regarded as typical. He was busy establishing himself as a playwright and, full of ideas for his new theatre, was not very interested in compromising his vision of theatrical reform in the service of someone else's theatre, even in the service of a director as extraordinary as Reinhardt.

Brecht does not seem to have been very enthusiastic about his first position as dramaturg, though he needed the stable salary that it offered. While working there, he was to a great extent immersed in developing his own career as a playwright, with productions in Munich and Berlin; he was to receive the Kleist prize for *Trommeln in der Nacht* (1922), *Baal* (1919) and *Im Dickicht der Städte* (1923). Herbert Ihering's review of *Trommeln in der Nacht* commented: 'The evidence of Brecht's genius is that his plays bring a new artistic totality into existence, with its own laws, its own dramaturgy' (cited in Hayman 1983: 91).

As a dramaturg, Brecht was involved in the development of the theatre's repertoire; for instance, he wrote to Barrett O. Clark concerning the theatre's plans to produce 'a number of American plays' (Brecht 1990: 82, 26 April). His most significant task, however, was to adapt *Edward II*, discussed above, which he eventually directed himself. The adaptation was written with Feuchtwanger, whose contribution, aside from his knowledge of English, seems to have been largely structural. As we have seen, it was a significant project for Brecht's development as a writer and director, though undertaken in the role of 'dramaturg'.

Brecht's next appointment as dramaturg was at the Deutsches Theater in Berlin. His friend and colleague Carl Zuckmayer suggests that he and Brecht were primarily appointed as 'ornamental additions of a progressive sort who would attach the younger generation to the triumphal chariot of the whole enterprise' (quoted in Schechter 1978: 59). Zuckmayer recollects:

> [Brecht] seldom turned up there ... Roughly speaking, what he wanted was to take over complete control: the season's programme must be regulated entirely according to his theories, and the stage be rechristened 'epic smoke-theatre', it being his view that people might actually be disposed to think if they were allowed to smoke at the same time. As this was refused him he confined himself to coming and drawing his pay.
> (Quoted in Willett 1984: 145)

This, as Joel Schechter comments, 'may be somewhat apocryphal' (1978: 58). Brecht did have some involvement in the theatre's work. His role again involved adaptation – he worked to desentimentalize Alexander Dumas's *La Dame aux Camélias* (1848) in a translation by Ferdinand Bruckner. It was agreed that Brecht's interventions into the text should not be mentioned either in the programme or to the translator: the result was that Bruckner sued the theatre (see Hayman 1983: 107). Brecht also seems to have had some input into discussions towards Erich Engel's production of *Coriolanus* (1925), also an adaptation. He and Zuckmayer also had some, minimal, input into repertoire (see Willett 1984: 145). Brecht is known to have attended some of Reinhardt's rehearsals, including productions of works by George Bernard Shaw and Luigi Pirandello, both of whom he found influential. One guesses that he is likely to have made some contribution in terms of discussing the work, but there is no record of this.

However, what Zuckmayer's recollections confirm is Brecht's sense that in order to change the theatre, the whole theatre-going context needed to change. The dramaturg's work needed to extend beyond the choice of plays or, indeed, their adaptation. It was necessary to address the theatre in its entirety, including its relationship to the public. Brecht's concern with the context of a performance meant that he needed to work with a company who understood and were prepared to critique the theatre event as a whole and to question its function.

He found a much more congenial working relationship in his third dramaturgical role, which had a direct influence on his later career. It was not surprising that he was drawn to the Marxist director, Piscator, who was setting up his own theatre company in 1927. Piscator, once a member of Berlin Dada, was committed to a political theatre that drew on montage techniques and mobilized all the technical resources of the stage to present life as a broad, contemporary, social span, rather than to present detailed, individual and perhaps, 'timeless' experiences.

In *Der Messingkauf*, Brecht writes: 'Piscator was one of the greatest theatre men of all time. He electrified the theatre and made it capable of grasping great subjects' (Brecht 1977: 67). He also comments that without Piscator's achievements, his own theatre, 'would hardly be conceivable' (Brecht 1977: 69). It was Piscator who was first associated with the concept of 'epic' dramaturgy, particularly in relation to his production of Alfons Paquet's *Fahnen* (1924). Looking back, he wrote that his formal aims concerned:

> the extension of the action and the clarification of the background of an action, that is to say, it involved the continuation of the play beyond the dramatic framework. A didactic play (Lehrstück) was developed from the spectacle-play (Schaustück). This automatically led to the use of techniques from areas that had never been seen in the theatre before. (Quoted in Piscator 1980: 70)

For Piscator, as for Brecht, conventional dramatic structures were too compressed and too closely focused on the individual experience. Piscator sought to broaden the scope of dramatic works, by showing the entire social context. Through his use of montage, he was able to present a layered, loosely knit presentation of the action as a series of clearly historicized events – using, for example, filmed interludes, projected text or documentary material. According to Piscator, the contemporary theatre did not offer scripts that exemplified this dramaturgy: therefore, adaptation was essential. In this, he echoes Brecht's dramaturg in *Der Messingkauf*, who suggests that in order to compensate for the dearth of appropriate plays it might be useful to take reports on real court cases as material, to adapt novels or to dramatize historical incidents. The adaptation of an existing play is clearly an alternative solution.

Though Piscator was not a *writer*, Brecht wrote that:

> The Augsburger [Brecht] claimed that apart from himself he was the only competent dramatist. He would ask if Piscator hadn't proved that plays can also be made by inspiring scenes and projects by other writers, supplying them with documents and scenic performances, and making a montage of them. (Brecht 1977: 68)

However, since Piscator was not a literary man, he needed dramaturgs to work with him in order to 'rework texts in the light of our political standpoint and to work out new scenes to suit my ideas for the production, and to help shape the script' (Piscator 1980: 194). This demand for a dramaturg who might 'co-operate creatively' was an extension of a role that was usually confined to decisions concerning repertoire, casting and any necessary editing of play texts. It was Piscator, too, who developed the model of the 'dramaturgical collective', somewhat similar to the teamwork of the Berliner Ensemble in later years. By his own admission, the ideal was not fully realized in practice and there remained tensions between individual desires and collective decisions.

Brecht was involved in several productions at the Piscatorbuhne, most notably the adaptation of Jaroslav Hašek's unfinished novel, *Osudy Dobrého Vojáka Švejka za Světové Války* (1922–3), as *Die Abenteuer der Braven Soldaten Schwejk* (1928), which Brecht later adapted single-handedly (1941–3). The collective's official starting point was a dramatic adaptation by Max Brod and Hans Reimann, but in fact they went back to the novel, while the playwrights' names remained attached to the production. Piscator comments that in Brod and Reimann's version, 'Hašek's satire had been lost in an attempt to construct a "well-made" play' (Piscator 1980: 255), while what attracted him was Hašek's 'view of life in its entirety'. Brecht seems to have undertaken much of the writing, though in collaboration with Felix Gasbarra, Leo Lania and Piscator himself. However, it was Piscator who evolved the key device that enabled the play's dramaturgy:

> Even when I read the novel, long before we even thought of dramatizing it, I had a mental picture of events following one another in a ceaseless, uninterrupted stream. Faced with the problem of putting this novel on the stage, this impression in my mind assumed the concrete form of the conveyor belt. (Piscator 1980: 257)

Piscator set Schwejk and other performers on one conveyor belt, while scenic effects could move past on a second belt or in projected backgrounds and cartoon film drawn by Georg Grosz. Gasbarra wrote:

> It seemed impossible to capture the epic movement of the novel with traditional theatre techniques. With a fixed stage, the flow of Hašek's plot was bound to be chopped up into single scenes, and this would falsify the fluid character of the novel. Piscator overcame this problem by replacing the fixed stage floor with a moving floor ... and this solved our

textual problems as well as our technical problems. The adapters no longer needed a framework other than the original story; they could limit themselves to choosing the most effective scenes in the novel and turning them into actable texts. (Gasbarra in Piscator 1980: 259)

Piscator's mechanism provided the means to present the whole social context, while the conventional dramaturgy of Brod and Reimann's adaptation tended towards a collapse of the novel's panoramic scope. When Brecht set out to write his own adaptation, without the use of the conveyor belt, he had to find alternative solutions and used very little material from the Piscator version.

Piscator's collective worked together in a hotel in Neubabelsberg, a village just outside Berlin. Piscator would practise marksmanship in the grounds and a physical trainer was employed to keep the dramaturgs fit! Brecht remembers that in Piscator's theatre rehearsals were accompanied by a bunch of playwrights conducting a 'non-stop discussion onstage' (Brecht 1977: 64). He also recalls first nights when he and Piscator would walk around the outside of the theatre involved in long and creative discussions.

Perhaps it is in these descriptions of his work with Piscator that we get the clearest impression of how important dialogue was to Brecht. He was to spend the better part of the 1930s and 1940s in exile from the German-speaking theatre. When one considers the pleasure he took and the creative energy he drew from these long days and nights of intense conversations one begins to realize how hard this exile must have been.

Piscator's use of the dramaturg seems to have influenced Brecht's later practice, though Brecht might seem to have less urgent need for the dramaturg's specific skills as a playwright (despite this his dramaturgs were, as we have seen, engaged in adaptation). Brecht already had a tendency to work in teams before he worked with Piscator: he had already established the idea of the 'Brecht collective', who would work together on his plays. Throughout his life, he worked closely with collaborators, often female: the most notable were Elizabeth Hauptmann, Ruth Berlau and Margarete Steffin, who Luckhurst suggests were, in effect, dramaturgs (Luckhurst 2006a: 121). However, it was Piscator who first made the 'dramaturgical collective' a structural element of a professional theatre company. For both Brecht and Piscator this emphasis on dramaturgical discussion arose out of the urgent need for a political theatre to address the issues of the age. They both saw their dramaturgies as engaging urgently with their contemporary context. In describing the playwrights' on-stage discussion during Piscator's rehearsals, Brecht adds, 'and this discussion continued right through the whole immense city in newspapers, drawing rooms, pubs and cafés' (Brecht 1977: 65). Though he and Piscator were temperamentally different, and though their aesthetics also differed in crucial respects, they were united in this desire to begin a discussion that could ignite the city.

Brecht's Dramaturgs: Later Dialogues

In 1948, Brecht returned to communist East Germany, where, in 1949 the Berliner Ensemble was established, first occupying the Deutsches Theater and then, in 1954, moving to the Theater am Schiffbauerdamm, where some of Brecht's early plays had been staged. At last, Brecht had his own company and could develop his ideas through the practical work of theatre production. He now had his own dramaturgs, as well as actors, designers, musicians, administrators and others.

As we have already suggested, a conscious engagement with dramaturgy was absolutely integral to the work of the Berliner Ensemble as a whole. Each member of Brecht's ensemble – actors, designers, directors and of course, dramaturgs – was also, at least potentially, a critic and even an 'outside eye'.

This level of teamwork led to lively rehearsals, as Brecht's chief dramaturg, Palitzsch recalls:

> Sometimes so many people – increasing numbers – participated in the rehearsals that finally, in order to put a stop to the constant comings and goings, Wekwerth and I urged that only those should be admitted who could and wanted to remain from beginning to end of a working period. (Palitzsch, cited in Iden 2005: 58: our translation)

Weber writes of Brecht:

> He asked everyone he trusted to come to rehearsal and constantly asked their opinions; he controlled his work through their reactions. In the fifties, his productions were always team-work, and he constantly used all the people connected with a production – assistants, designer, musicians (Eisler was at many rehearsals). Brecht asked the Ensemble's technicians to attend dress rehearsals and afterwards sought their opinions. (Weber 1967: 105)

The contributions of designers and musicians might be partly dramaturgical. For instance, in journal entries relating to *Antigone*, Brecht makes it clear that decisions about the design were dramaturgically significant:

> In modelling the set Cas and I stumble on an ideological element of the first order. Should we place the barbaric totem poles with the horses' skulls at the back between the actors' benches, thus indicating the barbaric location of the old poem which the actors leave in order to act (the de-totemised version)? We decide to place the acting among the totem poles, since we are still living in the totemic state of the class war. (Brecht 2003: 198, 4 January 1948)

Here, we can see how questions about the stage design become questions about the positioning of the company in relation to Sophocles's text. To what extent is Sophocles's social context paralleled in the contemporary world? Brecht and Neher decide that in fact their contemporary society still participates in elements of 'barbarism', albeit in different forms. Therefore, the actors cannot leave the totem poles behind them. This is a critical dramaturgical (and political) decision, rather than solely a matter of aesthetic preference.

Apart from designing the overall stage set, Neher would also produce sketch after sketch of individual moments of stage action, rather like a 'comic strip', or like the storyboards used in contemporary film production. These pictures were used in rehearsal and were a tool for the practical analysis of the play. The positioning of the characters was discussed in terms of the ways in which it revealed the social attitudes or '*gestus*' of those in the scene. Once the stage picture was agreed, it then formed the basis for blocking that part of the scene. Neher's contribution to Lenz's *Der Hofmeister* was so significant that he is credited as co-director.

What, then, was the dramaturg's role in a company where everyone, 'assistants, designer, musicians ... technicians' might also occasionally play the role of dramaturg? In fact, there was plenty of work for the team of dramaturgs to do. We have previously mentioned their involvement in historical/contextual analysis. This not only included entering into discussions of the work in progress, but also copious note-taking and compiling written analyses of the plays to be produced. They were also involved in contextualizing the Ensemble's work for the public, which included conducting archival work such as the compilation of the 'model books' as well as the writing of programme notes and other material. They were involved in contextual research related to the productions and plays in hand, including audience research and attending discussions with those responsible for design and construction. They were involved in outreach and audience development, leading workshops and directing performances with factory workers and so on. The dramaturg, then, was not merely a sounding-board for the director, but was involved in a wide range of demanding practical tasks, associated with a thorough, well-informed and imaginatively demonstrated ideological and intellectual grasp of the relationship between the play, the theatre, its historical context and its audiences.

When trying to establish Brecht's practical use of the dramaturg, Luckhurst cautions against too much reliance on the image of the dramaturg in *Der Messingkauf*, who is, she suggests, 'a composite configuration of various literary, critical, pedagogical and administrative functions, which were undertaken not by a single person, but by a team' (Luckhurst 2006a: 129). This is not to say that the dramaturg in Brecht's theoretical work is insignificant, since the character demonstrates Brecht's ideal of a writer, critic, scholar and communicator who is also able to take a practical involvement in the work of performance. In practice, however, Brecht spread dramaturgical roles between a large number of dramaturgs, some of whom had special responsibility for particular tasks. For example, Palitzsch was the dramaturg with primary responsibility for the programmes and public relations; Berlau was responsible for model books; Hauptmann was 'Brecht's personal researcher' (Luckhurst 2006b: 205) and a mentor to the less experienced dramaturgs. Brecht's dramaturgs were not, therefore, all-powerful, all-encompassing figures, though the scope of the work undertaken might be extraordinarily wide.

However, the dramaturgical team was much more actively involved in the production process than traditional dramaturgs might be, with the role sometimes sliding into that of the directing assistant or even writer. Palitzsch confirms this involvement, which differed from his experience as dramaturg at the Dresdener Volksbühne:

> There, a director was a director and a dramaturg was a dramaturg, whereas at the Berliner Ensemble, the dramaturg – or whatever you want to call them, we were all called 'assistants' – accompanied a production from the beginning onwards: when we did *Der Hofmeister*, I read Lenz's original version and all the additions to it, took part in the staging and was responsible for the Model Book. (Palitzsch, cited in Iden 2005: 49, our translation)

As the above quote implies, the job title, 'dramaturg', was not habitually used. Palitzsch was originally employed as an 'assistant', though his role later became identifiable as the Ensemble's head 'dramaturg'. Weber, who confirms that he was employed as a 'directing assistant and actor', was subsequently involved in dramaturgical work (Weber 2005: 1).

Luckhurst draws attention to a letter from Rülicke, addressed to an 'old-school' dramaturg named Heinen, explaining the situation at the Berliner Ensemble:

> Brecht only works with young people, whom he has trained himself. Dramaturgs, in the traditional sense, do not exist in our theatre at all. Our dramaturgs work as assistant directors and vice versa; our directors work in the Dramaturgy Department. This way of working has probably come about as a result of Brecht's activity as a writer, director and dramaturg. (BA 764/37, translated in Luckhurst 2006a: 130)

Thus Rülicke demonstrates the sense that the Brechtian dramaturg breaks with tradition, moving beyond the traditional confines of the role.

The letter goes on to stress the youth of the team. Luckhurst also clarifies the training system in place at the Berliner Ensemble, which was tiered, including students from universities and schools at lower levels, with six *Meisterschüler* from the Academy of Arts, each year. As laid out in a letter to Paul Wandel, an education minister, the *Meisterschüler* undertook a two- to three-year training, which might enable them to be dramaturgs, directors or theatre critics, and were expected to attend rehearsals and meetings with designers, direct amateur groups in factories and participate in making adaptations of plays for production (Brecht 1981: 73, 24 May 1951). These trainees worked alongside the dramaturgical staff of the ensemble, including Palitzsch, Hauptmann and Berlau, among others.

Despite the large number of dramaturgs (or 'assistants') the programmes for Berlin productions during Brecht's lifetime very rarely credit dramaturgs at all, though they name the director and sometimes assistant or co-directors, stage designers, actors and occasionally lighting designers. Certainly, not everyone involved in a production is credited, whether as 'assistants' or 'dramaturgs'. Given the numbers involved, this may of course have been simply pragmatic. However, Henrik Adler, a dramaturg with the Berliner Ensemble in more recent years, suggests that there may also have been a sense that the dramaturgs' contributions were towards objective, scientific analysis (in the Marxist sense), which did not depend upon an individual, artistic role, requiring personal recognition:

> It doesn't have to do with power ... It reflects something like objective truth ... Theatre work was something like scientific work ... The second thing is that the dramaturg in ... the Berliner Ensemble is something like – he is the theatre. There's nothing which is not dramaturgical. The whole thing – the whole thing is dramaturgy. (Adler 2005: 13–14)

Bearing this last point in mind, the dramaturgs (or assistants) were certainly kept busy. Rehearsals were preceded by a period of discussion and analysis, which Weber suggests lasted as long as six months (Weber 1967: 103). Tenschert suggests that again, the wider ensemble was involved in initial discussions (Copfermann 1960: 44). However, a smaller group, comprising the director, assistant directors and dramaturgs, took the discussions further. Examples of such scene analyses have been given earlier. *Theaterarbeit* gives us a detailed breakdown of the various stages of work, from the initial analysis and discussions of setting and casting, through the 'Reading Rehearsal', 'Positioning Rehearsal', 'Set Rehearsal' and 'Rehearsal of details' to run-throughs, dress rehearsals and previews (Berliner Ensemble 1961: 256–8, translated in Willett 1964: 241–2).

The editing of the theatre programme was also the job of the dramaturg and involved compiling a range of contextual material to assist the audience in appreciating the play. Palitzsch, who originally trained as a graphic designer, was particularly significant in designing publicity material and, indeed, helped Brecht to design the company logo that still turns on the top of the Theater am Schiffbauerdamm.

The Berliner Ensemble's programmes tend to contain extensive contextual material, though the approach differs for different plays. For instance, the programme for *Pauken und Trompeten* (1955) (adapted from George Farquhar's *The Recruiting Officer*) is visually engaging and the material is reasonably condensed, digestible and light in tone. By contrast, the programme for Erwin Strittmatter's *Katzgraben* (1953) is visually less stimulating and contains vast quantities of sometimes rather heavy contextual material, including quotes from Josef Stalin and Walter Ulbricht, newspaper articles, plans for land reform, and concludes on a triumphal note, with a quotation from one of Brecht's own poems. This is placed alongside fictional material that relates to the *fabel* of the play (letters or diaries written by the characters).

We are left in no doubt as to the political intent of this production or the eagerness of the company to ensure a thorough understanding of the contemporary setting. Of course, this play is rather different from all the others in that it is the only play by a contemporary German playwright, dealing with contemporary German issues, to be produced by the Ensemble during Brecht's lifetime. It has also been suggested that the production was politically motivated in the sense of attempting to secure governmental approval during a period where it was in some doubt.

One interesting letter in the programme is from a farmer, 'E. Trunte', who invites the company to visit his farm in Lower Lusatia (where the play is set) and, indeed, suggests that the play's author, Strittmatter, has already done so. The letter is addressed to Rülicke. While we do not know whether Rülicke or other dramaturgs took Trunte up on his offer (it was made rather late in rehearsals), we do know that Palitzsch and Von Appen had certainly made field trips to Lower Lusatia the previous year, in order to research the design of the piece. Strittmatter, as the farmer suggests, did visit and knew the area, while Brecht had visited it with the Ensemble, again in 1952.

This, combined with the copiousness of the programme material suggests a degree of original field research and a deliberate engagement with the situation of contemporary workers. 'Only the artists of the Berliner Ensemble, who are laymen in this matters, have shown any interest in these things,' says Trunte, ruefully (Programme for *Katzgraben*, 1953: 15, BA, our translation). There does seem a level of integrity about this research that goes beyond lip service to the Communist Party line. Though Brecht's official response to the June uprising shortly after the play opened in 1953 appeared to place him in support of the state and in opposition to the workers (although conversely, private material and recollections of colleagues suggest the opposite), yet his hope, however naive or self-deluding, was always that the two might work together.

The dramaturg was, as has been mentioned, one of those involved in attending rehearsals and offering comments on the evolving production, keeping a close eye on the emerging directorial line. If the dramaturg's role was a somewhat invisible one, many of the assistants seem to have increasingly worked as directors, often in teams. Some, such as Palitzsch, Wekwerth and Bruno Besson eventually became well known as directors in their own right. As already mentioned, in Brecht's time, there was an understanding that roles would necessarily overlap. As Adler suggests, 'Maybe preparing the work and directing are two stages of one work' (Adler 2005: 49). Luckhurst suggests that the roles of the Ensemble's dramaturgs and directors became more distinct after

Brecht's death, leading directly to the development of the 'production dramaturg' proper and a 'struggle for territory' between the directors, dramaturgs and playwrights (Luckhurst 2006b: 20).

In reflecting on his time spent working for Brecht, the director Besson comments:

> As far as I am concerned, I am unable to say what was given to me. In any case, this 'thing' – I can't name it – [was] perhaps a kind of attention to the world, a sensitivity, a sensuality. And also a respect for everyone on stage, a tactfulness, an enormous respect for actors. (Quoted in Walsh 1990: 115)

What emerges for us through an analysis of Brecht's production methods, including his use of dramaturgs and of the whole Ensemble, is a clear sense of the Ensemble's belief that theatre, if put forward with intelligence, clarity and humour, can reach out to its context to initiate social change. It is an engaged theatre, in touch with its world. All Brecht's dramaturgical ideas are concerned with facilitating this engagement, having an effect in the world, changing it. Adler, speaking fifty years later, wonders how Brecht's ideas can now be realized. He wonders whether anyone in Berlin still believes that theatre can have a significant political effect: 'I do not think that anybody really believes that theatre can change the world today, and we have to reflect on this hopelessness too. I'm not at the end of my thoughts about this problem' (Adler 2005: 25).

While Brecht's hopefulness may not have been handed down to later generations, theatre of the last sixty years would look very different without him. He expanded the dramaturg's role, effectively introducing what would later be described as the 'production dramaturg' – the dramaturg who works with the creative team in rehearsal. He made the dramaturg into a collaborator, rather than a distant figure in an office full of un-read scripts. Brecht's legacy in terms of dramaturgy, in its wider sense, is too enormous to summarize. In Britain alone his work had a huge impact on the development of socialist political theatre in the 1960s. This work, in turn, filtered into the mainstream via a number of routes, including feminist theatres and 'state-of-the-nation' plays at the National Theatre. At the same time, his work has reverberations in postmodern performance, where montage, loose-knit sequences, narrative devices, theatrical transparency (indeed, self-reflexivity) and various kinds of *verfremdungseffekts* are just some of the traces of Brechtian dramaturgy.

Brecht emphasized that the theatre is not only a place of entertainment but a moment of political action. While this thought owed much to Meyerhold, Piscator and others, his entire career was spent in examining its dramaturgical implications. His dramaturgy involves a whole range of strategies that aim to make it possible to engage an audience in an energetic, playful, yet critical analysis of its world. Brecht's work demonstrates that a new politics both requires and produces a new dramaturgy; this idea has itself been of considerable influence, as we shall see in the following chapter.

3 Names and Identities: Political Dramaturgies in Britain

As we have seen, Brecht's dramaturgy stresses the relationship between a work and its context; a play is an event taking place in time and must be viewed both historically and in terms of its relation to the current climate. Theatre is always in dialogue with its audience. The urgent concerns of the contemporary world drive the dramaturgical decisions that are made in preparing a play for production.

Brecht's influence is evident in the British political theatre of the 1960s and 1970s. Reminiscences of these decades often suggest the excitement and sense of urgency that artists experienced.

> We did think a revolution was about to happen. We really did think that. And for a moment, it looked like it would... it felt... like freedom, really. (Brenton 2001: 12)

As Brenton's comment suggests, within the UK theatre, much of the experimentation and, therefore, the emerging dramaturgies of these decades also seem to have been driven by political commitment. In this chapter, we will identify a few of the ways in which politics have spurred new dramaturgies within the British theatre over the past fifty years, attempting to provide some sense of the relationship between politics and dramaturgy. It is important to recognize that this is not a history of political theatre. New political plays, for instance, may make use of relatively conventional dramaturgical structures. We are specifically discussing the innovations in dramatic form that have arisen through political commitment or questioning of one kind or another.

As we discuss these political dramaturgies, we will also pause occasionally to reflect on the terms we are using. To delineate is also to limit: terms that label a work are invariably problematic. On the other hand, they can be useful tools for helping us to articulate the different strategies and groupings implicit in different dramaturgies. There are those who regard the dramaturg with suspicion, partly because they sense there could be a tendency to look for systems, rules, patterns. While it is useful to identify these patterns, an insistence upon them can be reductive. We need to be aware of the politics of dramaturgical analysis itself, the potential dangers, as well as the potential gains.

For example, our use of the term 'political dramaturgies' may prove insufficiently specific. While it would be possible to label as 'political', work by Bertolt Brecht, Welfare State, Deborah Levy, David Edgar and Desperate Optimists, these artists are more striking in their differences than in their similarities. They embody different political positions, different aesthetics, are influenced by different performance traditions and approach their work with different intentions. In other words, their dramaturgies are not remotely similar. It might therefore be helpful to find more precise words with which to differentiate between them and to open up the discussion of what it means, or might mean, to make 'political' theatre.

Given that there can be many different approaches to political theatre, what defines a work as 'political' in the first place? What do we mean by the term 'political'? We tentatively suggest that we are applying it to works that are substantially shaped by the conscious exploration of the needs of particular constituencies, with an articulated desire for social change, whether or not the work is aligned to a specific political manifesto or ideology. However, postmodernist theory suggests that all cultural discourse can be regarded as politically inflected and subject to systems of cultural control – with the result that there can be no such thing as a theatre that does not express a political perspective. Yet surely it remains important to differentiate between the political strategies used and levels of commitment articulated within different artists' work?

At the Berliner Ensemble, political dramaturgy began with a set of shared starting points and values, as well as with a shared vision of a specific socialist programme. When considering British theatre of the 1960s and 1970s, one might claim, with Margaretta D'Arcy, that 'a *political* group is one that has a definite *political plan*' (Theatre Quarterly Symposium 1976: 48). In other words, for D'Arcy, Brecht's theatre was political precisely because it aimed (to some degree at least) to promote a particular political ideology and process. D'Arcy, supported by her partner, John Arden, suggests that plays that tackle a single issue in isolation are 'social' or 'educational', rather than 'political', since they do not address the underlying problems of the political (capitalist) system. This prompts Micheline Wandor's rather dismayed response that 'one can't write about everything at the same time' (Theatre Quarterly Symposium 1976: 49) and, indeed, D'Arcy and Arden's position seems unhelpfully polarizing, if refreshingly uncompromising.

The aims and intentions of 'political theatre' vary; even where there is some consistency of political viewpoint, there are variations in what may be considered as political efficacy. Might the apparent 'failure' of the British avant garde's political project (see, for example, Howard Brenton, 1981 (1975): 91–2) be apparent only with reference to a particular view of what its success ought to have looked like? Did it indeed, despite D'Arcy and Arden's demands, ever have anything like 'a coherent programme or a single identity'? (Hewison 1986: 225). Perhaps the failure of the revolution to materialize does not mean this work was or is entirely without potency? Kershaw concludes, after Hewison,

> whilst it is obvious that alternative theatre did not bring about a political revolution, it is by no means certain that it failed to achieve other types of general effect ... it is my contention that ... the movement offered a significant challenge to the status quo, and may even have contributed to the modification of dominant ideologies in the 1970s and 1980s. (Kershaw 1999: 18 and 21)

One might take Peter Palitzsch's view that though theatre can change the world, it will be 'by millimetres' (cited in Iden 2005: 16–17). Or if, as Adler suggests, few theatre-makers now believe, like Brecht, that theatre can 'change the world', might its changes be local, personal, or gradual? Or perhaps, rather than instigate change, might theatre and performance support new lines of thought and action as they emerge? These questions may not easily be answered, and they are far from closed.

'Radical Populism' or 'Carnival Agitprop'

Despite the formal innovations of British 'alternative' theatre of the 1960s and 1970s (and already, we find ourselves using a problematic term), it appears that the most significant impulse towards a new dramaturgy arose from the left-wing political motivations of the post-war generation. This impetus is discussed in most historical accounts of the period, most notably in Itzin (1980), but also in Ansorge (1975), Edgar (1979), Davies (1987) and Kershaw (1992). This impulse, which led the theatre-makers towards working in new places, with new audiences, towards (fairly) clearly defined political ends, inevitably led to a rethinking of dramaturgical strategy.

This partly led theatre-makers to look for existing forms and traditions that might be put to use. Here we find the term 'agitation propaganda' one of the most immediately significant. Although little documentation was available to the later companies, the Worker's Theatre Movement's 'agitprop' productions of the 1920s and 1930s had an influence on their work. These drew on Russian and German forms of 'agitprop': didactic, broad theatre, which eschewed naturalism in favour of directness, caricature and comedy, to present an explicit political content. The movement found agitprop effective because it was mobile, immediate and direct: 'it can be taken to the people, instead of waiting for them to come to you. And it is a theatre of attack. "Naturalistic" theatre gives you the appearance of reality, but it does not show what lies beneath it' (Tom Thomas, quoted in Prentki and Selman 2000: 61).

Given the lack of an available archive, Steve Gooch suggests that a full sense of this tradition was not always immediately available even to those working within it. Gooch comments that this meant that the new companies had to 'learn by trial-and-error, making mistakes as they went along, instead of being able to refer to accounts of similar initiatives in previous decades where similar problems had been encountered and similar mistakes made' (quoted in Kershaw 1999: 90).

A number of factors provoked this 'trial-and-error' and led to some interesting experiments with new dramaturgies. While the term 'radical populism' is open to interpretation, as Sierz demonstrates (Sierz 2006: 302), it can usefully be employed to describe the impulse behind some of the dramaturgies that emerged. These attempted to argue for radical change, while drawing on popular forms – using 'popular' in its socialist sense, to mean forms that are current for the 'proletariat', the working classes.

One of the first requirements was a need to reach new audiences, perhaps by performing in non-traditional locations. For example, work was performed in folk clubs, working men's clubs, rallies and on the street. Many of these contexts necessitated forms that were immediate and drew on the types of 'popular' entertainment that were usually present in those locations. Brevity, clarity, humour and music are mentioned repeatedly as useful tools in reaching a working-class audience.

John McGrath warns against an assumption that this audience is less sophisticated than middle-class theatre-goers: indeed, he suggests that this is a very sophisticated audience, yet one that does not share middle-class expectations: 'it is the sophistication of the audience of the folk tales, able to shift ground with ease, if given secure guidance' (McGrath 1981: 29).

Some companies, in their desire to be 'popular' drew on forms of entertainment that already existed in working-class venues, while infusing them with 'radical' content. This included reference to the performance styles of entertainers such as Chuck Berry and Little Richard. Others drew on older forms, such as music hall, pantomime and comedy. Joan Littlewood's Theatre Workshop, for example, presented *Oh, What a Lovely War!* (1963), basing it on the Pierrot shows of the early twentieth century, incorporating popular songs of the First World War and setting these elements against stark, projected documentary material. McGrath's company, 7:84, drew on the Scottish form of the ceilidh, when presenting their 1973 production, *The Cheviot, the Stag and the Black, Black Oil*, which toured to venues in rural Scotland.

On the other hand, there was an interesting tension between the use of these traditional, 'popular' forms, and reference to newer, 'populist' forms, drawn from films and television. For example, David Edgar, writing for agitprop company, The General Will, argued that 'populist' forms had more currency among working-class audiences. His *The National Interest* (1971), referenced gangster movies in depicting the first year of the Conservative government, showing Tory gangsters manipulating tiny model workers.

Companies also discovered that work had to be direct, energetic and full of 'pace and movement', which McGrath compares to the complex and fast plot developments of film scripts (McGrath 1981: 31). Ronald Muldoon, of CAST, comments that, 'We soon learned that we had to work fast, cut fast, to get at least a laugh a minute, if we were to stop the bastards going for a beer in the middle of it' (quoted in Itzin 1980: 14). The AgitProp Street Players (later Red Ladder) gave performances for GLC tenants' committee meetings on rent problems, drawing on melodrama and music hall in sketches that aimed to articulate an account of the struggle so far. Kathleen McCreery remembers:

> The sketches had to be short, twelve to fifteen minutes was the maximum since they had to be fitted into the tenants' meeting – first restriction. With so little time to say anything, they had to be simple in the extreme: we could only put over a few ideas, clearly. Subtlety and

development of characters was out. They had to be topical and flexible since the situation of the tenants was changing constantly ... The criterion was: did it help the struggle or did it not? (Quoted in Itzin 1980: 41)

These companies adopted dramaturgies drawn from working-class culture, or which seemed to sit well within working-class contexts, using them to express a political content. While the term 'radical populism' is effective in describing this strategy, it may suggest, but does not precisely capture, an important tension between overtly propagandist political forms and forms that were imagistic, celebratory and carnivalesque. Kershaw suggests that British agitprop of the 1960s and 1970s differed from the agitprop of Germany, Russia or even Britain earlier in the century, suggesting that this 'new form of agitprop', was 'inflected by irony' and was therefore 'a principal route along which carnivalesque celebration and agitprop protest could meet' (Kershaw 1992: 81).

Kershaw describes this as 'carnival agitprop', proposing that companies of the period can be placed on a continuum between these two terms, where at the furthest points The People Show and early Welfare State could be primarily associated with 'carnival', and CAST and Red Ladder primarily with 'agitprop'.

For example, in contrast to the AgitProp Street Players' sketches for the tenants' associations, or their later, more sophisticated work as Red Ladder, based on issues concerning women at work (see below), the NHS, unemployment, industry and nuclear arms (Red Ladder 2006:1–2), Welfare State created works such as *The Loves, Lives and Murders of Lancelot Barrabas Quail* (1977), which told a simple story using giant puppets in an open-air performance, placing this within a circle of tents offering surreal and beautiful tableaux, a film, music, tea and hot potatoes (Coult and Kershaw 1983: 10–11).

Even at these ends of the spectrum, Kershaw suggests that these companies may be better understood if we appreciate the contemporary connection between carnival and agitprop, where the 'implicit opposition' of the former emerges in relation to the 'explicit opposition' of the latter (Kershaw 1992: 82).

For example, Kershaw's term helps us to understand that Welfare State, while emerging from the ambience of Albert Hunt's Bradford Art College and clearly creating celebratory spectacle and carnivalesque forms, can also be positioned in relation to agitprop, the dramaturgy of explicit political protest. As director John Fox explains, the company did, on occasion, 'lash out with propaganda in carnival guise', though usually preferring 'to make our politics more oblique and implicit' (Fox

2002: 34). When seeking to involve whole communities in celebratory events, these sometimes contained political themes or were constructed as elements of a specific protest. On the other hand, their primary political impact was the communal creative experience, which in itself proposed an alternative to conventional social relations: 'One objective of our big-scale community events is for participants to gain some control over their lives by accessing their creative potential and taking to the streets together' (Fox 2002: 34).

Kershaw's term challenges the reading offered by other commentators (he cites David Edgar and John Bull [Kershaw 1992: 68]), who have suggested that the 'alternative' theatre of the 1970s was divided into two camps, one characterized by celebratory aesthetics, the other by political commitment. The two terms each imply a set of formal strategies, from the anarchic disruption, 'topsy-turvydom' and spectacle of 'carnival', to the concise, explicit and direct political address of 'agitprop'. By bringing these terms together, Kershaw articulates a relationship, proposing that these strategies are complementary and related, rather than contradictory and distinct.

'Brechtian Dramaturgy' and 'State-of-the-Nation' Plays

David Hare's *Fanshen* (1975), written for Joint Stock, is an interesting transitional piece between the early agitprop and later political plays staged in subsidized theatres. It is also interesting in that it invites us to consider the idea of a British 'Brechtian dramaturgy'. Hare's play, an adaptation of William Hinton's novel about the Chinese revolution, is often compared to Brecht's work, both because of its theme and because there are clearly formal similarities (use of placards, epic structure, presentational style of performance and so on). However, despite its subject matter, Hare's version of Hinton's expressly Marxist novel is not itself fundamentally based in a Marxist ideology.

What did inspire its politics? To answer this, we need to be aware of the group's commitment to a democratic ideal. During the 1970s, political thinking about process and participation affected the organization of theatre companies themselves. For some, this meant an element of collaborative authorship, particularly in more visually based, agitprop work. Others, like Joint Stock, worked with a designated author, yet aimed to open up the writing process in some way. For example, Joint Stock involved the actors in research and workshopping, prior to a separate writing process. Through this work on *Fanshen*, the company made the decision to become a collective, responding to the play's questions about group organization and decision-making.

Hare wrote *Fanshen* after initial explorations with the company, during which 'the actors flung themselves at whatever bit they fancied, more or less in whatever style they fancied'. He comments: 'In shaping the play, I was very little influenced by any particular discovery in the workshop, but I was crucially affected by its spirit' (Hare, cited in Ritchie 1987: 108). He clarifies director Bill Gaskill's sense of responsibility towards the Chinese peasants, before adding:

> Although the subject-matter of the play was political, the instincts of the company were in essence moral. We were not revolutionaries ... In making *Fanshen*, none of us believed that we could duplicate the overturning we described. We knew any form of change here was bound to be different. But we all admired the revolution, and shared an obligation to describe it in a way of which its people would approve. The adoption of a rehearsal process based on the Chinese political method of 'Self-Report, Public Appraisal' might, in other hands, and with other material, have degenerated into a gimmick. But here it had weight and was surprisingly quick and effective. The self-criticism was real. (Hare, cited in Ritchie 1987: 108)

In searching for their own connections with the politics of the work, Hare and the company created a play about the moral and social issues of democratic process. In doing so, they revolutionized their own working process, but remained without unequivocal commitment to revolutionary socialism or the confident reference to Marxist thinking that underpins Brecht's work. Thus, although seemingly the most 'Brechtian' of early political theatre, and though certainly political in the questions it raises, *Fanshen* is in some ways typical of British political theatre, in its lack of allegiance to a specifically revolutionary socialist programme in Britain.

British political theatre did not grow out of a strong revolutionary worker's movement. Although it was founded in the envisioned alternatives of a counter-culture, this counter-culture was, as Kershaw observes, 'not at all programmatic' (Kershaw 1992: 80). Edgar, writing in 1978, comments on the problem this presented for British political theatre: 'the absence of a consequent mass revolutionary *culture* has obviated the growth of new theatrical forms ... The work of Brecht did not drop off the trees' (Edgar 1979: 29).

Hare's adaptation of *Fanshen* sought to make it relevant to a UK context and, in doing so, one could argue that he was following Brecht's example. Edgar, too, was influenced by Brecht's approach to adaptation and several of his late 1970s works were adaptations of biographies or novels. Painter places Edgar's adaptations in the historical context of work by Meyerhold, Piscator and Brecht, commenting:

> The strategy is that of intertextual commentary to assist analysis of history in relation to the present. A related point is surely that the individual's voice ... becomes a collective voice in the subsequent theatre collaborations, further rejecting the individualist position of our Conservative age. (Painter 1996: 53)

Edgar's *Nicholas Nickleby* (1980), implicitly questions Dickens' optimistic vision of the philanthropic capitalist, exemplified by the Cheeryble family. This immensely successful adaptation for the Royal Shakespeare Theatre Company was developed through a process similar to that of *Fanshen*, involving the company in its early exploration. Edgar commented, in 1980: 'It's not a personal statement; it's Dickens having been passed through a filter of 45 people and written down by me' (Edgar, quoted in Painter 1996: 69). The adaptation ends with the challenge presented by the 'new Smike', a small boy stranded in the snow; Nickleby steps out of the idealized Christmas card picture of the closing moments, to hold the boy up to the audience. Edgar comments: 'He is ... asking the audience the question as to whether the Cheerybles can exist, whether actually the solution is to be found in individual philanthropy, and the message of the adaptation is, no, it probably isn't' (Edgar, quoted in Painter 1996: 73).

Edgar, who began his career in journalism, has always drawn on documentary research in order to write his dramas. His early involvement with agitprop gradually gave way to a desire to work on an epic scale and with richer characterization. His term for his own dramaturgy is 'faction' (e.g. Reinelt 2004; Edgar 2007): real events become a model for a fictional story, in which the characters are caught up in recognizable social and political events. For instance, *Destiny* (1976) was based on two years of research and presents characters in a series of representative situations, in order to examine the roots of fascism in contemporary British culture.

Edgar has proposed, 'a synthesis ... of the surface perception of Naturalism and the social analysis that underlies Agitprop plays' (Edgar cited in Innes 2002: 182), which might enable a representation of individual psychologies (as in naturalism) in relation to sharply drawn social structures, based on real situations (as in agitprop). Plays such as *Destiny* and *May Days* (1983) are full of political speeches, but they do not carry an unambiguous political message. They examine, rather than exemplify, the dramaturgy of political rhetoric. Edgar's interest in the human predicament in tension with a political programme perhaps inevitably leads towards an exploration of ambivalence, contradiction and ideological crisis in relation to political activism. This is clearly demonstrated in *May Days*, in which the central characters shift from left-wing to right-wing politics. On the other hand, feminist companies adopted similar dramaturgical strategies, with quite different effects, seeing this tension (between personal and public) as the very location of political struggle and change (see below).

Yet, in many ways, *May Days* exemplifies a shift towards a somewhat more introspective approach to political theatre, mirroring the changing political circumstances, as it became clear that the revolution would not take place. It is representative of a series of 'state-of-the-nation' plays, which, as the term suggests, attempted to articulate a panoramic vision, often a pessimistic one, of contemporary society. Others, for example, were Brenton's *Weapons of Happiness* (1976), or Brenton and Hare's *Pravda* (1985).

As Brenton suggests, the excitement of 1968 gave way to disillusionment, sooner for some than others:

> I think what happened was that we did write a lot of good plays in the '70s and '80s because my generation came out of the '60s and knew clearly that the revolution wasn't going to happen in France. And then you'd think well, what's your relationship with the whole of this business? ... And so you began to write about that. We all wrote several plays about it. All of us did. And it became a theme. You were trying to understand the nature of the world, this distorted and blocked world and so you wrote Cold War plays, in fact ... Which meant they had quite broad appeal. (Brenton 2001: 12)

And so, as the 1970s progressed, British socialist theatre, at least within the subsidized London venues, tended to examine the position of the politically committed individual in the context of an alien political climate, striking a note of frustration, rage and disappointment, rather than political optimism. While it might demonstrate a Brechtian aesthetics, it lacked the Berliner Ensemble's buoyant confidence. The 'grand narrative' of Marxism was no longer tenable, nor could it be replaced. Rather, the narratives of different constituencies began to emphasize the plurality and hybridity of contemporary culture.

'Socialist Feminism' and a New 'Dialectical Dramaturgy'

It may be that we find a more truly 'Brechtian' dramaturgy in a theatre that took issue with some aspects of Brecht's own politics. Socialist feminism both challenged Brechtian thinking and responded to its political urgency and the strategies for making the theatre an instrument for change.

The term 'socialist feminism' is used to refer to the dominant strand of feminist thinking in Britain during the 1970s, which was strongly allied to a socialist/Marxist philosophy. While the term is descriptive of a tendency, and does not do justice to the wide variety of feminist traditions (as we shall see later), it is useful in that it identifies work that has emerged from the political theatre groups and traditions discussed earlier in this chapter. Women's theatre groups were gradually formed as a desire to focus on women's empowerment and concerns suggested a need to break with the existing companies. Useful accounts of the development of feminist theatre, including its appearance in the early twentieth century, can be found in Aston and Reinelt (2000).

Feminist companies were developing an idea that had emerged during the 1960s, that 'the personal is political'. As they opened up questions of individual identity they increasingly required a different form of theatre from the early 'carnival agitprop' – one in which the individual and the domestic were given greater prominence – and perhaps one that tended increasingly towards more formal diversity, reflecting the various concerns and backgrounds of its artists and audiences.

Socialist feminism, 'seeks to locate oppression in terms of the complex matrix of gender, class, race, ideology etc., and identify the historical sitings of such oppressions in order to radically transform society' (Aston 1995: 73). Given its origins in socialist theatre groups, early feminist work reflected many of the same dramaturgical tendencies that have already been mentioned – the use of agitprop and similar forms for political rallies, for instance.

As with the other political groups, Brecht was a major influence. While Red Ladder was never an exclusively feminist company, *Strike While the Iron is Hot* is an example of early feminist drama. Created collectively, it is itself a reworking of Brecht's *Die Mutter*, linking the socialist politics of that play with the economics of domestic life. Janelle Reinelt (1996: 40) describes its use of concrete physical images to demonstrate political perspectives as 'gestic' in the Brechtian sense. For example, in one scene, pint and half-pint glasses are used to demonstrate the relative rates of pay both between men and between the sexes (all the women have half-pint glasses). While Brecht's play moves the 'mother' out from her domestic setting into the political arena, Red Ladder brings these two loci together, adjusting the balance in an attempt to demonstrate that 'the personal is political'.

Both Elin Diamond (1988) and Reinelt (1994) have discussed the ways in which feminism has used Brechtian techniques to expose the construction of gender and the norms of representation. Perhaps the best-known example of this (and one cited by both critics) is Caryl Churchill's *Cloud 9* (1978). In Act One of this play, which is set in colonial Africa, the character of Betty is played by a man; Joshua, a black servant, is played by a white actor and Edward, the young boy, is played by a young woman. Through this combining of roles with bodies that do not match our expectations, Churchill 'makes strange' the demands that are laid on each character by the society they inhabit. It is suggested that Betty and Joshua have each internalized the values of the white patriarchy. Hence, each is played by a white man: one in drag; one, in effect, in an imaginary 'blackface'. However, the logic operates a little differently in the case of Edward, whose female body suggests, somewhat problematically, an 'inner' reality that refuses to conform to expectation and – again problematically – there seems an implication that his 'femininity' is somehow associated with his latent homosexuality, potentially confusing gender identity with sexual difference. Despite this, the play undoubtedly alerts the audience to the performativity and incongruity of social roles (often with great comic effect); as Diamond puts it, it enables the spectator 'to see a sign system *as* a sign system' (Diamond 1988: 85).

Gillian Hanna of Monstrous Regiment also cites Brecht's influence in terms of acting style (Hanna 1978: 7), suggesting that a kind of 'meshing' of Stanislavskian emotional memory with Brechtian epic acting enables an acting style that can both embody the personal and present it in its historical/social context. Reinelt comments of this, 'thus the feminist critique of the division between private and public concerns leads in the direction of both a new dramaturgy and a revised acting style' (Reinelt 1996: 46).

Despite Reinelt's suggestion that this work articulates a 'new dramaturgy', its structures have elements in common with Edgar's work, discussed above, and we would argue that much of this work can be framed by its references to a 'Brechtian dramaturgy', using many of its techniques and indeed, taking a dialectical approach to Brecht's own brand of Marxism. One could perhaps call it a 'feminist epic drama-turgy', or 'dialectical dramaturgy'. On the other hand, 'socialist feminist dramaturgy' is the more familiar, and perhaps therefore a more useful, term, and has the advantage of claiming its own distinct identity.

'Radical Feminism' and the Discussion of a 'Women's' Dramaturgy

As mentioned earlier, the term 'socialist feminism' does not do justice to the full spectrum of feminist positions. Indeed, in the United States, 'radical feminism' has been more dominant and it certainly has had an influence in the UK. These different strands of feminism have tended towards different approaches to defining new dramaturgies.

British socialist feminist theatre tends, like other British socialist the-atres, to be based on the play text, albeit ones that may seek out new ways of negotiating their contexts and contents. Radical feminism may also embrace the play text but has tended to generate more debates about theatre form and, specifically, a language or aesthetics particular to women. This is because radical feminism begins with the idea that the underlying cause of women's oppression is that society is based on patriarchal values, rather than seeing this oppression as rooted in an economic system reliant on a range of inequalities. It therefore sees it as necessary to prioritize women's experience as *distinct* from that of men, rather than to work alongside men to transform the multiple inequities of the existing social system. It proposes a feminist counter-culture, whereas socialist feminism proposes to transform the mainstream.

This is, of course, a simplification. As Wandor points out, most the-atrical works (and most feminists) do not unproblematically fall within one or other of these feminisms, but display a complex mix of attitudes and approaches, even where one appears to dominate (Wandor 2001: 147). While radical feminists have been criticized for suggesting an ahistorical and essentialist approach, most feminists have found it nec-essary to engage in counter-cultural strategies and to explore feminist alternatives to mainstream traditions. Writer Deborah Levy helps to clarify a potential shared position:

> If you talk about a female language for the theatre, all you're really talking about is attention, not intention. It's where your attention is as a writer. A

lot of women's writerly attention is in a very different place from that of male writers. (Levy 1993: 228)

One project that has brought together a wide range of women practitioners is the Magdalena Project formed by Jill Greenhalgh in 1986, originally based in Cardiff, but providing an international forum for women from all over the world (the project is documented by Bassnett 1996b and Fry 2007). The emphasis is on 'experimental' work, and Susan Bassnett comments: 'It became clear that whilst the traditional theatre had been going through a process of 'feminisation' with the advent of the women's movement, albeit on a very low level, the experimental theatre world had not undergone anything similar' (Bassnett 1987a: 227). It depends, of course, on what work is defined as 'experimental' and perhaps Bassnett overstates the case a little when she writes, in 1987, that, 'women playwrights have still not begun to question the play as a form' (Bassnett 1987a: 226). However, one of the project's initial aims was to '[articulate] the problem of whether there might indeed be some specifically female form of theatre that has never come into existence, but which might have been latently there through all the centuries of patriarchal domination' (Bassnett 1987a: 226).

Though no consensus emerged from the first (or even subsequent) events, this is perhaps not surprising, given the wide range of practitioners embraced in its original remit. Nevertheless, the project was, and continues to be, enormously stimulating and nourishing for women practitioners all over the world.

Radical feminism has explored (and continues to explore) the difficulties surrounding the use of language itself. French feminist Julia Kristeva differentiates between the 'semiotic' and the 'symbolic', where the 'semiotic' is defined as those pre-linguistic elements of expressivity (connected to the body) that precede the entry into the patriarchal 'symbolic' order of written language. Others, such as Hélène Cixous and Luce Irigaray, use this idea to propose a form of specifically female writing, or *écriture féminine*, which positions itself between the semiotic and the symbolic, drawing on the former in order to destabilize the symbolic through a range of strategies, including gaps, erasures, stutters, repetition and word-play. In performance, language may be further destabilized by the ways in which other 'texts' or 'textures' are deployed – the body, the voice, the instability of the performed identity and so on.

Within the UK, the influence of this thinking on feminist theatres of the 1980s and 1990s was most clearly seen in feminist work that contained a strong physical or visual dimension. The relationship between feminism, writing and devised work is discussed in Oddey (1998),

MacDonald (2000) and Heddon and Milling (2006); it is apparent that an interest in problematizing patriarchal linguistic and representational strategies was closely allied to, though not identical with, an interest in devised work – or, more commonly, in work where a writer worked in close relationship with a group to develop a new text. Devised work enabled women to find a collective voice, but it also lent itself to the development of non-verbal theatricality. Companies such as Scarlet Harlots (later Scarlet Theatre), Blood Group and, after them, Foursight Theatre are all devising companies, which have emphasized physical and visual imagery in exploring feminist themes. Blood Group's director, Anna Furse, 'was keen to explore the possibility of a "feminine" theatre language', focusing on 'the potential "language" of the (female) body' in performances such as DIRT (1983), which explored the relationship between the sex industry and theatrical acting (Heddon and Milling 2006: 87).

Levy is a writer whose 'practice evolved in the theatre space through a process of dialogue with the other participants in the theatre-making process – directors, performers, designers and composers' (MacDonald 2000: 240). She has acknowledged the influence of Kristeva and Cixous in her plays of the early 1990s (Levy 2000: viii). Her play, *The B-File*, was written in response to a workshop she led for the Magdalena Project in 1991, which was framed by three questions:

1. B is feeling homesick in her own home. Where does she want to be?
2. B is missing someone she's never met. Who is this person?
3. B wants to be someone else. Who does she want to be? (Levy 2000: 83)

While Levy hints at the 'formal ensemble choreographic sequences' of the first production (Levy 2000: 83), the published text leaves such possibilities open to new directors and performers. In the script, the protagonist, Beatrice, or B, is played by five different actresses and her identity is constantly shifting and questioned by the other Bs. The five Bs speak in different languages, take it in turns to act as 'Interpretor' and propose different versions of the character:

Interpretor: Is Beatrice a character?

If she is a character, is she dressed for the part?

Is Beatrice a persona?

If she is a persona, what are her voices?

One of the Bs gives [B3] a microphone.

B3:	Gracias.
B4:	My pleasure. *(Exits to the side.)*
B3:	Mi manca la persona che non homai incontracto.
Interpretor:	She says she is missing someone she has never met. Who is this person?
B3:	This person is Beatrice.

(Levy 2000: 92)

Levy comments, in 1993: 'How we invent ourselves will always be a major theme in my work' (Levy 1993: 226). While not exclusively associated with feminism, the concern with the construction of the self continues to be a driving force in creating new dramaturgies. If Levy's work disperses a persona across five women's bodies, voices and creativity, we might notice that in Sarah Kane's 'open' dramaturgy, as discussed in Chapter 1, the lack of clearly identified speakers challenges us to locate the boundaries of identity. Within explicitly 'political' dramaturgies, new forms have emerged in response to the problems of constructing social or collective identities, as we shall see in the next section.

'Cultural Hybrids'

Claire MacDonald's trilogy of 1989, *Utopia*, suggests the ways in which we use language to construct ourselves and our stories, despite its inadequacies. Throughout this trilogy, the action consists of an anonymous man and a woman in a hotel room, narrating stories through which they dream up an imaginary world. This world is created and destroyed through words alone. The woman suggests the importance of this struggle with text:

Woman:	She recognises it as a system, of course, but what she tries to tell him, painfully and with some difficulty it now seems, is that it may all be constructed – masculine, feminine, desire, sex – but you still have to live with it, and even in dreams, actions have consequences. They can get away from everything – almost. They can change all the rules – almost. They can hack it to pieces and end up in the burnt-out garden, BUT – they'll still be Adele and Bishop, still male and female. They can't change that. In the end, that's all there is, isn't there?

(MacDonald 1992 [1989]: 180)

The two characters are as anonymously 'man' and 'woman' as possible, in an anonymous, bland hotel room that could be in any country. Yet they can't alter the fact that they are 'man' and 'woman', they can only replay, reassess and renegotiate what that means, through the displaced selves of their own writing.

What does the word 'woman' mean? Theorists such as Judith Butler (Butler 1990, 1993) and others have questioned the very construction of the category 'woman', which is unable to describe the range of identities it is presumed to stand for. Ethnic, sexual and gender and class identities, among others, may be in conflicting relationship with one another. On the other hand, a temporary and provisional acceptance of a collective term may be useful in attempting to critique the social situation in which one finds oneself.

For example, the very existence of 'gay theatre' has been more-or-less continuously threatened. In such a cold climate, a collective identity may prove crucial and offer its own challenges. When theatre censorship ended in Britain, in 1968, it was suddenly permissible to make openly gay characters and relationships central to the drama. An important aspect of gay theatre has, since then, been the exploration of what kinds of narrative might or could be presented, from the shocking images of death camps in US writer Martin Sherman's *Bent* (1978), through the examination of a public school outcast in Julian Mitchell's *Another Country* (1981), via another American writer, Larry Kramer's, polemical, AIDS-related play, *The Normal Heart* (1985) to the celebratory warmth of Jonathan Harvey's *Beautiful Thing* (1993) to Mark Ravenhill's *Mother Clapp's Molly House* (2001) and beyond (historical accounts can be found in Osment 1989, De Jongh 1992 and Freeman 1997).

Most of the above plays (excluding Ravenhill's) adopt broadly socialist realist dramaturgies. However, for many, it is important to develop new forms with which to challenge the very assumptions, categories and groupings implicit in performance, both within and beyond the theatre. Thus, while Michael Billington wonders about the lack of gay plays in British theatre (2006), gay and lesbian live art is thriving. Live art, as opposed to theatre, tends towards a greater flexibility of form and context, and is less markedly associated with fictional characterization, moving easily between the 'authentic' and the artificial or theatrical. We find, within this broad area, a range of potential dramaturgies that invite the exploration and critique of sexual and gender identities.

One example of this is the use of drag, where the drag persona is presented as 'authentic' (i.e. not as a fictional character). At its most challenging, drag exposes 'the under-stated, taken-for-granted quality of heterosexual performativity' (Butler 1993: 237), by exaggerating and destabilizing the behaviours usually associated with femininity (or masculinity). Butler describes this as an example of 'hyperbolic cita-tion', a way of taking possession of oppressive stereotypes, in order to oppose them. This strategy, which has been employed by many solo lesbian and gay performers (often drawing on night club and cabaret traditions) is in many ways similar to Churchill's strategy of cross-dressing her characters in *Cloud 9*. However, a performer such as Lois Weaver is in charge of her own role-playing in a way that is not pre-sumed of an actress; thus her (lesbian femme) persona, Tammy Whynot, becomes more complex in its meshing of parody and self-expressive possibility.

Rosi Braidotti uses the notion of the 'nomadic subject' to suggest an exploration of gender that doesn't settle on a signifying label ('woman') but moves through layers of identity, looks at their interrelation: 'nomadic consciousness consists in not taking any kind of identity as permanent. The nomad is only passing through ... The nomad has no passport – or has too many of them' (Braidotti 1994: 33). This idea takes us to notions of hybridity, rather than the statement of a singular position. This has proved important, not only to feminism, or to gay and lesbian performance, but to the acknowledgement of hybrid cul-tural identities, which have also opened up new dramaturgies and con-tinue to do so.

A performance such as Stacey Makishi's *Fold* (2001) explores a spec-trum of identities, destablizing language in her narration of a story in which a young girl, Jamie Fukuda, grows up as a lesbian in Hawaii. When *Fold* was reworked to become part of Apples and Snakes' *Writers on the Storm* (2002) it entered into a fourfold work whose interweaving structure was musical as well as thematic. Hawaiian Creole and Standard English (with an American accent) met the accents of the Caribbean, London and Dublin (by way of Sweden and the United States) in the poetry of Crisis, Aoife Mannix and Patrick Neate. This musicality made its own political point, suggesting the fluidity of the English language and its transformation across cultures.

Within *Fold*, Makishi's use of language further explores its fluidity and transformational power. She not only slips between Creole and Standard English, but also makes her words slip between meanings, just as she transforms objects, folding pillowcases into origami chickens, injecting eggs with dye. Just as she can fold her arm, or her leg to show us the 'fold' of the vagina, so individual words ('chick', 'cock', 'rainbow') can be made to keep shifting their significance. For instance, the narrator, Iris, is clearly the 'eye' that sees. She is also the 'I' that speaks. She explains to us that Iris also means 'rainbow' and so Iris becomes identified with the rainbow, an image of diversity. Makishi's poetic work demonstrates the ways in which recent performance has brought together influences from queer theory, feminist theory and cultural theory to examine hybrid identities, rather than settling on a straightforward identification with a single category – black, female, lesbian and so on.

Those who identify themselves as black British, and/or British-Asian already position themselves *between* or *on the border* of two (or more) cultures. These terms, of course, are not without their own difficulties. Our use of black British as a broad term to include all British citizens of African and Asian descent reflects common UK practice, but risks generalization. Our occasional uses of the more specific terms, British Asian or British Afro-Caribbean do not avoid generalization either. Since the establishment of companies devoted to black British work in the 1970s and 1980s, there has been an increasing interest in hybridity. Terms such as 'intercultural performance' and 'cross-cultural performance' are problematic: the latter is potentially reductive, suggesting that cultures are distinct and separate identities, while the former, at worst, can imply dubious notions of 'universality'. 'Cultural hybridity', on the other hand, is helpful in suggesting the complexity of identities formed out of a range of different cultural contexts, which, while specific, are not necessarily unaffected by each other.

Yet this difficult negotiation between the importance of understanding both difference and relationship is the subject of much debate and controversy. According to Jatinder Verma, speaking in 1991, 'If there is going to be any point in using the term "black theatre", it has to find a theatrical form for itself' (quoted in Osborne 2006: 27). Felix Cross, in 1998 suggested that, 'it is only when black theatre develops something white theatre doesn't have that it will have the power and influence to move forward' (quoted in Osborne 2006: 27). A London Arts Board paper, 'Going Black Under the Skin' (Craze 1995), documents a New Playwright's Trust Project, 'Black Voices for the New Millennium' and suggests, again, the need to recognize the characteristics of a 'black dramaturgy', that might essentially differ from the norms of 'white dramaturgy'.

This paper pulls together a number of characteristics of black work, suggesting that black dramaturgy tends towards 'circular', rather than 'linear' structures, affecting its presentation of time, space and community; Bonnie Greer is cited as suggesting that Derek Walcott's use of stage time is experienced as circular and that this 'introduces a quite different dynamic to Western dramaturgy and instantly creates a tension which must make for hybridisation' (Craze 1995: 13).

All these notions, of course, like those concerning a 'women's drama-turgy', are problematic, if they tend towards generalization, either by tending to treat black experience as homogeneous, or by tending to exclude black practitioners from supposedly 'white' dramaturgies.

Alternatively, Dimple Godiwala identifies British-Asian theatre as 'one of hybridity' and lists a number of strategies exploited by British-Asian artists, which serve to challenge existing formal conventions. Many of these are paralleled in other black theatres, for instance, those referencing Afro-Caribbean experience. For example, they include the fusing of conventional British theatre forms with popular forms from black cultures, such as 'Bollywood' kitsch or Trinidadian carnival. British-Asian theatre also draws on the traditional performances and lit-erature of ancient India, while African rituals, histories and traditions inform the work of writers such as Felix Cross. Companies such as Tara Arts have revisioned classics such as Shakespeare's *A Midsummer Night's Dream* (c. 1595), while Mustapha Matura recently recontextualized Chekhov's play of 1900, in his *The Three Sisters* (2006), setting it in the Caribbean. Standard English use is sometimes challenged by the use of Indian languages or 'nation language' from the Caribbean alongside, or in hybrid forms, with English.

However, we must be wary of assuming that the idea of 'cultural hybridity' solves all our problems in attempting to name emerging dra-maturgies, since Bharucha also warns against the potential for valorizing 'hybridity', 'displacement' and 'migration' as essential aspects of 'the postmodern condition', which can lead to a dismissal of those who either do not, or cannot migrate (Bharucha 2000). Nevertheless, an explo-ration of the ways in which form can mirror a sense of hybrid identity has become increasingly important within British performance.

In her essay, 'Keep On Running: The Politics of Black British Performance', Catherine Ugwu (Ugwu 1995: 54) suggests that live art has offered the most radical possibilities for black performers, enabling them to 'own' their performances, present personal testimonies and break with the restrictions of established contexts for performance, pro-viding scope for the exploration of notions of hybridity and exchange, including a free movement between different genres, traditions, forms and spaces. Makishi's work, and that of many others, might be consid-ered in relation to this term, which is closely related to 'performance art', though seeming to resist the implicit theatricality of the latter.

It might be important to point out that the term 'live art' in UK arts practice has a distinct history and purpose. It became established through the necessity of describing forms of performance or art that could not easily be accommodated under the existing Arts Council England categories: 'Drama', 'Visual Arts', 'Dance' and so on. 'Live art' was established, paradoxically enough, as a category that resists the limits of categorization. The multiplicity and flexibility of practices implied by the term might best allow the fluid movement between identity positions, an exploration of cultural performance and performativity and a destabilization of existing forms of representation.

One of the many artists Ugwu refers to is Ronald Fraser-Munro. Within all his work, Fraser-Munro's playfulness and the mix of media is at one with his avowed aim, to reach a younger, non-theatre-going audience. This is one of the reasons why he deliberately cites role-play games and other digital imagery – avoiding the division between 'popular' and 'high' culture.

Fraser-Munro has explored a range of contexts for his work, from the theatre to the Internet to live, improvised interaction with the public. Much of it involves the 'hyperbolic citation' of media stereotypes of white and upper-class oppression. In *Quack FM* (1994) he plays a variety of roles, including that of a Klan member; he has performed as a Nazi, as a landowner and has frequently occupied the role of Catholic priest. Insofar as these stereotypes are defined by their exclusion of black identity, his enactments are immediately 'readable' as ironic. On the other hand, his occupation of these roles is double-edged, producing a powerful effect by borrowing their modes of authority and aggression.

'New Dramaturgy'

Political theatre in Britain continues to take many forms and any narrative of its development is bound to leave unacknowledged the full range of trajectories from the 1960s to the present. We may also become blinkered by ideas of forward progression, tending to overlook the work that continues to explore well-established but not discredited strategies. However, we tentatively suggest that whereas the dominant political dramaturgy of the 1960s and 1970s tended to be based in notions of a collective movement, grounded in socialist ideology, we have increasingly seen an emphasis on the plural and on the individual (and perhaps still more importantly, the individual body) as the site of political tension. The notion, significant in the 1960s, and of particular importance to feminism, that 'the personal is political', has led to the diffusion of politics through every aspect of cultural performance. There are many and complex reasons for these changes, which have occurred partly through the decline of socialist revolutionary politics globally and in Britain, partly through the desire to acknowledge a spectrum of shifting identity positions and partly through postmodernist critique of norms of representation and normalizing social constructs and conventions. As we have seen, it has been increasingly difficult to define our areas of enquiry, with terms such as 'cultural hybridity' and 'live art' attempting to open up areas that resist definition, to create a space for new ways of working. One might also mention 'performance writing' (Bergvall 1996, Allsopp 1999) as a term that seeks to acknowledge approaches to writing and performance that are outside the conventional limitations of genres such as 'playwriting', 'poetry' or 'literature'. Yet if there are new ways of working, we need to find ways of discussing them dramaturgically. For this reason, critics, dramaturgs and artists persist, despite the difficulties, in finding terms with which to describe the work that interests them.

For example, in looking at developments in the theatre, Hans-Thies Lehmann uses the term 'postdramatic' to describe work from which 'sense and synthesis has largely disappeared' (Lehmann 2006: 25) and which tends towards a subversion of traditional theatrical hierarchies. Lehmann's project is ambitious; although he dismisses the feasibility of creating a twentieth-century version of Lessing's *Hamburgische Dramaturgie*, openly declaring that Lessing's unifying project would be impossible today, he essentially attempts to gather a wide range of practices under this broad heading. The term 'postdramatic' is very close to the idea of 'postmodernist' theatre, but is more precise, in that it suggests a relationship (albeit an antithetical one) to the 'dramatic'. Admittedly, when one considers the broad spectrum of work gathered under this label, it comes to seem rather less precise, since Lehmann includes artists as diverse as Peter Brook, Pina Bausch, Tadeusz Kantor, Tadashi Suzuki, Complicite and Forced Entertainment (Lehmann 2006: 23–4). However Lehmann's work attempts to draw out threads of commonality between some of these late twentieth- and now twenty-first-century artists.

As discussed in Chapter 1, there have been other attempts to find terms for recent dramaturgies or 'new dramaturgies' that do not necessarily privilege the dramatic text. The apparent dissolution of hierarchies or, at least, fixed relationships, can sometimes, though not consistently or unproblematically, extend to working structures, and even to processes of analysis. For example, André Lepecki writes: 'In the new landscape, the choreographer claims a theoretical voice, the critic emerges as producer, the agent writes dance reviews, the philosopher tries some steps, the audience is invited to join as both students and practitioner' (Lepecki 2001: 29). We are thus reminded that, while we may try to define, encapsulate and categorize, this attempt could become ever more complex. Within postmodernist practices, roles and definitions are becoming increasingly blurred and in a constant process of redefinition and recontextualization.

There has been much debate about the political potential (or lack of it) within postmodernist theatre practices (Auslander 1992, Phelan 1993, Kershaw 1999 and Müller-Schöll 2004). If meaning itself is destabilized, how can such a theatre make any coherent statement, or intervene in any effective way? We might quote Lehmann's contention that theatre can 'deconstruct the space of political discourse ... through the dismantling of discursive certainties of the political' (Lehmann 2006: 177). While this raises the disquieting question as to whether the destabilizing of 'discursive certainties' actually produces a political effect, the work may perhaps offer, or confirm, alternative ways of imagining the world.

For instance, Desperate Optimists' *Play-boy* (1998) loosely connects stories of national identity and displacement, weaving these around the history of Synge's *Playboy of the Western World* (1907). While Desperate Optimists begin their performance by suggesting that they are going to tell us 'the facts', nothing in *Play-boy* can be described as an 'authoritative' utterance. Even in the seemingly authentic videos of friends and relations, the company invite their interviewees to make statements about a play that, as Joe Lawlor admits, some of them have never even seen. As the performance progresses, historical facts merge into fiction, one story displaces the next, fake blood appears on the performers' shirts, while on the video, a real gun goes off.

Synge's play was initially rejected because it was allegedly not *true to life*. It portrayed Irish people in a way that they repudiated as being inaccurate. Desperate Optimists' work seems to reject the very possibility of an accurate representation of a people, or of anything else. Instead, story-telling seems to become, as their publicity material suggests, 'a strategy for survival' and a way of critiquing the world without laying claim to it.

It is possible that such compositional logics suggest or require new modes of analysis. Maaike Bleeker, referencing Deleuze and Guattari, proposes a 'consideration of the interaction between stage and audience' in terms of *movement* (Bleeker 2003: 163). This, she writes, 'presents an alternative to representational thinking in which meaning is thought to result from the decoding of signs' (Bleeker 2003: 163). Meaning is considered, not as something that is static or fixed, but as something that 'takes place and results from the way the audience is moved by a performance or invited to move along with it or [is] even led astray' (Bleeker 2003: 163). The implication is that we might look for the politics of a work in terms of what it *does*, rather than what it *says*.

One could, for example, suggest that Desperate Optimists' work moves its audience between history and story, between the apparently real and the blatantly fake. It seems to invite us to take pleasure in this movement, to submit to uncertainty, to allow ourselves, with the characters in the stories, to be constantly displaced and wrong-footed. This is not, perhaps, a challenge to our political positioning, but rather to our sense of what a 'position' might be.

New dramaturgies, then, might suggest new ways of negotiating our roles as spectators and critics. This negotiation, this attempt to articulate and identify what we have witnessed, is itself a political act.

Part II

4 The Dramaturg and the Theatre Institution

In the first part of this volume, we discussed the concept of 'dramaturgy', seeing this as a term for the ways in which a performance work is composed and contextualized. We also suggested that it was connected with the ways in which one might try to articulate, analyse and name the strategies that are used in the construction of an artwork. Our conclusion was that it was intimately connected with the process of constructing a work and the interpretative analysis that was part of that process, and we cited Barba's metaphor of a 'weave' to suggest the way in which dramaturgy describes the integration of all the elements within a single work.

Although we have argued that 'dramaturgy' is not dependent on the existence of a dramaturg, in Part II, we turn our attention to this elusive figure. Writing in 1960, Günter Skopnik, then chief dramaturg at the Municipal Theatre in Frankfurt am Main, tells this anecdote:

> When Prince Schwarzenberg asked Heinrich Laube, the great Director of the Burgtheatre in Vienna, what a dramaturg really was, the latter could only answer hesitatingly and shrugging his shoulders 'Highness, that is what no one could tell you in a few words'. (Skopnik 1960: 233)

Laube hesitated, not because the dramaturg lacks specific responsibilities, but because there are many different ways of answering this question. Although we will attempt to sketch some broad areas of common concern, there are really as many different ways of operating as a dramaturg within a theatre process as there are processes or dramaturgs. Understanding is made still more elusive since the work of the dramaturg is not immediately visible to the public. As Lynn M. Thomson comments: 'dramaturgical skill is generally expressed in process, is about process, including those often undetectable contributions that transform moments in rehearsal or meeting rooms' (Rudakoff and Thomson 2002: 167). Nor is the role of the dramaturg without its problems and controversies. However, we must begin by reiterating the question, all the same, even if we know that there may be many answers and that they cannot be encapsulated in 'a few words'.

What is a Dramaturg?

In Chapter 1, we suggested that G. E. Lessing has often been called the first dramaturg. His role, as discussed in that chapter, was to act as an in-house critic and to advise the theatre on its artistic direction. Though Lessing also wrote plays in his own right, his role as dramaturg consisted of offering an intellectual and critical commentary *preceding* and *following* the performance, but not necessarily *accompanying* the process of making the performance. Thomson implies a distinction between dramaturg and critic: 'Lessing functioned essentially as a critic for the Hamburg National Theatre and was not involved as a dramaturg in theatre making' (Rudakoff and Thomson 2002: 165). Yet one could suggest that Lessing occupied a position *between* 'theatre making' and that theatre's reception. He tried to build bridges. Lessing's role as a public educator, his discussion of dramatic composition and vision for criticism was founded on his ambition to mediate between the work and the viewer, to help explain the work and the experience of the work.

However, if we think of Lessing as a dramaturg, we will need to be aware that he represents a particular kind of dramaturg: the dramaturg as critic and commentator within the theatre. He is, therefore, the precursor of those dramaturgs who play an important institutional role in advising on repertoire and representing the theatre institution to its audiences, and those who bring their skills as writers, editors and translators to the work of a theatre company.

In Chapter 2, we discussed Bertolt Brecht's dramaturgy, and the ways in which it necessitated a more collaborative involvement from the dramaturg. In *Der Messingkauf* Brecht gives us a portrait of a dramaturg, one which might be considered as an 'ideal' representation of the role. Brecht's dramaturg is a critical facilitator with an inherently collaborative sensibility, driven by an ideological commitment to realize the ideas of the philosopher in practical terms. He is described as someone who 'puts himself at the Philosopher's disposal and promises to apply his knowledge and abilities to the conversion of the theatre into the "*thaeter*" of the Philosopher. He hopes the theatre will get a new lease of life' (Brecht 1977: 10). While his commitment is ideological and philosophical, he is also represented as a repository of knowledge and information, who enters the discussion to offer analysis, concrete explanation and contextual framing of specific plays, aspects of theatre production and historical developments within the theatre. He makes a decisive step at the beginning of the work by moving the discussion out from the office full of unread scripts, onto the stage itself, seeming to propose that his own work is inextricably concerned with the live event. He also demonstrates that theatre itself can be used as an analytical tool. We may remember Adler's speculation, for the Berliner Ensemble, that 'everything is dramaturgy' (Adler 2005: 14). Brecht's theatre is, potentially, dialectical analysis in action.

As we have seen, Brecht's own use of the dramaturg, in practice, divided the various functions of the role between a number of different people, so that dramaturgs were sometimes concerned with research, sometimes with archival work, sometimes with press and education, sometimes with rehearsals for specific productions. While the dramaturg in *Der Messingkauf* is a composite figure, the dialogues do give a sense of the range of work and the overall function of his dramaturgs and Brecht's use of dramaturgs in rehearsal offered a prototype of the modern 'production dramaturg', a figure that became increasingly common in Germany during the 1970s and 1980s. This is the dramaturg as part of the production team, the dramaturg offering directorial support and practical collaboration.

Both Lessing and Brecht were, of course, German: their respective ideas of the role do not encompass all the possible functions of the German dramaturg, yet they frame the German understanding of dramaturgical practice. Nor are these figures the only significant dramaturgs in the history of the German-speaking theatre. From Schiller to significant contemporary figures such as Jens Hilje in Berlin, Carl Hegemann in Leipzig (formerly at the Berliner Volksbühne) and Wolfgang Wiens in Vienna, this theatre offers many examples to those enquiring into the work of the dramaturg. The role has a long history and has acquired its place in the structures of contemporary German theatre-making. The situation is very different in the UK and North America.

The dramaturg has originated within a particular set of working structures (those of the German theatre). This leads one to ask whether the role will have to be rethought or adapted to working structures in other cultural contexts. For instance, Anne Cattaneo reflects on the difference between the dramaturgs' working conditions at the Berliner

Schaubühne and her own: 'The theatre had a company available for a year of preparation – to research, think about and develop an interpretation. The dramaturg would gather a lot of information to start a process.' She continues, ruefully, 'What the dramaturgs did there is what I try to do here in the five weeks we usually have in American theatre' (Cattaneo 2002: 225–6). Esslin also stresses the significance of differences in the conditions under which work is created:

> Much more than the German Dramaturg who operates in a well-established structure, and above all, in a culture in which the theatre performs a well-defined and important social, cultural and political role, the American dramaturg not only has to do the basic job of finding and nurturing scripts, but has also to work hard on helping to create that basic cultural atmosphere in which a healthy theatre can operate. (Quoted in Jonas, Proehl and Lupu 1997: 27)

In some respects, such as the tendency towards short rehearsal periods, the UK theatre mirrors that of the US. Moreover, we often find that aspects of the dramaturg's role are shared between directors, programmers, education officers, marketing managers, literary managers, associate directors and others. As writer and lecturer Sarah Woods speculates, there can seem to be no room for the dramaturg (Woods 2005: 16). The title has only recently begun to be used and is often associated with the role of 'literary manager', itself a relatively new position. Given this association, there tends to be an assumption that the dramaturg is primarily involved with developing new writing, working closely with playwrights. Will this continue to be the dramaturg's principal role in the UK, or are the alternatives, already appearing, indicative of a new trend? Will UK practitioners prefer to define themselves as 'curators', 'creative producers' or as those providing 'an outside eye', while occupying roles that are comparable to those of dramaturgs elsewhere, or will the idea of the 'dramaturg' come to more prominence? What are the nuances of these particular terms and practices? These are not easy questions, but we seem to be seeing a growing understanding of the dramaturg's role, within an increasingly sophisticated discussion of its potential for development.

Across Europe and in North America and Australasia, there has been a push to extend the possibilities of dramaturgical practice. Dramaturgs are found working in devised theatre and across art-forms – for instance, in dance and live art practice. These newly defined 'production dramaturgs' have a rather different function from those working on theatre productions based on a dramatic script. For one thing, they may be significant in helping to articulate and structure a work that gradually finds its form through the rehearsal process. For another, they may need to possess a more acute awareness and understanding of different kinds of text – choreographic, sonic, spatial. We also find dramaturgs associated with programming new work across art-forms. Here, the role is closer to that of the 'curator' or the 'creative producer' in the UK. Notions of an expanded dramaturgy look beyond the conventional spaces for performance. Could one, for example, bring to city planning, notions of a 'dramaturgy' of public space?

If the job title 'dramaturg' covers a diversity of functions, we should also touch on the possibility that other theatre artists can, on occasion, be described as 'dramaturgs'. For instance, we have suggested that Caspar Neher might be considered as a visual dramaturg within Brecht's theatre. American director Anne Bogart describes her sound designer as the 'best dramaturg that I have ever had' (Bogart 2001: 35) and similarly Jean-Marc Adolphe proposes that when Dominique Bagouet, 'consulted Boltanski about *Le Saut de l'Ange*, Boltanski's contribution as a visual artist was to a large degree dramaturgical' (Adolphe 1998: 27). Is this a helpful use of the term? One might speculate that a 'true' dramaturg is not fully immersed in the creative process, but mediates between that process and its potential public, operating as a 'critical collaborator', or a 'creative critic'. However, there is a fine line between this and full creative engagement, since the artistic process itself involves moments of detachment and critique, while criticism may involve becoming temporarily engrossed in the work. Alternatively, one might suggest that the dramaturg is able to take an overview and to contribute to the conception of the whole. Yet it would be patronizing to suggest that other artists were unable to do this. Ultimately, it must be admitted that the dramaturg does not have a monopoly on 'doing dramaturgy' and that there are scenographers and sound designers who are particularly adept at contributing to dramaturgical analysis and development.

To return to our initial question will certainly be to admit that there is no definitive answer. However, we might attempt a provisional, multiple summary. In this multiplicity, perhaps, lies the excitement of the term. What, then, is a dramaturg?

The dramaturg may be someone who plays a key institutional role in the theatre, helping to develop policy and repertoire, while acting as critic, commentator and communicator. The dramaturg may be someone who brings analytical skills, knowledge and creative thinking to the preparation and rehearsal of a theatre production, offering support to the director and contributing to the understanding and structuring of the work as it evolves. The dramaturg may be someone appointed to a theatre that takes a particular interest in dramatic literature and could be responsible for translation, adaptation and even writing new work. The dramaturg may be a person who is concerned with the identification and development of new writing for the theatre. The dramaturg may be a 'creative critic' or a 'critical collaborator'. The dramaturg may be all these things or only one of them, or some of them. The dramaturg may be someone who brings some of these skills to devised theatre, dance or live art. The dramaturg could be a curator or a creative producer or a programmer. The dramaturg could be a sound artist. The dramaturg could be a city planner. The dramaturg could be a provocateur, a collaborator, an activist, a creator of networks. The dramaturg is bound to seek out new roles, expanding our sense of the many ways in which 'dramaturgical thinking' might be applied.

For the purpose of this book, we must reluctantly set aside some of the more speculative ideas about the role of the dramaturg, for consideration at another time. The next three chapters concentrate primarily on the function of the dramaturg in relation to the creative process itself. We naturally devote some space to discussing the dramaturg in relation to play – and playwright – development, since this is a very significant function in UK practice. Next, we consider the role of the 'production dramaturg', while going on to discuss the specific role of the dramaturg in devising.

Before we do so, however, it is important that we set the scene by considering the history of the dramaturg and the position in relation to the theatre institution. As we have suggested, the dramaturg may well be concerned with many other factors apart from the immediate process of developing, planning or rehearsing a specific play or performance and, for some dramaturgs, this institutional function may be their most significant one.

Depending on the particular country and context, there are many activities the dramaturg may undertake within a repertory theatre or other subsidized arts institution. The precise nature of the role will necessarily vary between organizations and from country to country, depending on the artistic team and working practices the particular context requires. It is therefore difficult to summarize the function of the institutional dramaturg; however, Cattaneo offers a useful starting point when she quotes Tony Hiss in suggesting that the dramaturg is 'someone who keeps the whole in mind' (Cattaneo 1997: 6). We will return to this idea.

Dramaturgs are increasingly appearing in varied capacities in the UK. Though many are freelance, they are also found in very diverse institutional contexts. For example, Edward Kemp as resident dramaturg at Chichester Festival Theatre (2003–5) brought skills as a writer and director to his involvement in discussions about repertoire, to making adaptations and translations, to writing new works on commission and to working as a dramaturg on productions of texts by past writers (Kemp 2005). Duska Radosavljevic, until recently worked between Northern Stage and Newcastle University as a production dramaturg assisting in devised work, teaching undergraduates and postgraduates and bringing the two institutions together through her development of the production context in terms of marketing, programming satellite events and developing educational activities. The Arnolfini Gallery and University of Bristol are mentoring and supervizing a postgraduate student, Ruth Holdsworth, who is examining the role of the dramaturg/ curator in the context of live art programming. There are also numerous people working as 'literary managers', whose work may often be comparable to that of some working as 'dramaturgs' in other countries: for example, Hanna Slättne, from Belfast's Tinderbox identifies herself as a 'dramaturg', as does the company's artistic director, though she is officially termed 'literary manager'. Slättne was one of the founders of the Dramaturg's Network, which provides a forum for dramaturgs to meet and to circulate information about their work.

Some of the key functions of the dramaturg within the subsidized arts institutions are also found in the work of freelance dramaturgs or dramaturgs within small independent arts organizations. However, if the dramaturg is someone who 'keeps the whole in mind', there are aspects of the institutional dramaturg's role that often extend beyond the 'whole' of the specific production or script to encompass the 'whole' that is the theatre organization itself, its context, its repertoire and its artistic policy. These deserve particular consideration and discussion, having been the cause of unease as well as of growing interest.

Politics and Artistic Policy

Some of the nervousness around the dramaturg relates to the identification of the role with the pursuit of a strict policy or agenda, whether reflecting personal tastes, an institutional mission, a wider notion of a 'national theatre', or government priorities. In the UK, a conference at the University of Bristol, 29–31 January 1999 that brought trainee dramaturgs and literary managers together with professional theatre practitioners was provocatively titled 'Mentors or Censors?' According to one of the organizers, Mary Luckhurst (others were David Edgar, Vicky Featherstone and Graham Whybrow) this title,

> encapsulated the suspicious polarising view of dramaturgs which many in the theatre profession have assumed: the dramaturg as dangerous controller (destroyer perhaps) of the writer's creativity; or the dramaturg as ideologue, secretly pressing their own agenda of what a play is or isn't. (Luckhurst 1999: 4)

The association of the dramaturg with ideas of censorship does have some historical grounding, though it should be stressed that this concern is greatly exaggerated in relation to contemporary practice, whether in the UK, mainland Europe or North America. Nonetheless, it is an interesting consideration, since it invites us to question where to draw the line between the *implementation* of an aesthetic strategy and the *imposition* of such a strategy. What or who legitimates the choices made when a dramaturg helps to shape a repertoire or develop a 'house style'? Should the dramaturg respond to public demand, to commercial considerations, to the theatre management's policy or to the funding bodies? Is the dramaturg's function partly to question and challenge the choices made by others, to support them, or to act according to personal aesthetic convictions? An institutional dramaturg may have to find their own answers to these questions.

Germany's key role in developing the idea of the dramaturg is not without its problematic aspects, particularly in relation to the idea of German nationalism. We have already mentioned Lessing's wish to help shape and define a distinctly German theatre identity or dramaturgy, both through his criticism and his plays. If we elaborate on German theatre history here, it is in order to unpack the underlying reasons for this nervousness around the German dramaturg, which may help us to negotiate the issues facing the institutional dramaturg today.

Lessing was not alone in his drive towards a 'national' theatre and, indeed, the very formation of the Hamburger Nationaltheater was an initiative in this direction. In the context of its time, this movement can be seen as a necessary and extremely productive effort to regenerate and unify the German theatre. It should be remembered that Germany was, until the end of the nineteenth century, a fragmented nation, that the German language was accorded little value in intellectual circles in the early eighteenth century and that French theatre was dominant, due to

French cultural expansion. Later, the movement was given new impetus in resistance to the French invasion of Prussia (including the capture of Berlin) in 1807.

Therefore, during the mid-eighteenth and early nineteenth century, many urged a move away from imitating theatre forms acquired from other countries and towards discovering forms that reflected a specifically German cultural life, language and identity. These concerns also strongly informed the early nineteenth-century Romantic movement in Germany. Apart from Lessing, many other significant writers, such as Johann Wolfgang von Goethe, Friedrich von Schiller and Heinrich von Kleist were inspired by the idea of a drama rooted in the life of the German people. Another significant dramaturg, Ludwig Tieck, was also a German Romantic, infused by a nationalist spirit. Besides a return to the Greek and Shakespearean dramas as alternatives to the French style, an interest in German mythology, folk tales and traditions, as well as in German history and heroes, is characteristic of this movement. There is a stress on the *Volk* (the people), from whose culture the new work is expected to grow. This early nationalism in the theatre produced internationally acclaimed works by German writers, alongside a rejuvenation of the arts in other fields.

However, in the later nineteenth century, Richard Wagner's opera house at Bayreuth became a centre for nationalism of a more extreme variety and here, despite Wagner's significance as an artist, we begin to see it connected to ideas of racial superiority and anti-Semitism. The emphasis on the *Volk* was beginning to take a more sinister turn. What had begun as a move towards emancipation had become a potentially more destructive force over the course of a century – and was to become actively destructive during the twentieth century. Though one can hardly blame dramaturgs such as Lessing and Tieck for later developments, one can see how it is all too easy to make a connection between their nationalism, their use of the term 'dramaturgy' (particularly in relation to the formulation of a unified 'German dramaturgy') and its use under Hitler's Third Reich.

In 1933, Joseph Goebbels created the office of the *Reichsdramaturg* (National Dramaturg) in order to implement National Socialist cultural policy. Rainer Schlösser occupied this post until theatres were closed (due to the war) in 1944, and was also made president of the Propaganda Ministry in 1935. This meant that, as John London puts it, 'in effect he was chief theatre censor for the duration of the Third Reich' (London 2000: 10). However, Schlösser's role was not merely to react and to prohibit, but also to promote Nazi ideology through the theatre.

Although there was a substantial reduction in new plays, Schlösser promoted those plays and artists that the regime wished to encourage – dramatists such as Richard Billinger, Hans Rehberg and Schlösser's colleague, Eberhard Wolfgang Möller, as well as dramas by classic writers such as Lessing, Goethe and Kleist. The Nazis actually increased already generous theatre subsidies in 1933, opening new theatres (Gadberry 1995: 10–11). The line taken was not necessarily to promote strident political content, since this was not effective propaganda. In fact, the policy was eventually to ban overt political reference and a depiction of contemporary events was often considered problematic. Instead, the strategy was a more complex initiative to promote an aesthetic philosophy and programme, rejecting both realism and expressionism and favouring romantic *Volk* dramas that presented patriotic subjects, as well as large-scale events such as the bizarre and unsuccessful scheme to promote the open-air *Thing* plays, which were a type of ritual community drama, celebrating German heroism.

While there is clearly an enormous distance between Lessing's critical and questioning dramaturgy and Schlösser's destructive imposition of political ideology (dramatic *criticism* was indeed, banned in 1936), one can see how the desire to promote a particular cultural strategy, especially in relation to the idea of a 'national' theatre, can have a positive effect and can also, in certain contexts, become distorted and extreme. In some situations, indeed, this commitment can become a double-edged sword: for instance, the post-war German Democratic Republic was the only country to offer Brecht the theatre he needed; however, his work was, despite this, subject to censorship (and possibly to self-censorship) on several occasions.

Brecht's own example, while significant, has also been problematic in the UK, where the young Brecht's autocratic demands as a dramaturg at Reinhardt's Deutsches Theater in Berlin are better known than his mature employment and training of dramaturgs. However, it should be remembered that Brecht was not accorded the total artistic control he demanded as a young man and spent much of his time as a dramaturg working on adaptations. Despite this, one British (US-trained) dramaturg writes, quite mistakenly, of 'Brecht's totalitarian reign as a Dramaturg in Germany's National Theatres' as a legitimate factor in discouraging the development of British dramaturgs (Veltman 1998: 7).

Perhaps partly in order to avoid accusations of didacticism or exclusivity, we find Tynan trying to disown the idea of an explicit policy at England's National Theatre in the 1960s: 'The first thing we said to each other was that our policy should be to have no policy, except excellence in whatever we did' (Tynan 1971: 44). However, this leaves the term 'excellence' waiting to be defined. Indeed, Tynan goes on to qualify this statement by citing the influence of a number of factors on the choice of repertoire, including Arts Council pressure, practical concerns and his own political convictions. He also mentions having drawn up 'my own list of all the plays in world drama that could possibly, conceivably be worth reviving in Britain in the second half of the twentieth century', going on to admit that, 'interestingly, it wasn't a very long list' (Tynan 1971: 44). Clearly, 'excellence' has some quite definite, if unspoken, parameters.

It may be easy to criticize Tynan, retrospectively, but the problem still persists in England, where a desire to maintain an open, liberal position may leave some principles of decision-making unspoken and unquestioned, perhaps even appearing to be unquestionable. For instance, in July 2005, Simon Zimmerman, then at Arts Council England South West, initiated a series of staff development events and discussions to tease out the meaning of the word 'quality', in relation to artworks, since individual arts officers were often left to make funding decisions partly on this basis. The author's own involvement in two of these sessions revealed a number of difficulties with this term in relation to contemporary practice, not least its habitual application to the isolated 'art object' rather than to the event of art's reception. This vague reference to ideas of 'quality' and 'excellence' cannot be considered as representative of theatres throughout the UK. Within Wales, for example, we find a different set of tensions. A desire for a national theatrical identity – as well as a stage for Welsh-language theatre – has led to fierce discussions surrounding the possibility of setting up a Welsh national theatre. However, there has been much debate about the appropriate strategy for such a theatre. For instance, Anna-Maria Taylor, writing in 1997, suggests that:

> The strength of Welsh theatre since 1979 (and indeed before) lies in the abilities of those ... who have tried to establish types of playing and repertoire that are culturally appropriate to a linguistically and geographically divided and often overlooked country. (Taylor 1997: 44)

She goes on to propose that 'A new state theatre in Cardiff may suit the architectural and economic aspirations of an undersized capital desperate to look towards Europe for a future,' but that it must,

> take into account the diversity of theatrical work that has grown up out of many groups' localized engagement with living in modern Wales ... the

possibility of Welsh theatre contributing to a mainstream of European cultural activity seems to lie in not emulating the centre but dramatizing and articulating the experience of surviving on the edge. (Taylor 1997: 44–5)

In 2003, Theatre Genedlaethol Cymru was established as a national Welsh-language touring theatre company, with a remit to produce work that was flexible in genre. However, the separation of English-language and Welsh-language theatre in Wales has been criticized, as has the underfunding of smaller companies (Theatre Worker 2005). For Wales, then, a national strategy cannot be loosely defined as a general pursuit of 'excellence'. The Welsh Assembly government's recent proposal to strip Arts Council Wales's strategic and policy-making function, thereby centralizing policy decisions, has been rejected by a recent review of ACW, but raised new concerns about the future of theatre in Wales.

If, then, it is impossible either to avoid having an artistic policy or for any policy to be absolutely inclusive of all work worthy of production, how can the dramaturg, involved in implementing theatre policy, best work to make this policy as flexible and productive as possible? Is it helpful to make the theatre's considerations transparent? Is it helpful to submit strategies to regular review? Should the dramaturg be a member of the team that creates and implements this strategy or a critic who raises uncomfortable questions about its limitations?

The dramaturg has a connection with the state-subsidized theatre and the institutional dramaturg almost invariably appears in this context, partly because the role is often considered dispensable where commercial considerations are an issue and partly because the dramaturg is considered helpful in the implementation of a clear strategy for serving the public. The fact that Germany has had subsidized theatre for so much longer than the UK is one reason why the dramaturg appeared in German theatre far sooner than in the UK. This connection with funding and funding bodies is likely to be a continuing source of difficulty for the dramaturg (as it is, indeed, for many artists), since the funder's requirements may not always be in accord with the theatre and dramaturg's notions of 'excellence'. Henrik Adler, formerly a dramaturg at the Berliner Ensemble and now working in a related role at the Berliner Festspiele, draws attention to current concerns that funding requirements may compromise artistic considerations:

The problem today is the situation of public funding, and the situation of theatre in a city is very – it has become very complicated … You have to give evidence of your existence. You ... have to give validation. You have always to show that your theatre is sold out; that all the people love your theatre; that the critics [the reviews] are wonderful. So for me, this is a real point we have to bring into our work today. If we make theatre, we can't only think about making wonderful theatre – wonderful intellectual theatre, politically correct theatre ... we have to sell our theatre all the time. So, as I understand it, we are corrupted by these thoughts of selling. We have to sell our house, necessarily, to people who give money. Sometimes industrial corporations. The City. The State. But ... we have to reflect on the fact that we do this, in my opinion. And, in the end, the production might be an exciting expression of this reflection, showing – in terms of its aesthetics, its self-reflection, ambivalence and irony – the contradictory state of the whole theatre. (Adler 2005: 25)

The question here is whether the presence of a dramaturg is likely to exacerbate the difficulties surrounding the implementation of theatre policy, or whether the dramaturg is likely to promote debate. Will the dramaturg, as is often feared in the UK, insist on the rigid implementation of an aesthetic, political or commercial strategy, or will the dramaturg look to constantly question, broaden and re-evaluate a strategy, developing it organically in response to and in conversation with the artists and audiences it serves? Potentially, at least, the dramaturg is the person who is best placed to question and to analyse, as well as to deliver, the artistic philosophy of a particular institution. Adler suggests that policy is often caught up in competing considerations and that the dramaturg may usefully help to identify these tensions, rather than insist on the right way forward: 'Perhaps [the dramaturg] can't be the voice – the big voice ... Perhaps he is the person who explains the contradiction' (Adler 2005: 31).

The dramaturg, then, need not be seen as policing an artistic policy, but as working in a dynamic and developing relationship with it. Chapter 5 discusses a number of ways in which literary managers and dramaturgs are developing plays within a clear context, yet are prepared to challenge and develop theatre institutions through this development of new writing. In other ways, too, dramaturgs are involved in a consideration of 'the whole', when working in an institution, not as humourless preservers of particular ideologies or inflexible 'house styles', but as people involved in developing and exploring the potential for their institution and the various kinds of work it may be able to engage with. We will go on to consider a number of practical activities carried out by the dramaturg, all of which involve a consideration of the institution as a 'whole'.

The Dramaturg as Programmer

It can often be the dramaturg's job to establish an overview and to build a sympathetic context for a performance or series of performances. This may mean selecting works that are interesting when considered in relation to each other, perhaps built around a particular show or project. It may mean making sure that a repertoire has sufficient variety to keep people of diverse ages and social backgrounds coming into the theatre, gradually developing the audience's capacity for enjoying new and challenging work – this is likely to mean working closely with the marketing department. It may mean commissioning and developing new work, while also contributing to the creation of a helpful working atmosphere for the artists involved – working with them, rather than dictating to them.

Karen-Maria Bille, chief dramaturg at Denmark's Royal Danish Theatre, gives a sense of the considerations of planning a theatre repertoire and the way this theatre organizes different types of work (and audience) between different venues:

> First of all, we start there – what do we want to say this year? But with twelve opening nights a year, you can't have just one concept, and we have many different audiences. So that is why we try to separate them ... say, the younger, more experimental stuff is over in The Power Station [Turbinehallerne] and the more conservative is within [the main] house. (Bille 2005: 5)

Bille explains that the constraints of the theatre spaces place some restriction on programming, for instance, preventing the company from producing plays that require an intimate playing space: 'one of our problems here is the total lack of a black box and intimacy' (Bille 2005: 5).

Bille's own key concern at present is the development of new Danish plays and a specifically Danish repertoire, since 'we don't have a very big tradition of playwriting in Denmark' (Bille 2005: 18). She explains that existing Danish plays have tended to be satiric, influenced by writers such as Ludvig Holberg and Johan Ludvig Heiberg. The 'romantic' mode, she suggests, is less well established, with existing plays being relatively weak: 'But I think they're valuable, and I think you should make certain to water those roots as well' (Bille 2005: 19). She suggests that this is necessary in order to encourage a breadth of Danish playwriting and the same motivation also affects her commissioning of adaptations: 'we also commission adaptations of novels – stuff like that, to sort of make a tradition that never was there' (Bille 2005: 19).

We can see here an attempt to build a national repertoire in ways that mirror Lessing's concerns, to some degree: 'The Danes – they want Danish culture, and so why not give it to them?' (Bille 2005: 21). At the same time, it should not be misunderstood as a policy that produces a repertoire limited to exclusively Danish work – the theatre's 2005–6 season included productions of work by Shakespeare, Brecht, Tennessee Williams, an adaptation of a novel by Simone De Beauvoir, as well as work by Danish writers and companies, including one entitled, *Come on Bangladesh, Just Do It!* (Tue Biering, original title in English). At the time of our visit (April 2005), a play by Scottish writer David Greig was just opening. However, as the theatre's website suggests, as Denmark's national theatre, there is a perception of a responsibility to create an appropriately balanced programme.

A very different set of concerns influenced Thomas Frank as dramaturg at Berlin's Sophiensaele (2005–7), a smaller theatre producing more experimental work. Frank has also worked at the Künstlerhaus Mousonturm in Frankfurt, where he curated the *Plateaux* festival, which aims to promote emerging artists.

Frank explains that at both the Mousonturm and the Sophiensaele, he did not work with a given production budget, but had to set up projects for which he raised funds. This meant that each commission was carefully considered a long time in advance. Both theatres place an emphasis on contemporary work and have a desire to encourage young and emerging artists. Both offer an international programme and seek to develop new forms, so Frank tended to work with performance artists rather than with more conventional theatre companies and genres. Frank commented in 2005, 'I like … to keep my institution as flexible as possible in order to make different art forms happen … and to be really open to them – to think my theatre in a completely different way in order to generate artists' prognoses' (Frank 2005: 4). Frank, now joint artistic director at DieTheater, Vienna, then described himself as a 'Curator and Dramaturg', suggesting that the former term, drawn from the visual arts, was appropriate because his job entailed:

> bringing certain approaches together and … creating a 'shell' or creating an exhibition … you have to think very carefully about how you present a show, how you put it on, what kind of environment you create, and to think about the profile of your programme, and I think this is very much an artistic decision, but I strongly believe this is very much a political decision as well. (Frank 2005: 4)

Rather than seeing himself as someone who simply set out an agenda, Frank worked closely with artists in order to develop the work. In fact, he described his role as that of 'a mediator between the artist and the institution' (Frank 2005: 6). In commissioning work for the *Plateaux* festival, he was involved in discussions with the artists to help to refine their original concepts, to identify the core of their ideas and to discover the best ways of making them work. In describing how he and the artistic team went about this task, he uses the phrase, 'we were in love with the idea': the point is not to reshape and reinvent the artist's original conception, but to recognize and to realize it.

Frank's involvement with the projects he set up went beyond these initial stages and continued through dialogue with the artists involved. Here, his role slipped between that of the curator/producer and the dramaturg, with no absolute dividing line between the two. For example, when working with the UK company Lone Twin, who were developing their piece *Sledgehammer Songs* (2003), he says:

> We went for lunch almost every day – two months long – and had a really good conversation about what it was and about what they focused on. That was just a very good dialogue between me, as dramaturg, and them, as the artists ... I'm probably rather the curator, but in both cases the important thing is that they – that the artists have a partner to give them a kind of faith that it's welcome – that's it's kind of accepted or that it's understood. That's probably the most important thing, that it's understood. (Frank 2005: 14)

Interestingly, Frank's role as described here does have an equivalent in the UK, in the recent development of the position of 'creative producer'. The 'creative producer' takes a role that is simultaneously administrative and engaged with the development of the artwork, combining a position as fund-raiser, organizer, promoter with a depth of understanding and dialogue with the artists and the artistic process. While creative producers may be found in an institutional context (for example, Helen Cole, who curates the Live Art programme at the Arnolfini, Bristol, terms her role 'curator and creative producer'), they may also work as integral contributors to a single company (for example, Nick Sweeting for Improbable Theatre) or as curators for a festival (for example Mark Ball from the Fierce! Festival, Birmingham). What links these people is their ability to be present as dialogue-partner during the creative process. In this respect, many of them could loosely be termed 'dramaturgs' in a mode similar to Frank, who acknowledges, 'I think anyway that you have plenty of dramaturgs around. It's just termed differently' (Frank 2005: 7).

Radosavljevic offers us a different model for the work of a dramaturg, in her former position in which she operated between a theatre company, Northern Stage, and an educational institution, Newcastle University. The establishment of her post as 'dramaturg' was facilitated by Claire Malcolm at New Writing North and part of Radosavljevic's role was to involve writers from the English department (there is no Drama department at present) in contributing to the theatre, through evenings of poetry, which she edited and rehearsed, often involving musicians and, on one occasion, members of the ensemble: 'it's a kind of literary event that fits in with the artistic vision of the company, and it's still compatible with everything else that's going on' (Radosavljevic 2005: 3).

For the theatre company, she was able to represent the interests of writers and yet had a feel for the 'European aesthetic' of the company's style. Besides her input as production dramaturg, she was also involved in planning events and creating a context for a central production – what she terms a 'project model approach' (Radosavljevic 2005: 1). This is described in more detail in Chapter 6.

In each of these examples, the dramaturg is involved in curating events, yet in very different contexts and with very different objectives. Bille, working for a national theatre, aims to expand a national repertoire; Frank, at the Sophiensaele, sought to support and develop experimental work, while Radosavljevic's curation aimed to provide a context for a specific production and to strengthen links between two organizations (university and theatre company).

The Dramaturg as Educationalist and Go-between

As we have seen, the dramaturg may assist in bringing a series of productions or other events together to develop a context within which each individual work is viewed. However, an important part of the creation of this context includes education and marketing, so dramaturgs are likely to find themselves working across the different departments of an arts institution. The dramaturg is often involved in writing and organizing programme notes and marketing material; writing press releases; communicating with the press; doing pre- and post-performance presentations; developing educational material and so on.

We have seen, for example, that Brecht's dramaturgs were responsible for putting programme material together and Palitzsch, trained as a graphic designer, is particularly well known for his input into the design of publicity material (including the theatre logo) and editing theatre programmes (see, for example, Monk 2005: 17).

Adler suggests that in Germany, within the smaller producing houses, there is sometimes too much emphasis on this role, which prevents the dramaturg from carrying out a fuller engagement with the artistic process:

> In lots of theatres you have the dramaturg and the publicity officer in one person ... Sometimes there's the notion that the dramaturg just makes public work – works as the press officer, and this is a big problem. In a small theatre, you haven't really time to work on dramaturgy. You have to struggle so that you can organise the production and you can bring the press people into your rehearsal. So, when I talk about dramaturgy, it's a very luxurious situation in The Berliner Ensemble, any of the big theatres here in Berlin. (Adler 2005: 38–9)

Radosavljevic describes the way in which her work with Northern Stage involved close collaboration with the marketing department, assisting not only with the programme material but in the way a particular production was 'pitched', keeping the style of the marketing continuous with the ideas behind the programming and artistic production.

This kind of integrated approach is consistent with current trends within British theatre marketing, which lend themselves to collaboration with a dramaturg. For example, the 'Audience Builder' approach (Morris Hargreaves MacIntyre 2005) has implications for programming a repertoire as well as for marketing styles. This system segments the audience according to two main factors: first, the highest level of 'risk' taken in attending an art event in the past year; second, the frequency of attendance. 'Risk' is defined according to the organizational knowledge of audience behaviour and is re-evaluated each year. This system was pioneered at Bristol Old Vic and here 'risk' was broken down as follows, with A events as 'high' risk and E events as 'low' risk:

> A – new writing; work by obscure playwrights; work that is outside the mainstream
>
> B – 'serious drama'; Ibsen, Chekhov, Shakespeare's tragedies and histories
>
> C – 'mainstream' work; plays that people know (*Look Back in Anger, A Streetcar Named Desire*) or productions featuring actors people know (Pete Postlethwaite, Tara Fitzgerald, Neil Pearson)
>
> D – 'Accessible' work – Godber, Ayckbourn, Coward
>
> E – family shows (Morris Hargreaves MacIntyre 2005: 2)

Once the audience is mapped onto a grid, according to the two variables, it is possible to focus on a particular segment and to use more detailed information to target marketing. The aim, for instance, would be to get those members of the audience that attend events rated as 'C', twice a year (C2), to take a risk on some 'B' events and to increase attendance (to move to B3, for example). Since this is partly an *educational*, as well as a *sales* tactic, it can be seen that the programming can assist in offering this audience an event graded as 'B', which offers something that might interest the C2 group specifically. Though this kind of approach does not necessitate the use of a dramaturg, it can clearly make good use of a dramaturg's skills. Conversely, one can also see the potential for conflict with a dramaturg, if the marketing manager and the dramaturg do not share the same priorities.

Interestingly, at a debate chaired by Thomas Frank, at the Goethe Institut in London, 2004, there was some disagreement between theatre curators/programmers about the emphasis to be placed when marketing work. Ball, for instance (Birmingham, UK), advocated a similar approach to that described above:

> I don't think there's enough effort to get under the skin of audiences, to try to understand who they are and why they come. To know what their motivations are … It's about education, it's about placing it into a context … it's about taking the risk of seeing risk-taking work as less risky, if you know what I mean? (Frank and Waugh 2005: 102 and 106)

On the other hand, Christine Peters, from Theater der Welt, 2005, Stuttgart, suggested that 'You have to rely on, or trust in an artistic work and an artistic concept and then you have to provide a space for that … And to explain to an audience why this is a valuable piece of art' (Frank and Waugh 2005: 106). Though these approaches are not incompatible, an audience member swiftly pointed out a difference in emphasis. However, as Ball responded, 'it's the work that speaks to the audience … I don't think we're challenging the integrity of the work by pursuing a particular marketing and audience development strategy' (Frank and Waugh 2005: 109).

Collaboration with the education department or engagement with educational activities is also, clearly, key. We have touched on Radosavljevic's work with Newcastle University. Birmingham Repertory Theatre's development of new writing has also built its audience and effectiveness through educational activities and outreach – as have many other arts organizations. 'Page to Stage', for example, was an initiative that linked students from further and higher education to the shows being produced. This scheme offered workshops, often run by writers at the studio theatre, The Door. There has also been work with Birmingham's Adult Education Service, through offering writing courses. Trevelyan Wright states that average total audience figures for a play at The Door rose from 611 in 1998 to 1700 in 1991. Although the quality of the work produced must be primarily responsible for this, he suggests that educational activities have played a key role: 'We are providing an individual connection for each person to the process of writing and producing new work' (Wright 2001: 9).

Whether dealing with the production team, press, marketing or education departments, the dramaturg is often described as a mediator or 'go-between'. Matthias Lilienthal, now Artistic Director at Berlin's Hebbel-am-Ufer Theatres, but formerly dramaturg at the Berliner Volksbühne, summarizes the role as follows:

> [A dramaturg] is just an adviser to the director of the theatre, an advisor to the director of a play, and it is a person who holds these city theatres together and gives the whole enterprise a kind of vision in its daily life. I would describe my function as a dramaturg simply as putting the right people together at the right time. The right director with the right actors, play or project. I'm not especially good in any one of the fields, but I'm okay in every one of the fields, and I see my role in organising this process. (Lilienthal in Frank and Waugh 2005: 45)

Once again, we are made aware that the dramaturg is the person who 'keeps the whole in mind' – in this case making the dramaturg a useful central point of reference across the theatre institution, its various departments and personnel.

The Freelance Dramaturg

If there are potential political problems and hurdles for the dramaturg working in an institutional context, one is bound to ask whether there are advantages to freelance work. Indeed, some dramaturgs do suggest that working on a project-by-project basis allows them to side-step the assumption that they possess the power to commission and are some-how gate-keepers to the theatre building. It also potentially frees them from the restrictions of a particular theatre's policy. On the other hand, a dramaturg who is not employed directly by an institution may have little or no influence upon it. They could then find themselves in the invidious position of, for example, mentoring and developing work by new writers, yet without being able to help them towards a professional production. Alternatively, one could argue that freelancers are particularly well equipped to offer assistance, since they are likely to have a wider range of contacts and links with more producing houses than a dramaturg committed to a single theatre building. It is also possible to work dramaturgically outside the centres of the theatre industry, for instance, in helping to establish artist-led initiatives that generate their own performances, dialogues and practices. As always, it depends on the dramaturg and the quality and nature of their working relationships.

In any case, the situation is rarely as polarized as the descriptions 'freelance' and 'institutional' might suggest. Freelance dramaturgs often have live connections with specific institutions (including theatres, universities and artists networks), while being able to work in more than one context. As freelance dramaturg David Lane suggests, for instance: 'You reach a point where you locate yourself with frequent project partners who come back to you' (Lane 2006b: 1). Potentially this means that they can become involved in a project as and when both parties feel this is appropriate, rather than occupying a permanent and relatively inflexible position.

Dramaturg Hanna Slättne, now working for Tinderbox Theatre in Northern Ireland, but previously a freelance dramaturg, comments that, in most cases, freelancers 'are asked to come into the projects' (Slättne 2005a: 4), whether by the writer, or others on a creative team, suggesting a positive decision to work with that particular dramaturg, rather than an acceptance of whatever is on offer from an institution. On the other hand, while writers may genuinely desire assistance from a dramaturg (and the evidence seems strong that many do), there is also some suggestion that there may be pressure from funding bodies to secure the input of a dramaturg. Lane observes, neutrally, 'I think it's sort of picked up from the Arts Council as a sign of commitment, professionalization of your role as a writer, that you've got a dramaturg' (Lane 2006b: 2), while in an article for Writernet, Jonathan Meth is more explicit about the concern that funding bodies could be pushing writers to use dramaturgs (Meth 2003: 1). However, Lucy Powell expresses some surprise that her own interviews suggest that writers are often the fiercest advocates for the role (Powell 2006: 2).

If the working partnerships experienced by the freelance dramaturg do tend to reflect a positive and voluntary decision to work with someone in that role, it may also be the case that the decisions surrounding ways of working and 'parameters for collaboration' are more carefully thought through for each individual project. Slättne suggests: 'That will make for a much more open and explorative work environment in my experience'. In institutions, on the whole, 'the flexibility is not there around the work practice' (Slättne 2005a: 4). Lane confirms the importance of such flexibility: 'Every project's different. I've never worked in the same way on different projects, ever. Because people are different. And the play is different. So with different writers on the same project you work in different ways' (Lane 2006b: 3).

Both Lane and Slättne emphasize that, 'You have to be careful about how you broker relationships and why you're there as a dramaturg' (Lane 2006b: 2). Slättne mentions some frustration when she has been asked to come into a process that has already begun, where the role of the dramaturg was not clarified at the outset and 'I didn't get to function as a dramaturg, basically'. Following such experiences, Slättne says, 'the director and I set out what I was there to do right from the beginning' (Slättne 2005a: 4).

Lane also comments on the possibility of perceived conflicts of interest. For example, this might arise where a freelance dramaturg is script-reading for a theatre (generally a free service), yet also offers their own script-reading service (probably requiring a fee). While Lane is conscientious about marketing his services to writers whose contacts are freely available (through Writernet, for example), it is not necessarily evident to the writer that the dramaturg is not accessing a theatre's database. Moreover, it is also possible that a writer could pay for a critique that might be freely accessible by another route.

To return to the positive aspects of this working structure, Lane emphasizes the diversity of his work experience as a freelancer. For instance, he found himself, on one occasion, working with a live artist to structure a one-to-one piece that incorporated significant elements of improvisation, while, on another occasion, he worked with Half Moon Theatre to develop work with eleven children, among whom there were those with learning difficulties, others with behavioural difficulties and some excluded individuals. He comments on the interesting dramaturgical challenges involved in this last project, where he worked with the children to develop scenarios, which were structured into a 'picture script': 'I had to think very differently about how to apply my skills as a dramaturg and as a writer ... That pushed me in a new direction.' Lane observes that: 'As a freelancer, I think you have more opportunities to push yourself ... It increases my pool of creative solutions, as I like to call it' (Lane 2006b: 2).

Lane is also keen to stress the importance of his teaching work, irrespective of financial imperatives. This offers an opportunity to advocate for the role of the dramaturg and to promote the discussion of professional dramaturgical practice. As Lane clarifies, 'the reason I'm a teacher is because I'm a professional dramaturg, not because I'm an academic. If I stopped being a professional dramaturg I'd stop being a teacher, because the two things go hand in hand' (Lane 2006b: 1).

On the whole, it does seem that the freelance dramaturg is able to be more flexible than the institutional one, and to avoid the hierarchical relationships produced in an institutional situation. On the other hand, precisely because 'each situation is different', each project is likely to present its own political challenges and will need to be carefully considered from the very outset.

The Multiple Roles of the Dramaturg

In this chapter we have looked at the dramaturg in relation to the organization. We have seen that the dramaturg's role in the arts institution may be both creative and, at times, contentious, while freelance dramaturgs do not entirely escape controversy by being at one remove from such organizations. We have also looked at the contextual work of the institutional dramaturg, operating as someone who has an input into repertoire and programming, who facilitates relationships across the company, who has an input into educational and outreach work.

These contextual activities are most obviously associated with state-funded institutions with a remit to offer certain services to both artists and the public. For instance, a 'new writing' venue might be in receipt of public funding, on condition it offers accessible systems for aspiring writers, making it possible, in theory at least, for anyone to have work produced. Some theatre companies, however, do not claim to offer such a public service and exist principally in order to present the work of a particular artistic team. For instance, while a company might be encouraged to engage with funding priorities concerning access and education, their remit may be primarily to develop their own artistic work in an interesting and exciting way. The dramaturg working in such a context is likely to have a less public role than that of the dramaturg in, for example, the National Theatre of Scotland.

On the other hand, both, on occasion, may be asked to speak for their organization. One might also mention dramaturgs connected with writers' organizations, such as New Writing North, which have a public role, though not one connected with a specific theatre's policy (Theatre Writing Partnership is discussed in Chapter 5). Alternatively the term 'dramaturg' could be used in relation to curatorial roles within artist-led networks, such as the Magdalena Project, which demonstrate that dramaturgical work can be politically radical, explicitly offering alternatives to the cultural 'mainstream'. In short, dramaturgs appear in many different kinds of organization, and the politics of each situation (as for the freelancer) may offer its own contextual challenges.

In the chapters that follow, we will turn our attention to the dramaturg's role in the creative process itself. We include in this the dramaturg associated with developing the writer's work, which in the UK is a role closely identified with that of literary manager. Here, the dramaturg might occupy a space somewhere between offering a public service and assisting the artistic project – a tension that makes the role particularly challenging. In the subsequent chapters, we discuss the different functions of the 'production dramaturg', who may be concerned with scripted work, devised theatre, or other art-forms, such as dance. The term implies an involvement with the construction of the live performance, the 'production'.

However, as Brecht has shown us, the work of the dramaturg always, necessarily, concerns both composition and context. The two cannot be separated. Thus, even the dramaturg whose role is invisible to the world beyond the theatre company, knows that the work takes its place in that world, not only proposing its own critique, but carrying its own responsibilities.

5 The Dramaturg and the Playwright

Definitions and UK Working Practices

Throughout Britain, the term 'dramaturg' is most commonly understood to relate to the development of new theatre writing. This is probably because the literary manager is often the nearest British equivalent to the German dramaturg within our principal theatre institutions – though the literary manager tends to place a stronger emphasis on supporting and nurturing the playwright's creativity.

It should be remembered that even the term 'literary manager' is still relatively recent in British theatre and is itself subject to variation and change. The first official appointment of a literary manager in England is generally agreed to be that of Kenneth Tynan at the newly formed National Theatre under Laurence Olivier in 1963. Tynan actually requested the title 'dramaturg' but this was ultimately refused by the theatre board (Cattaneo 1997: 4), after his brief was widened by the additional requirement to act as head of 'Public Relations' (Luckhurst 2006a: 160). The term 'literary manager' had been used by Granville Barker and William Archer in their proposals for a National Theatre (1904) and was chosen by Tynan as a substitute for 'dramaturg'. Neither role was well understood. At the time, one satirical paper dismissively dubbed him 'librarian for an obscure South London repertory company' (*Private Eye*, quoted in Billington, 2001: 2). As this description suggests, Tynan, already an influential theatre critic, was not exclusively concerned with new writing or writers, though he was concerned with the dramatic text and repertoire. He was indeed a dramaturg/critic in the style of Lessing, despite his aspiration to be more practically involved in rehearsal, which was the cause of some controversy.

Given the more recent focus on 'new writing', it may come as some surprise to find a literary manager stating in 1964:

> A year or so ago, I noticed that out of more than two dozen plays running in the West End, only three had been written before 1950. This is the kind of fantastic imbalance that the National Theatre exists to correct. (Tynan 1984: 362)

Tynan is clearly stating the need to stage more, rather than fewer, established plays. This desire to balance new writing with classical works is in sharp contrast to the situation some twenty-five years later, when it was generally felt that there was an urgent need to stimulate and encourage new writing above all else. Since then, those theatres that have a commitment to new writing have tended to prioritize the appointment of literary managers, with a particular remit to identify and develop new playwrights – and, through them, new audiences. There has been a growth in British literary management, to the extent that it has been termed 'a silent revolution' (Payne, quoted in Luckhurst 2006a: 201). The job is now very much associated with new writing. The situation in North America is somewhat similar, with the very introduction of the dramaturg being associated with new writing. Anne Cattaneo comments that Francis Ferguson and Arthur Ballet, 'the two Americans who presage the advent of the dramaturgy profession in America, were early advocates of American playwriting … During the 1960s … Arthur Ballet tirelessly read and recommended new American plays' (Cattaneo 1997: 4). As in England, both the position of the dramaturg and that of the literary manager only began to be established in the 1960s, and in America they quickly became crucial to the playwrights' movement of the 1970s.

Given this history, it is perhaps unsurprising that in Britain and North America, the titles of 'literary manager' and 'dramaturg' are often used almost interchangeably. As the latter term becomes increasingly familiar to the British theatre profession, if not to its audiences, we are beginning to see its more frequent use within new writing contexts. In England and Scotland, recent public discussions of the dramaturg have been led by those interested in playwriting, for example, the Playwright's Studio was instrumental in organizing 'Dramaturgy and the Word', together with Queen Margaret University College, at Glasgow Centre for Contemporary Arts, 1 April, 2004. There is evidently some excitement around the possibilities inherent in this term (or at least there is a sense that it must be engaged with); however, there are also tensions.

While theatre or performance texts (assuming that 'text' is a term that can be applied to both verbal and non-verbal elements) are, broadly speaking, the dramaturg's key concerns, an assumed identification with the nurturing of the *playwright* can sometimes give rise to confusion and even disappointment in contexts where the term 'dramaturg' does not imply this focus. Misunderstandings are easily created, as, across the rest of Europe and even in some British contexts, the playwright is not invariably the dramaturg's primary consideration – and in some cases, is scarcely his or her concern at all.

In cases where the association with developing 'new writing' and the playwright is indeed implied, the term 'dramaturg' can still be understood in different ways and is chosen for varied reasons, even across British theatre. Sometimes it is chosen to suggest a non-administrative or even freelance role, distinct from the institutional overtones of 'literary manager' or 'literary director'. Sometimes its use reflects an approach that is influenced by mainland European models, which, as we discuss below, has particular implications. On occasion, the term may be publicly avoided for fear of alienating those unfamiliar with or hostile to it, yet it may still be considered as an appropriate and privately acknowledged description of the role carried out by the person employed as 'literary manager', 'script editor' or with some other title. On other occasions, the writer may be further confused by finding themselves termed the 'dramaturg' when the word is used to imply a 'writerly' or dramaturgical role in collaborative creation, or in adapting a classic, as in some production dramaturgy. For instance, Phil Smith comments of his relationship with TNT: 'I was always described as the company "dramaturg" – a role which has been an elastic one. Sometimes I've been co-writer, sometimes almost the director. But never literary manager' (Smith 2005: 1).

There is therefore little consistency in the current British use of such terminology, even within 'new writing', and any attempt to distinguish clear and consistently implemented divisions between those termed 'dramaturgs' and those termed 'literary managers' in the British theatre is likely to be unsuccessful. It is therefore always important to discover as much as possible about the role and approach of any particular dramaturg before making assumptions. Often, as Luckhurst points out (Luckhurst 2005), discussions concerning the 'dramaturg' in a British context become caught up in a vain struggle to define the term, rather than in acknowledging and exploring its multiplicity.

This is not to deny that a theoretical distinction between the terms 'literary manager' and 'dramaturg' can be made – and some uses of the term 'dramaturg' are indicative of shifts and tensions in approaches to writer and play development, deserving further examination. These distinctions and tendencies are particularly evident where the use of the term is influenced by mainland European practice.

The 'German' Dramaturg and the New Play

As we have clarified, dramaturgs trained in the German tradition will not necessarily see themselves as being exclusively or primarily concerned with the playwright. However, it is also true that in many cases play development is considered to be a part of the continental dramaturg's role, often a significant one. There are also dramaturgs, such as Wolfgang Wiens, who see it as the very definition of dramaturgy to act as an advocate for the author (Wiens 1986: 18).

When working with a new play and playwright, the primary and crucial difference between the 'German' dramaturg and the British literary manager is that *the literary manager usually steps out of the picture once the show goes into rehearsal, whereas the dramaturg frequently does not*. Though not an infallible rule (not all dramaturgs have the time for involvement in production), this is the most consistent and straightforward distinction to be made between the two. This means that the dramaturg is more likely to be oriented towards the *practical* work of production, than to be a primarily *literary* critic and advisor. The dramaturg's involvement in rehearsal may be indicative of his or her commitment to assisting the director, to facilitating the production as a whole and to further exploring the verbal text through performance.

Martin Esslin comments on the very different structuring of the theatre establishment in Germany, where theatre publishers act rather in the manner of powerful literary agents, identifying and offering new plays to the theatres, initially published 'as manuscripts for internal use only':

> The leading theatres are in intense competition to secure premieres of important new work ... a powerful theatre publisher like Rowohlt will let a leading theatre have the first production of an important new play as part of a package – 'if you do this play you are so keen on, will you also do one or two new plays by our new and relatively unknown authors ... '.
> (Esslin 1997: 26)

Maja Zade, dramaturg at Berlin's Schaubühne, suggests that this system is not always constructive: '[publishers] pick plays that they think are going to have great chances at being played at as many theatres as possible, so lots of really interesting work doesn't get picked up' (Zade 2006: 21).

As Esslin comments, the relatively 'complex, not to say chaotic' systems of American theatre put a greater onus on the American dramaturg to identify and nurture new writers. Much the same could be said of the British theatre.

Despite Germany's clear structure for the identification of new work, the playwrights themselves may sometimes be excluded from rehearsal, and in these cases, the dramaturg will liaise with the writer, as appropriate. Even when a 'German'-style dramaturg is used in Britain, the playwright is likely to be included in the rehearsal process and, where appropriate, will work with the dramaturg to refine the script as the performance develops. However, the distinctions between the 'dramaturg' and the 'literary manager' may still be maintained. The emphasis on following the script through into production may still reflect the dramaturg's orientation towards the verbal text in performance, rather than the words on the page and to the ensemble, or director, rather than exclusively to the playwright.

It must be acknowledged that if British theatre is occasionally identified as a 'director's theatre' (e.g. Woods 2005: 19), theatre in other European countries has, in recent years, tended to emphasize directorial creativity to a still greater extent. Sanja Nikcevic gives a persuasive analysis of this (Nikcevic 2005: 255–7). She comments that from the 1970s to the mid-1990s, the 'big boys club' of European directors preferred to draw on classic dramas or texts from other genres, and in adapting these 'did not collaborate with playwrights but had dramaturgs to do their verbalising for them' (Nikcevic 2005: 256). This interpretation, of course, assumes that this 'verbalizing' cannot be accorded the same creative status as 'playwriting'.

Nikcevic suggests that whereas in Britain and North America there has been a commitment to developing the writer's craft through workshops, there has, until recently, been a tendency to dismiss this idea in other Northern and Eastern European countries:

[Mainland] European theatre doesn't allow the playwright to develop a play and improve it, to learn something from the production process. Yet in the case of staging the contemporary play, the playwright often cannot sit in on rehearsals because he is too disturbing to the creative team – which he is not considered a part of. (Nikcevic 2005: 257)

She acknowledges that this situation has changed to some extent, with an increasing interest in new writing during the mid-1990s. In the early

1990s, Thomas Ostermeier's acclaimed productions of plays by young British playwrights such as David Harrower and MarkRavenhill, at the Baracke stage of the Deutsches Theater, Berlin, were influential in interesting directors in new work and inspiring a quest for new German writers. Zade, who previously worked with literary manager Graham Whybrow at the Royal Court Theatre, suggests that although the Schaubühne, now under Ostermeier's artistic directorship, continues to support new writing, this interest is again on the wane, since audiences tend to favour productions of the classics (Zade 2006: 19). If German theatre is a 'director's theatre', it is perhaps unsurprising that this situation gives rise to anxieties among British playwrights who doubt the 'German' dramaturg's commitment to the playwright and fear the potential disruption of the often close relationship between British directors and writers.

Indeed, Whybrow associates the term 'dramaturg' with a rather aggressive idea of 'fixing' a writer's work and with a potentially intrusive presence in rehearsal. He comments, in 2006: 'I simply do not see the problem in British theatre that dramaturgy is supposedly here to fix' (quoted in Powell 2006: 2). Whybrow distances himself from the role of the 'German' dramaturg:

> I do not act as the production dramaturg in the continental sense: my role is to foster the relationship between the playwright and director and I worry that the Brechtian model of the dramaturg is born of defensive cultures which perceive the need for radical intervention between the writer and the director. (Luckhurst 2006a: 231)

The playwright and lecturer, Sarah Woods, questions to what extent the 'German' type of dramaturg is likely to be integrated into the existing structures of British theatre:

> What you've got is a literary department tradition which still is relatively recent, working with the writer, and then that takes you up to the director ... And then you get into the director thing and the literary department falls away and then the writer hands over to the director and the director drives the process and I don't think there's room for a dramaturg, particularly, apart from in that literary tradition. ... I think a director/writer relationship should be very, very close, to the point that, you know, you are creating the same thing, and what you're creating is neither the sole vision of the writer nor the sole vision of the director, but actually is a conflation of the two and something better ... it's just a different division of labour in this country, and I think we'll probably use a dramaturg quite piecemeal – differently in dancing and improvised work to scripted work. (Woods 2005: 16–17)

This suggestion that we may use the dramaturg in a way that is 'quite piecemeal', rather than as a clearly established hierarchical role, is significant and does indeed seem to reflect current practice. In 2005, at 'What is Dramaturgy?', a symposium held at Birmingham Repertory Theatre, Luckhurst also commented on the different division of labour in England compared to mainland European countries, and the resulting tensions in considering the dramaturg (Luckhurst 2005). However, she also suggested that the consequent discussions around theatre process are vital and timely.

There have recently been a series of interesting appointments of writers as dramaturgs in state-subsidized theatre companies (for example, Edward Kemp at Chichester Festival Theatre 2003–5, David Greig at the National Theatre of Scotland and Adriano Shaplin at the Royal Shakespeare Company). However, it is much more usual for the UK dramaturg to be assumed to be the person who works *with* the writer. An increasing number of higher education courses offer training in 'dramaturgy' in Britain and are influenced by mainland European and North American practices. At the same time, though not as a direct result of this, there is a proliferation of literary departments and dramaturgs in the professional theatre, offering workshops, courses and training programmes for writers. There are also increasing numbers of higher education courses in 'playwriting'. These developments re-open questions of what kind of facilitator, teacher, dialogue-partner might be useful to a new writer and what views of writing might be reflected.

Before looking at some examples of contemporary practice in the UK, it may be helpful to give some sense of the recent history of literary management and the role of the writer in the British theatre, by outlining its development in three major subsidized companies, England's National Theatre Company, the Royal Shakespeare Company and the English Stage at the Royal Court Theatre. Since all these companies are based in London, the emphasis will be on the English playwright, but not exclusively so, since Welsh, Scottish and Irish playwrights are also performed at these venues.

The Literary Manager and the British Playwright

We have mentioned Tynan's role at the National, where he played an enormous part in setting up the new company, helping to plan the repertoire and casting, acting as spokesperson for the theatre and as a valuable adviser on European drama. As we have suggested, Tynan's vision for the new theatre did not exclusively concern new work, but rather the possibility of encompassing a range of work, old and new. His proposed first season included works by Noël Coward, Arthur Miller, John Arden, William Shakespeare, Bertolt Brecht, William Congreve and Anton Chekhov.

Tynan had a vision of becoming a Brechtian dramaturg, involved in the process of making work, as well as in commenting on it. With this aim in mind, he sometimes came into rehearsals and wrote up notes, which he sent to the directors. This was not an entirely popular inter-vention. One row concerned his adverse comments on Samuel Beckett's influence during George Devine's rehearsals of Beckett's *Play* (1964). Devine, a guest director from the Royal Court, responded angrily, once rehearsals had finished. Tynan's response in turn suggests the difference he perceived between the ethos of the National Theatre and the Royal Court:

> You profess yourself 'shocked' by the idea that one's obligation to an author need not extend beyond a general loyalty to his script: there speaks the advocate of a writer's theatre ... I believe in neither a direc-tor's nor a writer's theatre, but a theatre of intelligent audiences ... I thought we had outgrown the idea of theatre as a mystic rite born of secret communion between author, director, actors and an empty auditorium. (Quoted in Shellard 2003: 292)

While Tynan undoubtedly had a great influence on the early years of the National Theatre, he equally undoubtedly had more influence on the development of new writing in his position as critic at *The Observer*, where he had spent the 1950s and early 1960s pushing for a transfor-mation of the British theatre and championing new work by Brecht, Beckett, Osborne, Arnold Wesker and many others.

Under the fifteen years of Peter Hall's artistic directorship at the National, the post changed radically. Instead of a 'literary manager' in the style of Tynan, John Russell Brown was an academic, was titled 'associate director' and was responsible for script-reading. Russell Brown, unlike Tynan, is emphatic in distancing himself from the role of 'dramaturg': 'I'm not a dramaturg ... my special task is to be in charge of the script department' (Beacham 1978: 39). Within the institution as a whole, there is no doubt that Russell Brown's role was less significant than Tynan's. Nevertheless, in the late 1970s, we see evidence of a grow-ing culture of writer development in the establishment of workshop productions for plays that cannot be staged. The National Theatre Studio was opened in 1984, for research and development work. The idea was that this was a space that could be used in creating work that might well be produced elsewhere. By this time, Nicholas Wright had succeeded Russell Brown and he comments: 'It was extraordinary: at the height of Thatcherism to start a place that wasn't going to sell any tickets, where there wasn't a guaranteed end result, and whose bounty would be shared out with one's competitors' (Costa 2005: 2). Despite this, it is consonant with the gradual emergence of a culture of 'play development'.

Nicholas Hytner is now artistic director at the National, where Jack Bradley has been head of the literary department since 1995, overseeing a substantial increase in the number of new plays put on at the National. Lucy Davies is head of the Studio, which has approximately twenty writers on attachment, all with offices and a weekly wage. The Studio continues to be used by both new and established writers, directors and companies; these include 'physical theatre companies' such as Frantic and Gecko. Associate director Tom Morris (former artistic director at Battersea Arts Centre) is employed 'to identify, develop, nurture the non-literary stuff none of us knows how to do' (Hytner, quoted in Neill 2004: 2). Thus the National's policy towards new work, as well as 'new writing', is broader than it has ever been.

At the Royal Shakespeare Company we see a similarly recent breadth and energy in the development and production of new work. Dominic Cooke, heading the RSC's new writing festival in 2004, comments, 'Weirdly ... new writing is what the RSC was formed to do: to forge a relationship between living writers and the Renaissance' (Costa 2004: 2).

While the work of early 'literary managers' or 'play advisers' did concern liaison with writers, they were also involved in adaptation, translation and input into repertoire. Russell Brown notes a shift in the late 1970s, when Howard Davies took over the RSC's Warehouse Studio (later the Donmar Warehouse), with Walter Donohue as his assistant (Beacham 1978: 38). Unlike the Aldwych, which produced a mix of new and classic texts, the Warehouse was 'a theatre for doing new British plays' (Donohue, quoted in Rosen 1978: 43). For instance, new works by Howard Barker, Barrie Keefe and Edward Bond were performed there. In an interview of 1978, Donohue distinguishes his work from that of the 'German' dramaturg because he is rarely involved in rehearsals (Rosen 1978: 45) and he displays, like many literary managers, a kind of generous vagueness about his reasons for endorsing new work: 'Why I think a play is good really has more to do with instinct than anything else' (Rosen 1978: 46). Donohue mentions play-readings as 'learning experiences' for writers, but admits that they are a compromise, given the number of scripts received (twelve per week in 1978) and the limited possibility of production.

There was a dip in the RSC's commitment to new writing at the end of the 1980s, while in the 1990s literary manager Simon Reade called a halt to the script-reading service altogether (see Luckhurst 2006a: 234), preferring to develop new writing through commissions. Paul Sirett was appointed as 'dramaturg' in 2001, though he describes his role as being essentially that of 'literary manager', suggesting to Mary Luckhurst, in an interview of 2004, that the workload and scale of the company limited the potential for him to be 'involved in the actual production processes ... practically involved in theatre making' (Sirett, quoted in Luckhurst 2006a: 235). Ensuing developments have seen an interesting division between the role of 'dramaturg' and that of 'literary manager' at the RSC. Jeanie O' Hare is now 'literary manager', while several writers have been employed with some dramaturgical responsibilities – two as 'writers in residence' and two as 'writer dramaturgs'.

These new developments emerge as part of a recent emphasis on new writing. In 2004, under the artistic directorship of Michael Boyd, and headed by Dominic Cooke, a 'New Works Festival' was established as the start of a five-year plan to 'regularly put new untried scripts on the main stage' (Cooke, quoted in Costa 2004: 2). In 2006, Boyd commented that the company planned to 'knock Shakespeare off his podium', with half of the company's output concerning new work (Higgins 2006: 1). In the same year, the company announced the appointment of writers in key positions, in a direct attempt to include them within the ensemble and encourage them to write for that specific company – rather as Shakespeare did for his own company. Overall, this suggests a substantial shift towards new writing at the RSC. Living writers may now, potentially, play a central role in a company that first emerged as a 'memorial theatre'.

The third theatre to be discussed in this section is the one best known and internationally respected for its work with writers. The English Stage Company took up residence at the Royal Court Theatre in 1956 under the artistic directorship of George Devine and Tony Richardson. From the first, the Court saw itself as a 'writers' theatre', with an artistic directorship committed to the supremacy of the writer as the central creative force in theatre-making.

The company's third production was the now legendary *Look Back in Anger* (1956), by John Osborne. This is still widely seen as a watershed production, establishing the tenor and the quality of new work at the Court and beyond for years to come. Yet Devine identified Peter Hall's 1955 production of Beckett's *Waiting for Godot* as being equally seminal for the British theatre and considered it part of his mission 'to introduce this other line, the line of Beckett and Ionesco and all that' (quoted in Roberts 1999: 57). Thus, in its first inception, the Court intended to place new British work in the wider context of all European drama. This emphasis fell away after Devine's directorship, but has been resumed in recent years.

In his provocative and enjoyable book, *1956 And All That* (1999), Dan Rebellato suggests that the Court played a key role in 'the professionalisation of the playwright', creating conditions in which the successful playwright was able to be part of a network, receive free admission to performances and, eventually, work full time on writing plays, rather than as a performer/playwright or playwright/novelist. This emphasis on the writer also implied a theatre that stripped away competing visual or physical 'texts', or directorial 'concepts' and presented the author's work in spare, direct productions.

In a bid to widen the scope of works produced, the company instituted Sunday Night Productions without decor – simple, one-off productions on a bare stage. This provided a way of trying out new plays and directors and might be offered as a substitute for full production. In later years, the 'Theatre Upstairs' came to replace the Sunday nights, offering a smaller venue, where new work could be produced with cheaper production and less financial risk. This split between two venues divided the company's work into two, effectively implementing a 'ladder of development'. This was an initially controversial move, though one that pre-empts the 'rehearsed readings' and 'work-in-progress' showings now held by many companies as a first stage on the way towards full production.

The first full-time literary manager at the Royal Court was Rob Ritchie, in 1979 (Luckhurst 2006a: 225). Before this, plays had been considered by a panel, which included a resident dramatist. A writers' group was briefly established in 1958, serving partly as a teaching session for writers, partly as a meeting place. Work with young writers has also taken place since 1966, now including a festival (established in 1973) and a separate theatre space, The Site.

Under Stephen Daldry, the 1990s produced a plethora of new writers that renewed the theatre's international reputation. Characterized by Aleks Sierz as 'in-yer-face' playwrights (Sierz 2001), while known across Europe as 'blood and sperm' dramatists, writers such as Sarah Kane and

Mark Ravenhill generated excitement and controversy in the UK and across Europe. In the early 1990s, Daldry dramatically increased the number of new works produced at the Court before handing over to Ian Rickson in 1994. Rickson rejuvenated the Court's commitment to international drama, establishing an international department in 1996. Graham Whybrow was also appointed in 1994. The role now included script-reading, dialogue with writers, helping to develop plays prior to rehearsal and fostering a close working relationship between the writer and director (Luckhurst 2006a: 225).

In 2007, Dominic Cooke has just been appointed as the new artistic director, fresh from his associate directorship at the RSC, where he headed the New Works Festival. Cooke has a track record at the Court (as associate director), potentially making him a 'safe pair of hands'; nevertheless, this appointment could herald some interesting changes. Billington, problematically opposing 'text-based' work, to devised, visual, physical and site-specific work, urges the Court to resist this 'hectic eclecticism', while continuing to 'fulfil its historic role: that of putting the writer at the centre of the theatrical event' (Billington 2007: 1). While Cooke is not likely to question the importance of the writer, he seems to see less of a division between 'text-based' work, devising and other innovative theatre practices. He argues:

> New writing has a way to go in terms of ambition ... You see devised work that opens up the possibilities of what can be done on stage, and I don't understand why that's quite rare with new plays. The writers I know are just as imaginative and original as the auteur-directors who are devising shows. (Quoted in Costa 2006: 1)

Although it is too early to gauge the effect of this and other recent appointments at the Royal Court, including that of Ruth Little, as Literary Manager, all three of these major, state-funded companies have changed and their changes reflect a shift in the climate. New work, always at the centre of the Court's endeavours, has increasingly become important to the National and the RSC. Meanwhile, the Court itself has increased its activities in developing and reaching new writers and has returned to a broader, international repertoire. All three companies imply a readiness to consider various kinds of 'new work', including the writer, but reaching beyond social realism to other dramatic and performance genres.

There have, of course, been other changes that have influenced the situation for British playwrights. In the 1970s, UK writers began to establish organizations and networks to support their own concerns and initiatives. As Edgar suggests: 'Young provocative theatre writers in particular sought to overcome their traditional isolation by developing all kinds of collective methods and institutions to fight for their interests and indeed to develop their work' (Edgar 2005: 299). These included North-West Playwrights in Manchester, Stagecoach in the Midlands and Northern Playwrights in the North East. The Theatre Writers' Union was founded in 1975, to negotiate contractual agreements and provide a forum for debate. Edgar suggests that despite the importance of the Royal Court, these groups put pressure on the producing companies and thus, 'without these informal, writer-led sites the history of post-1956 British theatre would have been very different' (Edgar 2005: 299). He suggests that the promotion of women playwrights in the 1980s was facilitated by such organizations, for example. Writing competitions (for instance, the Verity Bargate Award) and festivals (for instance, the International Playwriting Festival at the Warehouse in Croydon) have also provided outlets for identifying and promoting new work.

Aleks Sierz questions a direct correlation between arts funding and creative output, 'creativity is stimulated less by the amount of funding you get and more by the way you use it' (Sierz 2003: 36). Yet, while it is a complex matter, state funding has clearly been a significant factor in the development of new work, and continues to be so. The work of the three theatres discussed above would not have been possible without the establishment of Arts Council funding in the 1940s, increasing rapidly in the subsequent decades. Sierz also concedes the importance of Lottery funding to regional theatres such as Birmingham Rep. Despite the ebb and flow of funding, Arts Council England has provided opportunities for writers in the past, through writers' awards, and continues to do so with their Grants for the Arts. New work, and previously, new writing, have been a priority in recent years, giving rise to an increase in opportunities for writers.

For these and other reasons, it is clear that across the UK theatre there has been a phenomenal growth in the appointment of literary managers and in the number of writer development programmes. Recent interest in the 'dramaturg' is partly a reflection of this current emphasis on writing, but also of links with mainland European theatre. This interest in the dramaturg is increasingly opening up debates about the many and various ways of working with new writing and other new work. Theatre practice across Britain currently encompasses many different strands of thinking about these issues and we will go on to examine a few of them. It is to be hoped that our theatre continues to explore diverse approaches, since the potential of recent debates is to open up new possibilities, rather than to close down existing ones.

The Dramaturg as Mentor or 'Buddy'

Penny Gold has worked for many years as a literary manager, dramaturg and (formerly) commissioning editor and producer for the BBC. She is also a playwright herself. She is currently working in a freelance dramaturgical capacity for Kali Theatre, the Hampstead Theatre and the RSC. In her work for Kali, the company chose to term her a 'dramaturg', since 'literary manager' suggests an integral, organizational role. Here, the term 'dramaturg' does not represent an allegiance to German-influenced working practices, which Gold views with some disapproval, stating: 'the German theatre dramaturg has a far more controlling role over script development, even during the production period, than is usual in British theatre' (Gold 2005: 2).

In contrast, Gold advocates a very gentle, questioning approach, drawing out from the writer a sense of what their project is, what they are hoping to communicate and achieve, rather than offering an interpretation, frameworks and rules:

> Something I believe very, very deeply, is that it is the role of the script editor or the literary manager or dramaturg, or whatever you want to call them, to subdue themselves to the spirit of the writer they are dealing with and not to impose some kind of prescriptive notion of how plays ought to be. So your endeavour is to try to find out what the writer hopes for; what he or she is trying to explore; what he or she wants to say ... and help them to make it what they want it to be. (Gold 2005: 12)

Clearly, Gold accepts that there is an element of craft involved in the writer's work and that it is important to 'point out very early on ... if somebody is not thinking in feasible stage terms' (Gold 2005: 24). However, she also cautions that, 'One has to be careful about saying, "No, this is impossible"' (Gold 2005: 24), citing Beckett as an example of a playwright who breaks the rules.

Gold's non-doctrinaire approach is particularly important in the context of her work with Kali, a company specifically dedicated to supporting Asian women writers. Here, not only is Gold frequently working with vulnerable first-time writers, but she also finds that their work, reflecting the writers' ethnic communities, examines concerns and cultural practices which may sometimes be unfamiliar to Gold herself.

Noël Greig has worked as an actor, director and playwright as well as encouraging new writing, particularly in the context of work for and with young people. Speaking at the 'What is Dramaturgy?' symposium in Birmingham, he suggested that the ideal dramaturg might be considered the writer's 'buddy', characterized as a more experienced explorer, helping a novice through a dense 'forest' that is unfamiliar to both. He suggested, like Gold, that 'another playwright' is likely to be the starting point in the quest to find such a 'buddy'. He painted a picture of an intimate relationship that went 'beyond the details of crafting' suggesting that the conversations 'around the campfire' might focus on 'the well-springs of the story': 'It's the intangibles that are the well-springs of creativity' (Greig 2005a).

Greig's book, *Playwriting: A Practical Guide* (Greig 2005b) is consistent with this approach, while at the same time offering concrete enough exercises designed to prompt the writer to push his or her own ideas and techniques further. The tone is encouraging and non-doctrinaire, playful and open to both solitary and collaborative writing.

The main chapter headings suggest the elements Greig considers to be key to playwriting: 'Theme'; 'Issue'; 'Building a Character'; 'Finding the Story'; 'Location'; 'The Individual Voice'; 'Second Draft'. 'The details of crafting' relate, as one might expect, to basic principles for constructing dramatic fictional narrative. While the book is very open and encouraging about the possibility of rule-breaking and of stretching certain 'universal underlying principles' to their limits (Greig 2005b: 59), it does imply that all theatrical experimentation can be framed according to the ways in which it negotiates or challenges 'the rules' (see, for example, Greig 2005b: 84, 99, 102).

The advantage of this approach is that there is no insistence on one particular type of narrative structure. The disadvantage is that it does not acknowledge the possibility of a different set of starting principles, and this could impose its own limitations within an increasingly inter- and cross-disciplinary field. There is also, perhaps understandably in such a practical work, little analysis of the philosophical and political implications of form and a resulting tendency to present experimental works as exciting oddities, rather than as serious challenges to prevailing modes of making meaning.

Both Gold and Greig are well established and have proven their capability as British dramaturgs, who might as appropriately be termed 'literary managers' or 'mentors'. Both have taken significant part in the development of a British theatre (not to mention TV and radio) that produces writers who are well respected (and produced) across Europe and North America. Though their approaches are not identical, they share many ideas, not least that the writer needs a supportive, experienced mentor and champion, who is probably another writer. Their dramaturgical work also positions the writer as the primary creator in the theatre and tends towards an organic, writer-led approach in developing form and structure.

Some recent tendencies in writer development redefine and, to some extent, challenge, these notions of the British dramaturg/literary manager. Some of these changes reflect the very proliferation of literary managers and dramaturgs and the growth of new writer development into what Gold calls a 'cottage industry', fuelled by UK and Irish success in new writing since the 1990s and perceptions that the future of theatre lies in the discovery of new plays and the development of new audiences. Others, perhaps more recently, are due to mainland European and North American influence on the role of the dramaturg and on working practices in general.

Writer Development and the Theatre Industry

Since there is a suggestion that the rise of the dramaturg is associated with the establishment of an 'industry' in writer development (with negative implications of commercial and utilitarian interests), it is worth examining some of the more positive ways in which 'new writing' is being developed in relationship to the requirements of specific contexts within the UK theatre industry.

Esther Richardson, who formerly ran Theatre Writing Partnership (TWP) in the East Midlands, worked in a role that was initially oriented towards the development of writers for a specific regional demand. Her organization began as part of a script-reading venture to discover new writers for five of the principal building-based theatres in the region: Derby Playhouse, Leicester Haymarket, New Perspectives, Nottingham Playhouse and the Royal and Derngate Theatres in Northampton. However, Richardson's own role, commencing in 2001, was one of more active involvement with writers, and from the outset Richardson saw her job as being to fill the gaps left in a region without a designated new writing or experimental studio venue, including a need for 'work that is ... led by a commitment to the artist primarily' (Richardson 2005a: 5). In this respect, despite its link to the theatres, TWP is similar to other regional organizations that aim primarily to support writers, rather than to serve theatres – for example, Writernet, North West Playwrights, Yorkshire Playwrights and others. In 2006, TWP became an independent organization, though still maintaining an established relationship to the regional venues.

Thus, while the context, in terms of regional opportunities for writers, is not without its restrictions, this does not mean that the aim is to produce writers to write a particular 'type' of play, suitable for the five companies. On the contrary, Richardson suggests that what theatres need is 'somebody who challenges the system a bit' (Richardson 2005a: 43).

Richardson expresses some impatience with the criticisms of the growth of development programmes around new writing, pointing out that theatre is a 'collaborative art form' (Richardson 2005a: 23). She resents the suggestion that dramaturgs seek merely to 'meddle' in writers' work, which implies that they have no right to work in conjunction with writers to explore and develop new possibilities. She sees the development of new writing as being connected to ideas about collaboration and creative dialogue: 'If we're going to be a live, fantastically exciting, eclectic theatre culture, isn't it important that we do try different ways of working, and we do allow people into the process?' (Richardson 2005a: 25).

Although she suggests that most writers need to learn a craft, her vision of the dramaturg is less as a teacher of 'rules' than as a creative collaborator and she laments the situation in Britain, where literary managers tend to play down their own creative roles, speculating that, ' "dramaturg" seems to describe an artist, whereas a "literary manager" seems to describe a sort of administrative activity' (Richardson 2005a: 27).

Richardson does describe herself as an 'artist' and in her work as theatre writing director for TWP she sometimes brought together directing and dramaturgical skills, in order to workshop and develop new plays. She suggests that it is possible to work on a new play *as* a dramaturg, while fulfilling a director's function, though she acknowledges that 'it's a very delicate thing', which requires a particular combination of skills and necessitates 'self-awareness' and restraint, since the director/dramaturg must resist imposing too much on the developing text. She also suggests that the writer needs to have developed the work by themselves to a certain extent, before actors are invited into the process.

One key project for the partnership has been Amanda Whittington's *Satin n Steel*, which began as a play for *Get Shortie*, a season of short works, and ended as a full-length work that was shown at Nottingham Playhouse and Bolton Octagon (2005). Despite its acceptance for the main stage at the Playhouse, the work was not developed with this as an initial goal, though the selection of writers for the short festival aimed to identify 'writers whom I wanted to work with and who I felt were right for the theatres' (Richardson 2005a: 5). The success of Whittington's short play led to its subsequent development, though the writer 'didn't want to be locked into some kind of commission with one of the theatres' (Richardson 2005a: 6), and so the process was led by an interest in developing the story, characters and form, rather than being oriented towards meeting the brief of a particular theatre context. It was developed, Richardson explains, 'with the intention always of producing it at the end, but never with the intention of worrying about how it might be produced' (Richardson 2005a: 6).

The workshop process involved the actors in improvisation and creative input, yet Richardson emphasizes that the writer remained the author of the whole text. When the writer merely transcribed rehearsals, the resulting script did not work, but there were many points when she was able to pick up on discoveries made in rehearsal and make them part of her own creative context and structure.

There was clearly a tension in Richardson's work between the desire to develop writers' talents and support networks and TWP's close relationship to particular theatres, with the power to offer commissions. Speaking of the Eclipse Writers' Lab, a more recent project involving ten black writers, she suggested that although she knew that there would be likely to be a commission at the end of the project, it seemed important to separate this possibility from the lab itself: 'Is it possible to create genuine lab conditions if there is an end point the participants are competing for?' (Richardson 2005b). The project was therefore conducted in two phases, with the ten writers initially becoming involved in networking, seeing work and developing a scene, which was then presented to a small group. Each writer was then offered a 'seed commission' to develop work and theatres were then able to decide whether or not to offer full commissions – five were offered. Although Richardson admits to a consciousness of being, to some extent, a 'gate-keeper' (Richardson 2005b), her intention was to stimulate the production of exciting new writing within the region, and she describes the TWP as 'writer-led' – with the potential for professional and commercial success as a secondary priority (Richardson 2005a: 6).

Ben Payne, working for Birmingham Repertory Theatre as 'Associate Director (Literary)', also sees his relationship with a large theatre as a positive one, despite being much more closely tied to this organization than Richardson has ever been to the five East Midland theatres. Payne sees his theatre's size and substantial subsidy as offering an opportunity to support a whole range of work, developing new audiences, making links across new contexts and taking risks, besides 'enabling ... things to happen, even if they don't necessarily all happen here' (Payne 2006: 3). He has been working to develop new audiences at the studio theatre, The Door, since the late 1990s and has moved from a position of needing to prove that there is an audience for new work, to a more established situation where the work and its audiences can become more diverse. For instance, he suggests that there is an energy around work being made by black writer-performers and that this new work can be supported by the theatre, just as well as plays by new writers. Although Payne has become increasingly able to diversify and to take risks, when I first spoke to him, in 2000, he was even then interested in encouraging writers to develop into new areas, and was then working with Sarah Woods to develop a play about ballroom dancing, incorporating the dance into her concept and vision of the work.

The Rep supports young writers (twelve to twenty-five) through its 'Transmissions' programme, which operates on an annual basis as a festival of staged readings of new plays. The theatre also has an Attachment programme, which offers a more established writer the possibility of a continuing dialogue with the theatre, hopefully resulting in a commissioned work. In the 2006 season, Arzhang Pezhman's *The Bolt-Hole* was in production at The Door, an example of a continuing relationship with a writer whose earlier work, *LOCAL*, was developed through Transmissions and produced at the Royal Court in 2001. Pezhman has also worked with the Rep's Youth Theatre. After its run at The Door, the play toured other venues, including schools and colleges in the region, expanding the range of its audiences.

The policy at the Rep sees the development of new work as intrinsically bound up with the development of new audiences – as opposed to being a recipe for reducing audience numbers, which it can sometimes appear to be. However, the vision of 'new work' is wider than straightforward commissioning of play texts, while this is likely to remain an important part of the company's work.

At the Oval House symposium, 2005, Payne and Amber Lone discussed their work together on her play, *Paradise* (Payne and Lone 2005). This took place partly through an e-mail correspondence, with Payne offering continuous feedback as they discussed the play, which looked at the experience of growing up in a Muslim-Kashmiri household. Payne suggested that it was important to consider ways of retaining the play's immediacy, finding an appropriate form for the work and negotiating the changing political context. It seems a dialogue that was handled with some sensitivity.

If Birmingham Rep is a theatre that is famous for the controversies surrounding *Bezhti*, by Gurpreet Kaur Bhatti (2004), which offended some Sikh audiences, this particular issue needs to be placed in context. The theatre is continuously producing works for culturally and ethnically diverse audiences; in 2006 alone, at least nine separate works could be identified as directly targeting black audiences in some way, while clearly, other productions did not exclude a diverse spectatorship. In this theatre, the emphasis is less on 'new playwrights', but on the potential of new forms, contents, artists to engage on many levels, with many different kinds of people. 'Writer development' is therefore closely linked with both 'audience' and 'art-form' development, rather than seen as an end in itself. This is not a case of manipulating or moulding writers for particular ends, but of taking a broad view of new work, one that sees it as integrally linked to its context. As Payne says, this brings us back to the initial concept of the repertory theatre, as a building that is 'for everybody' within the city (Payne 2006: 8).

European Influences on UK Practice

If there is suspicion of the term 'dramaturg' as one that suggests a new writing 'industry', there is even more tension surrounding its association with European practices. It is therefore worth considering how these influences might be informing British theatre practice today.

Frauke Franz, dramaturg for Polka Theatre, works alongside literary managers. She suggests that while the literary manager tends to give feedback 'in the line and in the language' (Franz 2005a: 1), she believes she is more inclined to think about the whole stage picture. She looks at the text in terms of the spaces it offers for other things, such as physicality. She speaks of the need for the dramaturg to work beyond the writing process and into production to get the director and the writer to talk to one another, to facilitate a common understanding, but one in which the director is given the freedom to interpret the text.

For Franz, the dramaturg's work with playwrights might reflect a move away from the playwright as primary creator and towards the sense of a production team. The dramaturg's approach *joins* the writer's work to the production process, helping the playwright to develop a play not primarily as a work to be read, but as a text for performance.

Polka's *Playgrounding* is a year-long scheme to develop plays for children's theatre. Through this scheme, five writers were first attached for a year in 2003–4. Franz explains that her German background, combined with her experience of working 'mainly with devising theatre companies' in England, led her to develop (with Artistic Director Annie Wood and Associate Director of New Writing Richard Shannon), a vision of a project which would 'open the theatre to new ways of working, a place to experiment. We wanted to give the writers a chance to experience the theatrical process during the writing process, to embrace physicality and visual images' (Franz 2005b: 6).

The scheme began with two 'masterclasses' that were open to all. These involved writers directly in physical work, directing, music, design and puppetry, as well as demonstrating ways in which actors might physicalize a story. Writers were then invited to submit a synopsis and five pages of dialogue. Five writers were then selected for the programme.

The group of five then attended a week-long workshop, again incorporating practical skills and demonstrations. There was also feedback and mentoring for the writers and, in fact, Noël Greig took each of them for tutorials on their work. Franz describes the way that each writer was able to take away 'early design sketches and music ideas for the pieces' and, over the following six months, 'attended one-to-one dramaturgy sessions' including 'discussion about theatricality … how much dialogue is necessary to tell the story and how much can be told by other media like design, physicality, light and music' (Franz 2005b: 7).

Each play was given a workshop performance in January 2004 and the plays were directed by established professionals who were, however, new to directing children's work. This was therefore an event that forged new relationships, as well as showcasing the work of the scheme. Two of the plays were subsequently commissioned for production.

In the subsequent year, the scheme followed a similar pattern, but with the introduction of a two-day workshop between first draft and final draft, in which the dramaturg and actors worked on key ideas and scenes, which, Franz explains, 'gave a great insight into the dynamics between the characters and how the physical language will shape the play' (Franz 2005b: 9).

This very intensive, collaborative process, despite its embrace of more traditional 'mentoring' as part of its structure, suggests a much closer engagement between the writer and the theatre company. As Franz puts it, the writers learn about theatre and about 'writing as part of a collaborative process' (Franz 2005c). Franz suggests that her role involves helping them to write 'an open text', to 'create space' (Franz 2005c). She comments of the difference, again, between a literary manager and a dramaturg:

> When you work as a dramaturg in UK building based theatres, they often use you as a Literary Manager ... as soon as you go into the rehearsal space, they often don't care to involve you any more, which for me is hugely frustrating because I think that's where the real work of the dramaturg starts. In the production process. (Franz 2005a: 2)

UK dramaturg Hanna Slättne, at Northern Ireland's Tinderbox Theatre, also identifies the difference between the dramaturg and the literary manager as being, 'that the dramaturgs have a continued presence into the production and the rehearsal period' (Slättne 2005a:6). She comments:

> I find it frustrating being involved in the textual development of a script and then handing it over and not being part of the continuation of it ... the literary manager/dramaturg should be part of the production process to see what happens with the script, what works and what doesn't work. Additionally, when you go back to your desk and continue to read scripts you continue to engage with them with the live theatrical medium in mind. (Slättne 2005a: 6)

Though Slättne was trained in the UK, her views are influenced by the practices of her native country, Sweden, and, like Franz's, reflect an understanding of mainland European models and practices where the director tends to have greater significance. While her job title at Tinderbox is officially 'literary manager', the role is understood to be essentially that of a dramaturg, as Slättne defines it. This not only involves work on productions for Tinderbox, but, through *The Joint Dramaturgy Project*, Slättne's input is also offered to other theatre companies who are funded by the scheme to develop new projects. Her job does entail script-reading and mentoring, but she suggests that the approach is 'more dramaturgical' in the way that writing is workshopped with actors and becomes part of an explorative process 'around the ideas of the play, as well as the text of the play' (Slättne 2005a: 7).

Slättne identifies some of the resistance to the idea of the dramaturg (from both writers and directors) as being a resistance to the idea of collaborative creation: 'the issue, I suppose, then, for me is how to show the benefits of that more collaborative way of working which still places the writer in the centre and safeguards the integrity of their work' (Slättne 2005a: 3). When she runs workshops, she suggests, she does not aim to 'teach people to write. I can teach people to think about theatre, to experiment with structure, to experiment with the medium' (Slättne 2005a: 7). Slättne comments particularly on the openness of Northern Irish theatre writers, but is sanguine that this is a growing approach among literary managers throughout the UK, who are increasingly moving towards the role of the (mainland European) dramaturg.

Conclusion

It is often difficult to unravel the fundamental differences between approaches when much of the rhetoric around writers will appear superficially similar at different institutions. Most literary managers or dramaturgs will acknowledge that theatre is collaborative; most will accept the importance of the writer's individual creativity. Most will acknowledge the importance of both inspiration and craft. What is hard to ascertain, unless through direct experience of the work of each dramaturg or literary manager, is quite where the balance is to be struck.

Perhaps the fundamental question that divides the above approaches, is this: to what extent is playwriting a social or an individual activity and are 'the well-springs' of theatrical creativity to be found in the verbal text or on the rehearsal floor? This might be countered with another question: need there be a definitive answer or a choice between one extreme or another? Perhaps these issues need to be negotiated differently in every case. No one is proposing a 'one size fits all' concept of dramaturgy. Indeed, Slättne says, 'I like the word "dramaturg" because I think it's open … it's not easy to define, so it can open new doors to the future and new ways of working' (Slättne 2005b).

Working with a dramaturg (or not) is generally a choice. For some, this has undoubtedly been helpful. It is difficult, if not impossible to generalize about which working structures are most helpful and may best be considered in specific cases. Slättne emphasizes the importance of the freelance dramaturg, an elusive, but increasingly significant figure within UK theatre culture and one for whom the relationship is defined anew for each particular project.

Within new writing contexts in the UK, the use of the term 'dramaturg' does seem to reflect some shifts in approaches to work with writers. The development of new writing has become an established professional field. In many cases, there is now a more practical approach to workshopping and production than is suggested by terms such as 'literary manager' or 'mentor'. The word 'dramaturg' seems to acknowledge the creativity of the facilitating role in ways that 'literary manager' does not and it also seems to give scope for the development of new work that is not necessarily script-based. One must be careful not to suggest that these changes are ubiquitous, since in many cases, the word is simply co-opted as an alternative label for the 'literary manager' or 'script-reader/ editor'. Even in such cases, however, the term brings with it a new history, a new set of associations and vocabularies, which must be considered, even where they are rejected.

Recently, there seems a growing interest in considering and questioning the established structures of writer development, asking whether it might be possible to imagine alternatives that could produce different kinds of work and nurture different qualities in new writing. For example, David Lane, now a freelance dramaturg and previously a dramaturg at the Soho Theatre, has devised projects that seek to challenge and develop the notion of the 'rehearsed reading' (Lane 2006a) and is also developing a project to initiate dialogues between writers and non-theatre artists (sculptors, composers and so on), with a view to extending the writers' awareness of theatrical possibilities.

A discussion held at Arts Council England Yorkshire, 20 March 2006, initiated by Alison Andrews and Claire MacDonald, suggested a new range of possibilities for supporting writers. The group speculated on the possibility of initiatives that might open up the potential to write across art-forms and in new collaborations, rather than for established theatre forms. A research project and organization, 'The Space Between Words', was set up by MacDonald to pursue this further, first meeting at the University of Aberystwyth, 2–4 February, 2007. MacDonald writes:

> The Space Between Words aims to look at ways in which the support for writing for performance can be developed in radically inclusive ways, that is in ways that foster the exchange between literary and visual cultures, and that move beyond the convention of play-reading and revision, to include other kinds of textual and performance work around writing. (MacDonald 2007: 1)

The idea of 'radical inclusion' might be worth serious consideration in this context. Projects such as these and others raise the question of whether the UK dramaturg's work with writers might in future become more diverse, and more inclusive, operating in live art contexts and perhaps working with poets, story-tellers or writers working in interactive media. The development of new writing in Britain has always had a political edge, often aiming to promote a wide range of 'voices' and to develop new audiences. It now seems timely to ask whether there remain underlying assumptions about form, dramaturgical process and notions such as those of 'quality' and 'excellence', which might serve to limit an intended inclusivity. The politics of work with writers, as well as the work of writers, may need to be constantly articulated, analysed and reconsidered.

6 The Production Dramaturg

In Between

When working on a production as a dramaturg, the question often asked is whether one is working specifically as a *production dramaturg*. This question has two implications. First, it acknowledges that there are different ways of being a dramaturg. Second, the implicit question is essentially: 'So, do you get to go into the rehearsal space at all?' Practising dramaturgs and dramaturgy students alike will recognize this last question as particularly crucial, because many dramaturgs are likely to define themselves as creative thinkers and practitioners, directly involved in the creative process. Indeed, as we pointed out in Chapter 1, dramaturgy and dramaturgical analysis entail the attempt to bridge theory and practice; to move from the theoretical idea to the practical implementation. Many dramaturgs would therefore consider working on a production, from its earliest conception through to the end, as the essence of dramaturgical work.

In Chapter 2 we described Brecht's use of the dramaturg, suggesting that this was a forerunner of the contemporary production dramaturg. Here, we will take a closer look at the ways in which production dramaturgs work. Our intention is to give a sense of the role, not from an historical perspective, but through a discussion of current practice. Apart from a few isolated examples, there is no established tradition of production dramaturgy in the UK – not, at least, of collaborators with that title. The tradition of having a production dramaturg, working from the beginning of a project through to the end, is not that well established, though there are a few exceptions. We have already mentioned some of them, such as Edward Kemp, formerly for Chichester Festival Theatre, Duska Radosavljevic, formerly for Northern Stage, and

Adriano Shaplin (of Riot Group, New York), who was one of those recently appointed as dramaturgs at the RSC (Powell, 2006). There are also dramaturgs working in devising contexts – however, we will discuss these in our next chapter, in order to examine the specific challenges of these processes. Rarer still, are dramaturgs working in dance, but here we are also beginning to see developments: for example, Ruth Ben-Tovim has worked with Vincent Dance Theatre as a dramaturg. In order to get a more comprehensive perspective, this chapter also looks beyond the UK, drawing on conversations with Danish, German and US dramaturgs, including Kitte Wagner (Betty Nansen Theatre, Copenhagen), Bettina Masuch (dance curator, Hebbel Am Ufer, Berlin), Maja Zade (Schaubühne, Berlin), André Lepecki (Tisch School of Art, New York), Anne Cattaneo (Lincoln Center Theater, New York) and Christian Parker (Atlantic Theater Company, New York).

No two dramaturgs, collaborations or productions will be the same, and the dramaturgical role will always depend on the needs of the particular project. For this reason, it is impossible to describe a representative process, since, due to the very contextual nature of the production dramaturg's work, all processes will be different. It should also be noted that although most of the dramaturgs we talked to are now connected to an institution, freelancers will often occupy the role of production dramaturg, invited in by a director or company seeking a dialogue partner who can help shape the project from beginning to end, not least with feedback during the rehearsal period. Dramaturgs' rehearsal and production documention can also be found in Mark Bly (1996, 2001).

While there have been attempts to summarize the work of the production dramaturg, they can only ever be generalizations, however helpful. Some of these seem based on a Brechtian idea(l), which does not always reflect the work of the dramaturg in practice. Lloyd Trott argues for the dramaturg in production; however his argument remains theoretical, rather than illustrated by practical examples (Trott 1999: 32). While it is often assumed that the production dramaturg researches the play and/or its background, acting as a resource for rehearsals, not all directors or choreographers are interested in stacks of (historical) research or long, pre-rehearsal conversations about a play or an idea. In fact, Hildegard de Vuyst comments of her work with choreographer Alain Platel that she does not always do library research, 'because it's not going to be used' (Delahunta 2000: 23). Similarly, some directors will not be interested in historical research, but may be interested in research that looks at readings of the text, or analyses the text in terms of its treatment of key themes. Thus the research might take a number of different forms. One could, for instance, structure research around ideas and impressions that arise in the first contact between the actors and the play, without relying on any preconceived ideas about the play.

There is sometimes a sense that the dramaturg might be an encyclopedic authority, hovering darkly over the rehearsal, wielding Casaubon's *Key to all Mythologies*. For instance, Martin Esslin depicts the dramaturg as someone who attends rehearsals, provides background material about the playwright and the play's social or political implications, makes cuts in the play and helps with translations. Apart from this, the production dramaturg is consulted about difficult or unusual words (Esslin 1978: 49). This is not inaccurate in terms of some of the classical dramaturg's activities – for instance, Kemp recalls 'researching Molière's world' for Stephen Pimlott (Kemp 2007) – however, contemporary practitioners propose that the production dramaturg might be seen as a 'supportive, but questioning force' (Bly 1996: xxiv), whose work 'can function in a multi-faceted manner, helping the director and other artists to interpret and shape the sociological, textual, acting, directing and design values, as well as culturally sensitive aesthetic approaches' (Bly 2001: xv).

Although processes differ and will require different things from the dramaturg, it is possible to summarize some general tasks of production dramaturgy. These include pre-production work such as casting; research (of various kinds); discussion of the performance context; textual analysis; editing; translation; and planning rehearsals. In some cases, this role can also involve preparing a production or 'case' book (Bly 1996: xxiii). Other responsibilities might include the preparation of programme notes, and press releases.

The defining feature of production dramaturgs is their presence in the actual theatre-making process, in the rehearsal room. Quite how this might manifest itself is again dependent on the needs of the director and the production. Zade, for example, suggests that when working on Schiller's *Maria Stuart*, directed by Luk Perceval in 2005, she would come in every day for the first two weeks, then she would attend rehearsals once a week and then again every day for the last two weeks (Zade 2006: 6). In contrast, when working with director Benedict Andrews on David Harrower's *Blackbird* (2005), she would attend every single rehearsal. André Lepecki, who has primarily worked in dance, usually prefers to attend every rehearsal, even if very little happens. Thus, attendance depends on the particular working structure. For example, the dramaturg might attend more rehearsals in devised or dance processes, because he or she is actively helping, like a co-writer, to shape the dramaturgy.

From Theory to Practice

As we have discussed earlier, the production dramaturg could be said to emerge through Brecht's practice at the Berliner Ensemble. Hence, the prefix 'production' could be said to be a legacy from Brecht, who wanted to bring the dramaturgs out from behind their desks, away from the piles of scripts and books and into the rehearsal room. In the Brechtian conception, the dramaturg helps to develop a conceptual framework for the production, or, as Richard Pettengill puts it in terms of his own practice, the dramaturg 'questions and interrogates the proceedings with an eye to deepening the conceptual approach' (Pettengill 2006: 299). If the production dramaturg was born out of Brecht's urgent need for a practice informed by political discourse, this may be why he or she often sits on the fault line between theory and practice in the attempt to allow the two to inform one another. Eleonora Fabião reflects on her work as dramaturg with Mabou Mines Theater, commenting:

> Different from the other 'roles' I played before, I had the opportunity to emphasize a connection between artistic practice and theoretical thinking; through the dramaturg's viewpoint, practice and theory are emphatically experienced as complementary references, as different appearances of a unique matter. However, it is important to stress that the dramaturg is alchemically combining these references to make the scene richer in terms of dynamics and meaning; my dramaturgical purpose is not a project of intellectualizing the scene. (Fabião 2003: 29)

Fabião seems to suggest an interaction between idea and form. This interaction or oscillation is also found in the production dramaturg's concern with looking at the process whereby a play becomes a live production or an idea is realized in performance. The production dramaturg seeks to identify strategies for opening up the material, whether it be a play, a concept or a theme. Heidi Gilpin, who has been a dramaturgical collaborator for American choreographer William Forsythe, comments that she would help Forsythe to translate ideas that that could be linguistic, mathematical, or scientific into another form, that of dance (Delahunta 2000: 22).

In conducting a literary analysis we might view a play as a self-contained system of meanings, whereas in doing production dramaturgy we consider what possibilities and challenges the play opens up when thought of as a living composition in time and space. As Freddie

Rokem comments of his collaboration on *Oedipus Tyrannos* with director Leif Stinnerbom, dramaturgical analysis can 'create the basis for a specific production, exploring different options which the director develop[s] into the specific mise-en-scène of the production' (Rokem 2006: 261). Indeed, although the dramaturg's work is multi-faceted, ideas of bridging, translating, framing and contextualizing run through most of the dramaturg's work. Cattaneo comments that dramaturgical preparation of text involves finding a concept that 'embraces and adjusts the heart of the play for a twentieth-century production' (Cattaneo 1997: 7) For Cattaneo, however, this still involves a balance between looking at the play in its own context and the context in which it is produced. Kemp suggests that in working on an older text, he is attempting to act on the (dead) writer's behalf, to lend the text some of the resources offered by the contemporary world (Kemp 2007, 2005).

Creating a Context

As we saw with Brecht, the dramaturg is concerned with 'context', attentive to the bigger picture. The dramaturg attempts to place the work in context and articulates why and how a given work, or genre, might be important. On a concrete level, this concern is manifest at the very beginning of the process with the selection of the play, text or idea for production. Decisions concerning how the play (or idea) is to be realized are often connected with the reasons why it is chosen in the first place. Maja Zade sees it as her role to both pose and answer questions concerning the reason for producing a particular play in a particular time and place. Zade comments, in relation to the production of classic texts, that it has to be clear why and how a production might differ from other productions of the same play. The dramaturg has to help the theatre company to articulate a rationale for producing the work, relating it to contemporary society and the particular cultural or political climate.

This does not always have to lead to highly politicized productions, but it sometimes has done so. For example, as we have discussed earlier, in some European and North American contexts, the play is seen as an open resource to be 'exploded', deconstructed and recontextualized. Although this approach has its vehement critics, the argument is that classic plays are not dead museum pieces but need to be made vibrant and vital in the contemporary world. Thus, the 'radical' reworking of plays does not necessarily imply a disregard for the playwright, but it does imply that we cannot take a play's currency for granted.

Dramaturg Stefanie Carp comments:

> You must always know why you plan something, why you have to tell
> something on the stage. It also becomes daily more and more important
> to deal dramaturgically in the political sense, in the framework of a politi-
> cal ethic. I mean, theatre is after all a public meeting-place, and there you
> encounter, or have to encounter statements, public statements. Even to
> avoid live social experiences would be a statement. (Quoted in Kaynar
> 2006: 257)

Carp implies that politics are everywhere and everything is political.
Even non-engagement, or as she puts it avoidance of 'live social experiences', is a political act of refusal. The adaptation and recontextualization
of plays can clearly be provocative. For example, one thinks of the
Wooster Group's *Route 1 & 9 (The Last Act)* (1981), which included a
radical reworking of Thornton Wilder's *Our Town* (1938), critiquing
the play itself. Some condemned the production for its controversial use
of 'blackface' make-up, though others, such as Baz Kershaw, have
argued that the Wooster Group's use of 'blackface' can be 'interpreted as
opening up a critique of racism' (Kershaw 1999: 72). Kershaw is actually referring to a subsequent production, *LSD – Just the High Points*,
but he implies that the strategy is similar for both productions. Former
dramaturgical collaborator with the Wooster Group, Norman Frisch
describes this deconstructive approach to plays as exposing: 'the plumb-
ing, the wiring, the termites, the "invisible" world that existed inside the
walls of the structure' (Frisch 2002: 277).

Relocating a play naturally brings up aesthetic considerations: if one
wants to talk about the world today, is it necessary to modernize the
aesthetic? Is it appropriate to clarify the play's historical context, with
references to the debates that originally informed it? For Cattaneo it
seems important to 'honor and preserve the way the play worked in its
own time' (Cattaneo 1997: 7); how do we know how a play originally
'worked'? And why is this important? These are dramaturgical questions
and different dramaturgs are likely to have very different answers. The
more radical reworkings of classic texts, such as the Wooster Group's
work, or that of German Director, Frank Castorf (described below) are
often the source of controversy, since they effectively transform the play
text in order to construct an essentially new work. We may remember
that Brecht did the same and that he, too, was criticized for this.

To give an example of a radical reworking, Castorf's production of
King Lear (1992) reworked the play for a reunified Germany. According

to Rouse, 'Castorf cut a fair amount of Shakespeare's text. He kept lines and exchanges in which Shakespeare's play evoked something of the emotional tenor of a 'post-GDR' condition – the existential experience of a world falling to ruins' (Rouse 2000: 83). In this production, Goneril and Regan were seen scrubbing the floor 'like good German housewives', Cordelia 'tested the French King's devotion by pissing in a bucket, then demanding he drink from it', Lear, a friendly but 'seemingly senile' figure evoked Erich Honecker, while Kent became 'a collective character dubbed the "Seven Samurai", embodied by seven actors wearing breast-plate and helmet over long johns'. Rouse continues:

> There was nothing 'universal' about this use of Shakespeare's play. The production addressed itself to participants from an ex-East-German public sphere, and it endowed these participants with the power to shape their own destiny in a reunified Germany, rather than treating them as helpless losers. (Rouse 2000: 84)

A production such as this is no longer preoccupied with examining or recreating the play within its original context, but is using it as a vehicle to provoke questions about the context of the performance.

Speaking about her work on Maxim Gorky's *Datsniki* (*Summerfolk*) (1904), Wagner explains how she worked closely with the director, Peter Langdal, to re-imagine the play and to emphasize the parallels between its original context and the current one (Wagner 2005: 5). It was necessary to ask questions such as, 'What would this play speak of today? What can it tell us? What has it got to do with the world we live in? What could be the dramaturgical parallels between the play and a contemporary world?' Rather than seeing Gorky's play as being solely about Russian peasants threatening the aristocracy, it could be resonant of contemporary issues to do with globalization (Wagner 2005: 4). The process of bringing out such themes can require extensive rewriting to bring action and language into the current context. Wagner becomes an active *co-writer* in what she describes as a dynamic and playful dialogue with director Langdal, where dramaturgical discussion about the play is mixed with rewriting the scenes in a contemporary idiom (Wagner 2005: 6).

Thus the dialogue between the dramaturg and director concerns the search for the language, the ideas and the dramaturgical themes that can frame the production. The dramaturg develops the directors' ideas and helps to re-imagine, edit and rewrite the text. Wagner describes herself as someone who develops and enhances ideas, and who tries to locate these within a conceptual framework (Wagner 2005: 2). One could say that the dramaturg analyses how ideas sit within a larger structure, whether in terms of considering details within the architecture of the production or in considering how a theatre production sits within its cultural context. Stephanie Carp comments on the production dramaturg's attention to what one could call micro and macro structures:

> I expect the dramaturg to read the daily papers, to be versed in what is going on in the world at large, and in the theatre world in particular. This is the essence of production dramaturgy – to study, to develop a very narrow and a very broad long-distance view. (Quoted in Kaynar 2006: 257–8)

The production dramaturg can also help to develop a context for and around a production, by framing it with other events or discussions. When Radosavljevic worked with Northern Stage she was involved in curating and producing events to tie in with the company's current production. She describes this as follows:

> If we are producing a show, we have tried over the last few years to create an entire festival around it, so we would have … a musical programme, and a film programme … it's also been facilitated by the fact that Newcastle has got this cultural scene that's quite incestuous and everybody works with each other and they work across the arts forms, and so we've been able to also programme dance events in relation to particular productions. (Radosavljevic 2005: 3)

In 2003, Northern Stage presented a two-week 'Gypsy Festival' around the core production, *The Black Eyed Roses* (directed by Alan Lyddiard). Prior to and alongside this, Theater Pralipe, a Roma company based in Germany, presented *Carmen*. There was a day of musical events, incorporating a matinee of the Northern Stage production and an early evening performance of *Carmen*, as well as a panel discussion on UK traveller culture. As Radosavljevic explains, there were also films, another guest company from Spain, a dance programme and a programme of educational activities, happening city-wide. This was one of Radosavljevic's first projects with the company and she was very much involved in putting this selection of work together. She describes meeting people across the city, sharing ideas and references and 'trying to collate' this material 'into a meaningful core' (Radosavljevic 2005: 4). Again, the dramaturg's concern with 'the whole' ensured coherence across a varied programme. A festival, or series of events, such as this can draw attention to a production, provoking debate and discussion in conjunction with the production's theme or subject matter.

Pre-production

We often find production dramaturgs involved in 'pre-production', that is, the preparation of a project. Cattaneo describes this as preparing 'a concept or a way "into" the play' (Cattaneo 1997: 7). There are different ways of approaching this. For example, in preparing for Lone Twin Theatre's *Alice Bell* (2006), David Williams wrote a lengthy analysis of Michael Ondaatje's novel *In the Skin of a Lion* (1997), which was one of the initial stimuli. Here he found inspiration in the idea of the musical band, the sense of a 'mural', which evoked the idea of 'a falling together of accomplices … a wondrous night web' (Williams 2006b).

One could say that Williams's analysis inspired practical and philosophical starting points, because he offered not only a literary critique, but thought about the novel in terms of its spatial and dynamic potential. This kind of preparatory dramaturgical analysis potentially offers a structural and thematic framework for the production, and could give the director(s) some starting points, ways to think about the material, and 'find a way "into"' the work.

The more complex or imaginative or evocative the perspectives that the dramaturg brings to the initial text, the more exciting it may become for the director to imagine it as a stimulus for performance. Different staging possibilities emerge from different ways of reading the text, whether phenomenological, socio-political or deconstructive. Rokem describes his dramaturgical conversations with director Stinnerbom in preparing for *Oedipus Tyrannos*. Having observed the paradox created by Oedipus's answer to the Sphinx's riddle – on the one hand Oedipus had 'given the correct solution' yet this had led him to his mother's bed – Rokem describes how this provided a way into the play and its performance:

Very early in our discussions we decided that this paradox, the tragic outcome, even after giving the 'correct' answer to the riddle, had to be addressed in some way by the performance. The way to confront this issue was by trying to provide additional solutions to the riddle through the performance itself, at the same time as the performance itself attempted to give an additional solution to Sophocles' drama as a textual riddle. Proceeding in this way, it became clear that we were dealing with different levels of riddling, and dramaturgical analysis was a way to tackle the complex interactions between these levels. (Rokem 2006: 262).

One can, however, imagine dramaturgical approaches where there is no attempt to 'analyse' the work, but rather a generation of ideas about performance. For instance, composer and director Heiner Goebbels proposes that one can imagine the text as a 'landscape'. He asks: 'Can the punctuation marks tell us something? Or particular spellings? Capital letters? Breaking of lines?' (Goebbels 1997: 61). This offers a formalist approach to the text, rendering it a space for exploration, rather than a container of meanings to be decoded. Naturally, such a radical approach will not always be appropriate; however, one can see how it might prove useful in identifying rhythmic, structural qualities, which can be explored in an essentially musical treatment.

We should remember, however, that 'pre-production' need not always concern a verbal text at all: this is the case with most dance practices. Bettina Masuch points out that in these instances, pre-production work is about shaping material and finding a way to begin. While a play can provide a starting point and the initial dramaturgical questions revolve around 'finding a way "into" the play', in dance practices the first explorations are very open, and often begin with an idea or a concept. The dramaturg then has to assist in finding a working structure for the exploration.

For example, Masuch described her work with choreographer Meg Stuart on *Alibi*. The themes of *violence* and *aggression* provided the initial starting points. Masuch gives an account of a very extensive preparation period before the rehearsals, where she, Stuart, the video, set and sound designer, would meet up every three or four weeks for a few days to discuss ideas, research, cast and the overall shape of the project. Masuch comments that research is especially relevant at this early stage. This research might include identifying resonant points of reference: plays, films, texts, exhibitions, catalogues, music, images, articles, sounds and so on. However, Masuch may also help the choreographer to find a structure, both for the process of exploration and for the piece itself. She tries to help the choreographer find what she is looking for, both through facilitating the plans for rehearsal and by planning a number of workshops for the performers:

For example we decided to do a shooting class and then we decided to do training with a shaman from Bali, because Meg had this idea that the piece would end with a shaking scene and this idea came from a meditation training that she had done and then we invited that teacher to work with us on this idea. (Masuch 2006: 12)

Here, the dramaturg becomes a kind of artistic advisor, who looks to develop and deepen the conceptual approach through suggesting practical solutions as to how the theme could be explored. There is a simultaneous engagement with research and finding practical ways into the work; if the choreographer/director may be often engaged with looking at specific performance ideas, the dramaturg can help to create a practical and conceptual framework in which these ideas could be developed and understood.

Attending Rehearsals

In rehearsal, the dramaturg helps to implement the ideas discussed in pre-production. In Chapter 4, we suggested that the dramaturg can be a mediator, both within the institution and between the institution and its audience. We could argue that the dramaturg represents the audience within a rehearsal process, able to identify the potential gap between what is *intended* and what is likely to be *received* and to give the artist a perspective on what they are creating. Ben-Tovim, for example, describes her role as a dramaturg on Vincent Dance Theatre's *Broken Chords* (2005) as an 'outside eye'. She was there to give rehearsal feedback and to reflect back to the choreographer and dancers the overall meaning she saw conveyed in the performance. Her concern was therefore with analyzing how the semiotics – or actions – of performance were orchestrated into an overall structure. This would also involve discussions about the dramaturgical consequences of decisions made. For example, when working on *Broken Chords*, the 'fourth wall' was broken twenty minutes into the performance. The question arose as to whether or not this principle should be set up earlier in the performance, and Ben-Tovim discussed the timing of this break with Charlotte Vincent, in order to establish the effect on the overall meaning of the performance (Ben-Tovim 2007).

The production dramaturg attends the rehearsals as a supportive first audience. When working closely with the director or choreographer, the dramaturg is placed between maintaining an awareness of the overall project and its aims, and attempting to 'read' the work with fresh eyes. Masuch explains that while the dramaturg attempts to be clear-sighted about what is being communicated, he or she also needs to help the choreographer or director to find new and better ways to articulate their work. Masuch comments that it is about 'seeing what is actually there, and what is still missing' (Masuch 2006: 6).

Thus, the dramaturg helps the director or choreographer to refocus or, at least, to experience the work from a different perspective. The director might not always be able to maintain an objective perspective, and the dramaturg can help by sustaining a wider perspective, a long view, in the day-to-day struggle with the details of production. Indeed, seeing the work from a different perspective can help to provoke the development of new layers within the performance, adding more dimensions that can enrich and enhance. De Vuyst implies that she does not aim to give her 'opinion', so much as to describe what seems to be going on in the work and to relay these observations to the choreographer. She comments:

> A dramaturg is a mirror: you reflect – literally mirror – what you see. In my view this is the absolute basis of my work. However, I think the challenge is to be intellectual without being guilty of intellectualism. To reflect and provide insight in the most transparent way without getting in the way yourself. Without having to prove how clever you are, without taking a normative approach. (Vuyst 2006: 134–5)

How does the dramaturg negotiate this need for simultaneous empathy and distance? How is it possible to know the work intimately and yet observe it as if for the first time? For some, intimacy with the work is of primary importance. For instance, Lepecki suggests that the dramaturg needs to be as 'close as possible' (Lepecki 2006: 3). If the dramaturg is too much of a 'distant observer', there may be a tendency to give feedback only in order to resolve structural problems. Instead, Lepecki proposes that the dramaturg might see him or herself as someone who has a memory of the process and can draw on that memory creatively. He comments:

> The distant observer doesn't know that three months before, there was this improvisation that actually could fit perfectly in the moment in which the energy breaks. So he has no memory of the process because he is distant. But if you're close, you've got to remember not only the people off stage, but you are also going to remember the movie that we all went together to see after rehearsal and there was this great thing, and why don't you bring that in, or the thought that someone else had, or the dream I also had, that could be put into that scene. So for me dramaturgy is about proximity. (Lepecki 2006: 3)

Others take a different view. Wagner, for instance, considers physical distance to be important. She suggests that it is important not to become consumed by the daily politics of the production, to be able to ask questions and to respond when the performance does not make sense according to its own logic (Wagner 2005: 13).

These perspectives might reflect a difference in the performance-making process. While Lepecki works in a dance context, Wagner is usually concerned with plays. Where the work is devised or choreographed, there may be a need for the dramaturg to work very closely with the company, to shape the emerging piece.

When Masuch worked on *Alibi* she was in rehearsal for almost the whole process. During this period, the choreographer, dramaturg, video artist and sound artist were working together in the space, trying things out and developing the piece organically. Masuch comments: 'We created like a collage of material where you see whether something fits or not and then you re-work it – and that never happened separately. It always happened during the working process [working together]' (Masuch 2006: 14). Interestingly, Masuch was not a passive observer in the rehearsals, but took part in the workshops with the dancers and Stuart. After each rehearsal she and the choreographer would then go over the video-recorded rehearsals, analyse the footage and extract material:

> What was special about this piece was that we already from the first or second week did run-throughs from all the material we had and we then constantly worked on the order of the material. I would say it was a constant process of writing and rewriting the material. So you had worked on a movement sequence and then you decide that maybe it shouldn't be a solo, but a duet or maybe everybody should do it, or only the men should do it, or only the women should do it. So you start with a sequence and then somebody else does it the other way around. So you have the material but you constantly shape and re-shape. (Masuch 2006: 13)

Even when working on a text, it is possible to work in an open-ended way, so that the dramaturgy of the piece emerges through the process. Zade describes one such process when working on *Maria Stuart*. From the outset, Perceval was interested in discovering the dramaturgy of the play *through process*, and had therefore no interest in developing or defining a predetermined conceptual framework for the project. Instead, the casting and the 'bold cuts' in the text shifted the play in a particular direction (Zade 2006: 5).

Again, we find there is a balance to be struck: on the one hand, there may be a need to remember and preserve the original concept, but on the other hand it will always be necessary to allow the exploration to be, to some degree, open. In the process Zade describes, cuts are not made on the basis of a pre-rehearsal dramaturgical premise or concept. Instead the text is made open to exploration and cuts are made in rehearsal. Here the dramaturg helps to clarify what possibilities are emerging from the rehearsal process and facilitate discussion about dramaturgical consequences of the decisions. Zade comments that it is a process of 'stripping away everything that you don't need' (Zade 2006: 5). Zade describes how, as she and the director cut more and more of the text, they found themselves focusing the dramaturgy on the love triangle between Mary, Elizabeth and Leicester. This was not a preconceived result (Zade 2006: 5).

In this instance, there was no pre-production dramaturgical analysis, or, it would seem, any particular need for historical research to inform the dramaturgical focus. Rather, Zade describes an exploratory process where actors, dramaturg, director and other collaborators work towards identifying the dramaturgy of the production through practice.

Despite the excitement of such processes, we should note that not all dramaturgs would be comfortable in opening up the text to such radical treatment. In some instances, particularly where the company is working with an older text, the dramaturg may be seen as providing a writerly perspective and is sometimes even envisaged as a substitute for the writer. For example, Kemp echoes Wolfgang Wiens (1986: 18), when he describes himself as (on some occasions) acting as 'the writer's representative in the rehearsal room' (Kemp 2007). When the dramaturg occupies this role, we might expect a more cautious (though not a prohibitive) approach to textual alterations, and a particular responsibility for the verbal aspects of performance.

Casting – Shaping a Dramaturgy

In many cases production dramaturgs play an integral part in conceiving and facilitating the productions, and casting can become one of the first critical decisions. Indeed, the dramaturg can be involved with matching plays with directors, actors with directors, directors with dramaturgs, choreographers with dancers, projects with artists and so on. The initial process of finding the right team of people to work on a project will determine that project's possibilities and final shape. Zade describes this process:

> It starts with matching directors with plays that you want to do, trying to find the best combination, and then finding a set designer and doing the casting with the director. All the practical things that then have such a big impact on the end result, and quite often you kind of get the concept by doing the right kind of casting. (Zade 2006: 4)

Zade's conclusion is shared by Masuch, who comments that casting is particularly crucial because no matter whether it is a play or a dance production, casting is 'the first image' that is given to something (Masuch 2006: 20). Vuyst has pointed out that dramaturgy is involved in the choice of dancers working on a new piece. The idea of 'difference' informs Platel's dramaturgy, hence he selects dancers with very different backgrounds, colours, religions and personal stories (Delahunta 2000: 23). This collage principle is interestingly also reflected in Platel's performance dramaturgy which involves a multiplicity of contrasting stories, disciplines, emotions and narratives.

Dramaturgical research can also shape casting. Cattaneo explains that her research affected the dramaturgical interpretation and hence the casting for Mark Lapine's *A Midsummer Night's Dream* (1982) for the New York Festival. Her observation that the Elizabethan playwrights' fathers were close in class to the play's mechanicals inspired Lapine to see the mechanicals as 'regular citizens' (Cattaneo 1997: 9). She explains: 'Titania's seduction of Bottom was not ridiculous but became an almost plausible dream of emancipation, and the production allowed Theseus at the end to recognize Bottom for a moment as an equal' (Cattaneo 1997: 9). Thus, the casting reflected the fact that the characters were no longer buffoons, but more like real 'working class Americans' (Cattaneo 2006: 12).

The Dramaturg as Intermediary and Collaborator

A production involves a network of people working together towards creating a performance. The nature of the organization and the working structure will affect this network and its composition. It is not unusual for the dramaturg to become the person who holds this team of people together, acting as bridge-builder on the production itself. One will often find the dramaturg as the production's mediator or go-between, both in terms of communicating with the institution and audiences and in terms of mediating between the members of the creative team.

Zade suggests that she will often spend much time talking to actors, especially if they are working with a director for the first time. She explains that the theatre invites a range of different directors to work with the ensemble and there can be vast differences in directing style and approach. Here, Zade's job is to help the actors to understand a director's particular style and motivations. It may sound strange that the dramaturg should play the part of intermediary in a situation like this, but actor–director relationships are often complex, and it is far from unusual that misunderstandings or conflicts arise. It is therefore not unusual for the dramaturg to become a buffer or, indeed, a sounding-board.

The dramaturg holds a curious position: often there can be an understanding that he or she tries to maintain some neutrality. It is therefore not unusual for the dramaturg to become a mediator when there are conflicts, which do often occur during a production process. If the dramaturg is someone who gathers together material and ideas for a performance, it is also interesting to think of the dramaturg as someone who gathers information from everyone on a production. While the director may be preoccupied with other things, the dramaturg comes into contact with most people during the production process and is often in a good position to 'take the temperature'.

Lepecki comments that his role can be to ensure some kind of collaborative cohesiveness on the production and to be an intermediary between the collaborators and all parts involved in a process, 'making sure that the sound designer understands what the lighting designer is trying to do and that they are both speaking the same language' (Lepecki 2006: 17). Similarly, Henrik Adler comments that as a dramaturg, 'You have to be the integrator and the communicator, and you have to mediate between all these parties' (Adler 2005: 20). This can also entail establishing a link between the artists and the public.

This link can be established in a number of ways, but typically this will involve writing programme notes, or even press releases. In very practical terms, the dramaturg knows the work intimately, but will also command the language to describe the process. After all, a lot of the dramaturg's time is concerned with finding ways of articulating, discussing and framing what is going on in the rehearsal space. It therefore makes sense that the dramaturg becomes a kind of 'spokesperson' for the process. As we saw in Chapter 4, Radosavljevic worked closely with Northern Stage's marketing department, as well as preparing programme material. The dramaturg can therefore become a go-between, not only between production and public, but also between the artistic direction and the producers. Karen Maria Bille describes how she is the person the theatre turns to, if information about a specific production is required: 'We help them. Because normally, we're the ones that know ... We have all the information' (Bille 2005: 32). This information can then feed into ideas concerning marketing and presenting the performance to the public.

Lepecki believes that press material and programme notes are 'super crucial', because, as he says, they facilitate the transition from private process to 'public life' (Lepecki 2006: 19). Similarly, Cattaneo stresses the importance of press material and notes: 'You try and shape, to some degree, the perception of the audience seeing the play in what ever way you can' (Cattaneo 2006: 6). On the other hand, Radosavljevic suggests that this work can sometimes help to focus her thinking about a production: 'Suddenly I know what the show is about because I'm forced to write the programme notes' (Radosavljevic 2005: 22).

So what kind of collaborator does the production dramaturg make? There is sometimes a fine line between co-creation and facilitation. Sometimes the dramaturg can become an involved collaborator and co-creator. Lepecki, however, makes a very clear distinction between a co-director and a dramaturg. For him, dramaturgy is ultimately about facilitating the artist's work, and even if he does have a 'co-director's' role at times, he maintains that the final decision is the choreographer's.

Zade comments that the dramaturg and director can make decisions in close collaboration. She suggests that although this might sound daunting to directors unused to working with dramaturgs, in practice the directors understand that she is there to help: it is ultimately the director who has the final say (Zade 2006). While the dramaturgical presence in rehearsal could be considered threatening by some directors, for others this presence and input is welcome.

Norman Frisch, who has collaborated with the Wooster Group, among others, comments that he is not required to invest the process with his own creative ideas: 'They are looking to me to help shape or maintain a process in which ideas and perspectives other than their own are flowing. Even in ensembles that have worked together for a long time, this can be a challenge' (Frisch 2002: 274).

It seems that in Frisch's conception, production dramaturgy is a facilitation of ideas, which, perhaps paradoxically, means that the dramaturg is someone who helps keep the process open, while at the same time being aware that decisions have to be made in order to shape the material towards performance. As a facilitator, the dramaturg, it seems, is also one of the only people on the production that might not claim 'ownership'. Imschoot cites Kerkhoven's suggestion that the dramaturg is a 'modest figure ... at the service of the artist whose vision he or she helps support by giving feedback' (Imschoot 2003: 57). The dramaturg is therefore a curiously invisible person or, as Masuch proposes, the dramaturg is located in the 'in-between'. She cannot point to any single element of the performance as being distinctly her own. Thus the work of the dramaturg manifests itself in the, 'dialogue between the directors and the artists ... there's no representation of the work' (Masuch 2006: 16). The dramaturg is there to facilitate someone else's vision, or maybe more accurately is there to facilitate the production's vision.

The question of 'ownership' is interesting in terms of production dramaturgs. Though dramaturgs have different ways of articulating what they do, there is a shared sensibility about how they see themselves in relation to the director, ensemble or writer. It is true that while some dramaturgs believe that it is also their role to take an active part in coming up with creative solutions, others might not see things this way. Cattaneo, for example, believes that when working on a new text, it is not her role to 'offer specific solutions to the problems in the text' (Cattaneo 1997: 13) whereas Canadian dramaturg D.D. Kugler, for example, comments that his role is to test choices and assumptions, but also to propose possible choices (Kugler 2002: 97).

Yet many dramaturgs, in most contexts, are clear that they do not 'author' the work *per se*. There are, of course, exceptions. For instance, Lynn M. Thomson filed a court case in 2003, claiming a share of the royalties for the musical, *Rent*, on the basis that she had played a significant part in developing the work. The case was eventually settled out of court and has, perhaps, done little to allay fears that the dramaturg may take power away from the director or playwright. But although most dramaturgs do not claim to author the work, there still is a strong artistic and personal investment as the best dramaturg–director relationships also seem to be developed out of a genuinely shared artistic vision between director and dramaturg. Christian Parker points out that it is necessary to have an interest in the work in order to have something to contribute (Parker 2006). For him, that means a personal investment in both the story being told and a belief in the artistic team and the collaborative approach that is being established by them and the producers (Parker 2006).

But if it is clear what an actor or a designer, a writer or a director contributes to the process, how then does one qualify or describe what a dramaturg contributes? Of course, we know that dramaturgs offer notes, feedback, research and suggestions; however, these become subsumed into the fabric of the work itself. Michael Boyd, at the RSC, emphasizes the possible democratic nature of dramaturgical work, arguing that it underlines 'the core collaborative values of theatre because it disturbs all those outmoded ideas of authorship ... theatre is a group endeavour. It always has been' (Powell 2006).

So what does the dramaturg own? Anne Bogart, director of New York-based SITI company, observes in relation to work on the devised piece *American Silents*:

> I think with dramaturgs there is usually this really bizarre question of ownership of something, a director has ownership of staging, a [sic] actor has ownership of the acting ... well, in the best case, usually in a new play the role of a dramaturg is not to have ownership. But if you look at *American Silents*, there is a huge amount of ownership and it's called ownership of archival materials and of structural ideas. (Coleman and Wolff 1998: 27)

While it may be unclear as to how one can 'own' a set of 'structural ideas', Bogart seems to suggest that in this instance the dramaturgs' principal artistic contribution concerned structural thinking. Cattaneo comments that dramaturgs are often good at thinking structurally, are sensitive as to how something is shaped and how this shape or structure affects interpretation. In her experience, actors tend to be less concerned with the overall arc of a play, and directors might not always have time to examine the structural logic of the play in great depth (Cattaneo 2006: 26).

Structural thinking might also be evident in the dramaturg's concern with how to *facilitate working and collaborative structures*. As Frisch comments, sometimes his job involves 'constructing circles of dialogue, so that a project is not emanating from a single perspective or clique'. He adds that he works hard 'to expose the ideas underlying the work at hand and extend the circle of input and discussion' (Frisch 2002: 275). This seems to suggest that the dramaturg constantly looks for ways in which the process or the work can be enriched with different points of view. In coming into the rehearsal space, the dramaturg might be useful to the whole production team, engaging in an imaginative and conceptual discussion about the significance of the work, in order to clarify and contextualize it for its makers. This not only concerns the director or choreographer, but also the performers and technicians as well.

Ben-Tovim, for example, points out that when she worked on *Broken Chords* the dancers also appreciated her dramaturgical feedback, which gave them another layer of meaning, a sense of the world they were creating on stage (Ben-Tovim 2007).

The Production Dramaturg in Dance: An Emerging Field

Most of our discussion throughout the book has revolved around dramaturgy and the dramaturg within practices that centre on the dramatic text. However, in this chapter, we have also cited dramaturgs from dance practices, notably Lepecki, Masuch, Gilpin and Vuyst. While the theatre and dance processes can be very different, there are similarities in the essential role of the production dramaturg across dance and theatre. Indeed, Masuch, as well as Brian Quirt, artistic director of Canadian company Nightswimming (2006), maintain that there is no difference between working in dance or theatre. Masuch comments, 'You don't need a text to invent a structure for a piece. The structure can be scenes that have no verbal dialogue. You can have a physical dialogue' (Masuch 2006: 8). While the dance dramaturg is not found as frequently as the theatre dramaturg, there are and have been a number of significant dramaturg–choreographer collaborations. Imschoot (2003) offers a helpful overview of dramaturgs in European and North American dance practices.

Scholars and artists are increasingly taking up the challenge of investigating the relationship between dance and dramaturgy. This discussion can be found in Gilpin (1997) and Adolphe (1998). Gilpin, for instance, is emphatic that dance and movement-based performance also involves dramaturgical processes, and is surprised that, 'the process of dramaturgy, specifically for movement performance, has been largely overlooked by literary and theatre critics' (Gilpin 1997: 85).

It might therefore be worth considering whether there is such a thing as specific dance dramaturgy. Although we will not have the space to expand on this very broad question, Gilpin's suggestion that movement work confronts the audience with 'many differing vocabularies (text, image, movement, sound) and disciplinary perspectives – none of which play a hierarchical central role' (Gilpin 1997: 85), suggests affinity with the non-hierarchical, 'new' dramaturgies we discussed at the end of Chapter 3.

This idea is also to be found in the recently organized *Dance Lab: Dramaturgy* at the dance festival *Tanz Plattform* (Stuttgart,

February 2006). The intention behind the three-day lab was to examine the relationship between dramaturgy and dance. Conceding that the field of dramaturgy and particularly dance dramaturgy has hardly been 'touched upon by academic discourse and research', the intention was to explore the principles of composition in contemporary dance, particularly located in dance dramaturgies' work with simultaneous perception and multiple perspectives' (www.Theaterhaus.com). If many contemporary dance practices lend themselves more to multi- or cross-disciplinary dramaturgies, one question for future consideration might be whether these dramaturgies require a different kind of dramaturgical practice. Research into this is already being carried out (see Hansen 2005).

Conclusion

Often closely involved in conception, processes of research, facilitation, shaping and discussion of the work, the production dramaturg is aware of the inner logic of the performance, and is able to take critical stock of whether the production follows its own logic. Consequently, the dramaturg's feedback and presence might also help to establish 'red threads' (lines of connection) through the work.

The dramaturg is particularly concerned with the way in which the detail relates to the whole, and with strengthening the conceptual framework by considering the process, material and ideas from different perspectives and angles. This includes seeing the work from the perspective of the audience and the context in which the performance is presented. The dramaturg might offer dramaturgical analysis, often informed by research, reflection and consideration as to how the play places itself (or might be placed) within a current context. This analysis might provide a way into the play or concept, in order to help the director or choreographer to deepen their thinking around the material.

A question that could be raised from this chapter is to what extent this work is visible. Clearly the dramaturg's work is visible to the director or actors who discuss the play, concept or process with them. But analysis, feedback, support, critical perspectives and research leave no trace, other than by the way they help to shape the work itself, or the depth of the enquiry.

Where most other roles within the theatre-making process tend to be more easily defined, the dramaturg is often situated between many different tasks. The dramaturg is an advisor, facilitator and sounding-board, someone who contributes with different and diverse perspectives and further attempts to enhance and deepen the conceptual and practical approach in many different ways. Sometimes a co-creator, but more often an artistic advisor, the dramaturg offers feedback and reflection on the work. It is paradoxical that the dramaturg should be one of the most invisible, but at the same time most controversial figures in the theatre. Brizzell and Lepecki, for example, observe that it is not uncommon to encounter 'a diatribe against dramaturgs' and that 'those directors who dare work with a dramaturg, are always depicted as "weak", suspiciously not strong enough in their authorial independence and intellectual certitude' (2003: 15). Terry McCabe argues that directors should inhabit their 'natural authority' and do the dramaturg's work themselves (McCabe 2001: 64–73, esp. 71) Also relevant is Imschoot's analysis of the dramaturg as a 'political agent' and 'figure of complicity in a wider systemic range' (Imschoot 2003: 57).

On the other hand, although the dramaturg arguably wields more actual 'power' in some (most notably German) theatre contexts than in others, the role might also seem peripheral compared to other roles within the process. There might often be a sense that the dramaturg adapts to the demands of the production. At the same time, it is important to emphasize that however 'modest' a facilitator the dramaturg might be, dramaturgical practice, like any other, is naturally driven by personal interests and ideas. Thus, most collaborations between dramaturgs and directors or choreographers stem from a mutual interest and respect.

7 The Dramaturg and Devising: Shaping a Dramaturgy

An Emerging Role

In the previous chapter, we discussed the figure of the dramaturg as someone who translates ideas into practice and production, facilitating feedback, discussion and research. We now turn our attention to devising processes where the dramaturg is involved in shaping and creating the performance from the outset.

As mentioned earlier, Sarah Woods suggested that, in the UK, the dramaturg might be used in a way that was 'quite piecemeal', including an involvement of dramaturgs 'within dance and improvised work' (Woods 2005: 16–17). It remains to be seen whether UK practice will continue to develop the role of the dramaturg in 'new writing', or whether there will, in fact, be an even greater interest in the dramaturg's function within devised work.

Whatever the future holds, it is certainly possible to find dramaturgs working in contemporary devised performance in the UK. In this chapter we will discuss the particularities of this role, using examples from current UK practice, drawing on discussions with dramaturgs Steven Canny (Complicite), Louise Mari (Shunt), David Williams (Lone Twin Theatre), Frauke Franz (Primitive Science/Fake Productions) and Nell Leyshon (Platform 4). We will discuss a few of the devising dramaturg's key tasks, and highlight some of the critical qualities that the dramaturg brings to the work and the process.

This is by no means an exhaustive account. In fact, the conversations we had in the process of collecting interview material for this chapter encompassed a wide range of information and ideas, not all of which can be included here. The chapter does not provide a chronological account of devising processes, but tries to give a sense of the kinds of interventions and contributions that the dramaturg can make during them.

In a sense, dramaturgical practice is already integral to most devising processes. After all, devising companies have always found ways of discussing the content, structure and direction of their work. Total Theatre and CSSD's publication on dramaturgy (1999) includes articles by Twitchin, Butler and Harradine, who discuss the way dramaturgical practices are naturally integral to a devising company's way of working. Similarly, Elizabeth Lecompte comments that in the Wooster Group she has dramaturgical dialogues with everybody in the production and that 'dramaturgy goes on during breaks in rehearsal ad hoc'. The dramaturg is 'more like an assistant director, a good stage manager, a confidante' (Lecompte 1994: 204). Many companies involve someone as an informal dramaturg, or an 'outside eye'. This could be a role played by performers taking turns to sit outside the performance to give feedback. In other instances, it might be the designer who makes dramaturgical observations. Anne Bogart comments that the best dramaturg she has encountered is sound designer Darron L. West (Bogart 2001: 18). Herrington writes in an article on the SITI company's *Cabin Pressure*: 'Those who observe SITI rehearsals sometimes define West's role as that of dramaturg, sometimes even co-director. Certainly he is a key collaborator, responsible not only for the aural layers of the play, but also for input into the text and many ideas on staging' (Herrington 2002: 134). Sometimes a director might ask a trusted colleague to come in to observe a rehearsal.

However, what is particularly interesting about our examples in this chapter is that the dramaturgical role is acknowledged as an explicit function and not as something that happens informally or as an adjunct to other roles within the process. By inviting the dramaturg into the rehearsal, the companies or director welcome a more formalized engagement with dramaturgical discussion, analysis and reflection. While this analysis is not dependent on the dramaturg, the decision to use one might imply particular emphasis on such discussions. For example, Steven Canny suggests that Complicite, as a company, values relatively structured dramaturgical discussions where a group of people have post-rehearsal conversations about structure, meaning and overview (Canny 2006: 12).

No two devising companies or processes are alike. However, even though the processes discussed in this chapter vary considerably, there is a consensus between the dramaturgs as to the general nature of their work, despite the fact that they also admit the difficulty of defining the work precisely. For example, although David Williams describes himself as a 'dramaturg', he recognizes that his precise role is dependent on the specific context, the collaborators and the material (Williams 2006a: 1).

The dramaturg within the devising process is in the peculiar situation of having a job that is difficult to define, multiple and diverse. If 'dramaturgy' is a term that suggests a concern with making connections and linking ideas within a larger structure, the dramaturg can seem to be a connecting force, involved in all aspects of performance-making, with a view to assisting in the process of finding cohesion in the artistic work. Thus, paradoxically, the dramaturg's role is both quite specific and entirely uncertain.

But it is perhaps in devising that we see one of the clearest manifestations of the usefulness of the dramaturg's role. Devising, in the strictest sense of the word, implies a process where '*no* script – neither written play text nor performance score – exists prior to the work's creation' (Heddon and Milling 2006: 3). This notion of devising, in its purest form, informs other useful titles such as Oddey (1994), Lamden (2000), Bicât and Baldwin (2002). In truth, many (perhaps most) companies do use some form of script, verbal text or score, sometimes as a starting point, sometimes introducing it at a point during the process. Sometimes just a few elements, such as key exchanges or speeches will be scripted. Devising is therefore not a fixed style. However, we could suggest that devising implies that the dramaturgy of the work is not defined before the work commences.

A play does much to define the structure and content of a performance from the outset. However, in devising, the content, form and structure are determined as the process unfolds. The performance text is, to put it simply, 'written' not *before* but *as a consequence* of the process. Devising processes tend to reflect the particular places, spaces and people involved and the immediate contexts of the work tend to be woven into the performance. The compositional challenge is therefore to define and shape the material from the living process and from the dialogue between the people involved.

Devising is a process in which form and content may be shaped and generated simultaneously: thus, the deviser searches for structural parameters *while at the same time* creating new material. Williams, speaking about his own dramaturgical role with Lone Twin Theatre on *Alice Bell* (2006a), describes the process as 'a conversation in which you try and find the shape of the thing that you think you're after' (Williams 2006a: 8). While Williams is speaking about a specific process, this might encapsulate the general predicament of the deviser. As Williams suggests, within this simultaneous action of searching and shaping, 'you don't really know what's being sought' (Williams 2006a: 4). A very lucid, practical example of how dramaturgy is shaped through rehearsals, is given by Watson (1993) where he discusses Odin Teatret and their process.

A devising process might therefore require, on the one hand, a search for structure, while on the other hand, the facilitation of possibilities. The need to keep the process open can make it seem chaotic because one idea might lead to an exploration of parallel stories or ideas which in turn lead to other ideas and before long the process is going down different, perhaps disparate, avenues and paths. It is easy to get lost in the creative turmoil of devising. Indeed, if we were to draw a map of a typical devising process, it might reveal a labyrinthine journey of blind alleys, dead ends, associative leaps, mysterious paths and links between passages. Furthermore, and especially within the UK, it is not unusual that the deviser has to research, source, generate, evaluate and structure many diverse ideas in a very short space of time.

Paradoxically, this seemingly free and open-ended process might require an even stronger sense of structural organization and overview than a production of a conventional play would demand. This may be one reason for the use of the dramaturg in devising. We have already explored dramaturgy in architectural terms, and Williams compares the dramaturg's preoccupation with all things compositional to an architectural process:

> So you look at how logics are set up and maybe forgotten and look at possibilities and you look at how this bit makes sense in terms of the logics that you've developed, and maybe this [bit] doesn't makes sense in relation to that bit. So, I think it's very related to architecture, which is certainly how I understand it for myself. (Williams 2006a: 38)

When trying to articulate the shape of the thing being sought, the dramaturg's concern for how and why ideas might connect into a structure could prove crucial to the devising process. For example, creative producer Kate McGrath collaborated with Filter on their performance *Faster* (2003), directed by Guy Retallack. During the public seminar 'Structures in Devising' (2003) where directors and dramaturgs exchanged different approaches to structuring devising processes through case studies, McGrath and Retallack discussed their process. McGrath was invited to work on the production in a dramaturgical capacity. Although McGrath was very modest about her dramaturgical contribution, Retallack commented that her input and dramaturgical, structural overview was invaluable when it came to pulling together the different strands and elements. Retallack pointed out that it was immensely useful to have someone who could come in with fresh eyes to make observations on structure, dynamics and communication. Retallack described vividly how McGrath helped to keep the project on track, was able to retain a wealth of information, and helped to ensure that all collaborators were working according to the same artistic agenda.

Speaking at the same seminar, director of Primitive Science/Fake Productions Boz Temple-Morris argued that that this kind of dramaturgical overview is needed because a director might be so preoccupied with the complex details of the work that he or she could find it difficult to see them in context and as a whole. The dramaturg, he maintained, is in a good position to see the arc of a piece, emotionally and dramatically.

One senses that both these companies have been involved in a dynamic process, in which the dramaturg's role has gradually emerged as significant and necessary. This is a recurring feature of UK practice. Because there is no well-established tradition of dramaturgical work, the role can seem newly invented or discovered, emerging as a possible solution to the difficulties inherent in the devising process. As Canny points out, working as a dramaturg in the UK without any precedents gives him the freedom to define the role or tasks anew. However, with this freedom also comes uncertainty. Throughout our interview with him, Canny gave an inspiring narrative of how he began to understand the possibilities and implications of the dramaturgical role as he began to understand what the process *needed* from him as a dramaturg.

Indeed, the dramaturgs we spoke to frequently talked about their role with a real sense of having discovered, through practice, the particularities of their own function within the process. Having worked as Simon McBurney's assistant director and later associate director, Canny found that his 'work with Complicite developed over a period of time into a dramaturgical role with greater concern for dramaturgical structures' (2006: 2). However, it was when touring with the company in mainland Europe and meeting dramaturgs there that he realized that this role actually had a title (Canny 2006: 2).

Similarly, Louise Mari suggests that she 'fell into' the role in the London-based company Shunt, having initially wanted to pursue her passion for writing. Although the company works very collaboratively, and did not set out to have a dramaturg *per se*, Mari has naturally gravitated towards the more analytical dramaturgical role within the company, and could now be said to be the company's dramaturg. Williams initially entered the collaboration with Lone Twin Theatre as a kind of artistic 'mentor', but, as mentioned earlier, he sees the term 'dramaturg' as a useful one to describe a role that is actually redefined for each process. In contrast to all these, Franz, working with Temple-Morris found it natural to develop a dramaturg–director working relationship, since both had experience with the dramaturgical role in mainland Europe.

Similarly, Catherine Church, artistic director of Platform 4 was very clear that she needed a dramaturg's help with structure, narrative and feedback when she invited literary manager and playwright Leyshon to take on this role when working on *Claustrophobia* (2005). In our conversation with Church and Leyshon we discussed the distinction between playwright and dramaturg. If most dramaturgs are likely to define themselves as collaborators within the devising process, the question of authorship could become awkward if the dramaturg also happens to be a playwright. In the UK, where the two roles are often seen as intrinsically connected, this could become a common concern. The need to clarify the distinction might become particularly pressing in processes where notating, shaping and structuring work become the function of the dramaturg.

Beginnings

The dramaturg involved in devising is essentially a particular kind of production dramaturg, attending rehearsals. Thus, like other production dramaturgs, the devising dramaturg is involved in research, giving feedback, documenting the process and structuring material. However, a key feature of the dramaturg's work in devising is to keep track of a fast-moving process, to maintain an overview, take stock and to help the company to construct or 'wright' the performance. If devising processes are open-ended, a major contribution could be the identification of tangible and practical strategies for developing the work, particularly at the beginning of a process.

In Mari's work with Shunt, the process can begin with attempting to identify a dramaturgical starting point based on the many diverse interests of the company. She describes how Shunt, when embarking on a new project, will 'meet and present ideas of what subject we are going to explore. So we just look for a starting point and it normally involves what people like best and what excites them' (Mari and Uprichard 2006: 1). Mari is, from the outset, involved creatively in the project, in that she too brings ideas to the table. However, her role is twofold in that she will not only offer up her own ideas, but also try to establish a coherent starting point for the ensemble.

As ideas are presented, Mari will try to think of interesting connections between the different ideas. She describes how in *Amato Saltone* (2006), when looking for a meeting point between the different ideas, she began to consider the novel *Rear Window* by Cornell Woolrich. Many of the starting points offered were suggestive of this work. She decided to gather together new stimuli around this theme. Well-versed in Woolrich from a previous show, Mari identified aspects of the text that 'had something performative about them', and created a collection of different scenes, descriptions, images and ideas for the company to take away, respond to and, as Mari puts it, 'present some ideas around' (Mari and Uprichard 2006: 1–2). This then became a new, shared starting point for the company.

Franz finds herself in the same dual role, playing with ideas, yet making sure there is an alignment between her interests and those of the director, working together to find a practical starting point from among the many different possibilities. Having worked closely with Temple-Morris on developing performance concepts in the past, Franz is as much a creative collaborator as a facilitator of the directors' ideas. But part of her role is to suggest the potential for different strategies, identifying the structures and narratives implicit within the material or ideas presented.

As with Mari's work, her task might be to discover how three or four disparate ideas could connect and generate possibilities for further narrative threads. For example in the case of *No, It Was You* (2003), Pablo Picasso's painting *Guernica* was a starting point. While this painting might be the initial source, Franz's research process involved exploring what other stories might be behind *Guernica* and could run parallel to each other within a layered structure. This kind of research can be a lengthy process, but Franz's concern is to filter out what is unimportant, selecting material for exploration.

Franz and Mari both describe processes where the devising starts with a set of disparate ideas; however, devising can also involve stage adaptation. Speaking specifically about the process of adapting Haruki Murakami's series of short stories *The Elephant Vanishes* (2004), Canny comments that having made a decision that this could be interesting, one then has to explore, on a dramaturgical level, the question of whether the project is at all possible or how it might become possible. As Canny says, the questions are often simply to do with: 'Can we do this? Is there anything in this work that could transfer to the stage?' (Canny 2006: 3). For example, it is necessary to consider how a short story dramaturgy becomes a stage dramaturgy and how one might link a set of unconnected short stories.

With this project, there were also questions concerning the context of the work, written by a Japanese author, translated for an English market and concerning stories set in 'different worlds', semi-abstract locations in an unnamed city (Canny 2006: 4–5). Questions concerning how one translates one form into another also lead to questions concerning what kinds of stories one wants to tell, why and where.

While Canny is involved in casting and assembling a creative team, he will also, on a very practical level, begin to think about how to facilitate rehearsals. In this instance, for example, he had to consider how Murakami's complex stories and images might be translated into quite concrete starting points for exploration by the performers and other artistic collaborators. With no script to bring to the rehearsals, Canny details the process of setting up a task, discovering possibilities, setting a new task and then gradually beginning to find an emerging pattern that could lead towards what he calls a 'template' for production. It is worth quoting at length, to give a sense of this initial process:

I was literally ... underlining things in the book, picking out ideas that I thought would work, then putting them on pieces of paper, putting them on computer files under different tags so that we had everything in order. We had bits of old box files with things in, labelled under themes and with ideas, with pictures, thoughts on other writers' words on similar topics, research into elephants, etc. ... And it then became absolutely clear what my job would be ... I started to cut apart Murakami's book into very, very short chunks that I knew I could give to an actor, and that they could create a scene from or have a thought about. I would take little chunks of text and give it to the translators and they would re-translate it into Japanese. They would then give that text to the [Japanese] actors who would then present the scene to us and we would then talk about it, and Simon would rework it. And we would then have a thought about the structure or we'd put two pieces together that had been done on the same day or we'd put a piece that had been done a week before that into it and then the translators would translate it back into English and I would then shape it into something resembling a text that I'd know Complicite could work from in English. And this went on for the next twelve weeks where the computer became the most critical tool in the room, where for now you forget all the things to do with light, sound, etc. So you assemble a text through that long process, and you're still only on a template for your production. (Canny 2006: 6–8)

Canny gives us a vivid sense of the magnitude of this adaptation process, suggesting the way in which initial rehearsals concern finding ways into the text, teasing out the text's theatrical potential, all the time asking what, why and how different elements might be brought together. As Canny explains, this is a constant process of facilitation, exploration, reflection, drafting and redrafting. And all the while he has to keep an eye on the potential overarching architecture or dramaturgy that emerges from this process. It seems an exciting, exhilarating and exhausting task, requiring, it would seem, considerable powers of organization and a sensitivity to the whole.

The Dramaturg as Map-maker and Compass-bearer

It is evident that this kind of process will involve much risk-taking, days where certain characters are explored, or a certain idea is interrogated, sometimes to no avail. As improvisations, rehearsals and discussions generate new ideas, directions and developments, it is also natural that others are forgotten and even the original impulse can seem remote. Sometimes, explorations are merely detours, but the dramaturg needs to be the navigator, who differentiates between what might be an important pathway and what is probably a false lead, keeping in mind the overall journey and direction. At the same time, the dramaturg must bear in mind that new ideas can develop by chance, from 'mistakes', detours and free associations: these can sometimes change the direction of the piece entirely.

Shunt company member Heather Uprichard describes the dramaturg as 'a compass', helping the company to find its way through the morass of ideas and material (Mari and Uprichard 2006: 16). She suggests that whereas the director 'takes snapshots on the ground', the dramaturg 'holds the map of the process' (2006: 16).

A key tool in this 'map- or memory-making' is the dramaturg's extensive record of the process, often a hybrid between rehearsal journal, research archive, documentation, dramaturgical analysis and creative reflection. The dramaturg might spend many hours in rehearsals just watching, listening, writing, possibly drawing and recording. While this quiet documenting and organizing of information might sound like a fairly dry and uncreative act, the dramaturg's creative imagination is very much involved in this ordering process. In a devising process, anything and everything can become significant and it takes a creative eye and sensibility to be able to pick up on the potential and the poetry of what is going on in the space: a certain look between two performers, a sudden hand gesture, an accidental entrance or simply a particular feeling about the timing or duration of a moment might provide an exciting shift in direction.

On a more pragmatic level, it is important to retain and organize information: the dramaturg's production book can become a treasure chest of ideas and an enormous resource for the director's work. Mari explains that she writes down everything from improvisations to observations and exercises. The director and the company can then consult this book when they need to, or look to it for renewed inspiration. As Mari comments, her documentation becomes both a creative resource and also 'the memory of what's been going on' (Mari and Uprichard 2006: 31–2).

Tracing, tracking and mapping the process from the beginning can become vital in identifying and articulating an emerging pattern in the material. Remembering and returning to things can provide a key to understanding the work at difficult moments. Williams comments that, in recording, documenting and reflecting on the process, he is aware of what might have been lost, forgotten and abandoned, since some of those things could unexpectedly be brought back into the process and prove useful (Williams 2006a: 24).

In describing work on *Alice Bell*, Williams recalls that an early observation became crucial at a later point, helping to determine the overall compositional and dramaturgical framing of the work. As mentioned in Chapter 6, Michael Ondaatje's novel, *In the Skin of a Lion*, provided an early starting point for the piece. In his analysis of the novel, Williams had suggested that the way in which a band of musicians structures a performance (for instance, the emergence of solos, the reprisal of themes and so on) could possibly be used as a core dramaturgy for the production (Williams 2006b: 2). It could, he thought, be useful as a way of suggesting 'the relationships between individuals and a collective' (Williams 2006b: 18).

This written analysis got left behind early on. However, Williams comments: 'Near the end of the process I went back to it and said, "You know, this is where we started. This is what we've ended up with. Shouldn't we keep looking back at our starting points?"' (Williams 2006a: 20).

In some ways, the process had gone full circle and by the end, the company had returned to some of these early ideas. Such discoveries can be helpful in working out the structural logic of a performance, or at least in identifying and articulating the structural or compositional logic as it has developed. They can provide an anchor.

As mentioned earlier, André Lepecki suggests that the dramaturg's activity in documenting the work could be seen as a way of 'creating the memory of the production' (Lepecki 2006: 18). The dramaturg's gentle insistence on referring back to earlier starting points can provide moments of pause in the flow of the work, moments in which the devisers can take stock and reconnect with their original intentions. Mari explains:

> I'm constantly reminding myself of where we've come from and remind-
> ing David. It's like, 'Why were we doing this?' And I know where it's
> come from and why and what could possibly follow it. If we go back to
> where it came from, it seems easier to find something to follow it rather
> than having to look for something. There is a danger that everything can
> move away from you all the time and you never bring it down to any-
> thing. So something will happen and evolve into something else, which
> again evolves into something else and then everyone will wonder how
> they can contribute to that because they're not quite sure what it is or
> that they understand it. And then I can say, 'It came from this' – and once
> everyone knows where it came from, they can contribute, so it makes
> the ideas accessible to everyone rather than just being in the director's
> head. (Mari and Uprichard 2006: 32–3)

Canny also describes how his documentation and analysis of rehearsals for Complicite's *Light* (2000) became a useful map of the process. Although the director might have a clear conception of the work, Canny points out that it is impossible for any director to keep 'a document of moment by moment, what led to that revelation by an actor' (2006: 26). This 'moment by moment' documentation can facilitate continuity in the devising, and can reveal an emerging pattern and superstructure.

While the dramaturg may keep track of the details, he or she is constantly relating them to the larger picture. This is evident in Shunt's working relationship between director and dramaturg. Where Rosenberg, as Mari puts it, is 'more interested in the particular parts', she is concerned with how the particular parts join up, connect and ultimately synthesize. Talking specifically about the process for *Bear Dance*

Bear (2003), Mari exemplifies her line of questioning when trying to create an overall dramaturgy and line through the material:

> We had lots of completely different things that were happening, and we knew what they were worth. This is this bit. This is the bit where we do this, and this is the bit where we do this, and then the audience goes from here to here, but *why* is that? Why are the audience moving now, and why did somebody just say that and now you're in here and now they're saying that. So it's about finding the links between the parts and that's what I'm particularly looking at and interested in. (Mari and Uprichard 2006: 16)

So Mari initiates – and often insists on – discussions about the potential line through the material and the logic of the 'world' the company is creating. Similarly, Williams looks for ways in which a dramaturgical logic can be defined, seeing this as a matter of helping the company to understand the logic that they are in the process of developing, pointing out radical discontinuities, indicating ways in which moments might be woven together by cross-referencing with a word or an image established earlier, weighing up how a new development 'configures in relation to what we know the architecture of various other things are shaping up to be' (2006: 10). Like Mari, Williams observes that the artists, intensely involved in creating the material, may not be able to see things in perspective. His role may then be to intervene and to offer up alternative suggestions. He is able to consider the material,

> in relation to their body of work and … in relation to the architecture of what's taking shape around it. And it's about trying not to be so close up that the detail kind of blinds you to its possibilities, or its problems, in relation to either a sequence or a bigger chunk. (Williams 2006a: 14)

The dramaturg therefore helps the company to maintain a wider perspective. Leyshon describes a situation on *Claustrophobia* where she facilitated a dramaturgical discussion and exercise in helping Church and writer Anna Murphy pull together the different strands into a structure:

> We had a great piece of paper with Blu Tack on the wall and I made them structure the story in terms of scenes, characters and what happens … And then through conversations I literally wrote on each of these pieces of paper what would happen in each of the scenes – as detailed as possible – and I just kept firing questions at them … and at

the end we had ten scenes and I literally wrote the scene numbers on them … And that's the most difficult part of writing a play, to order that information and to go from an organic idea to a very, very firm structure. (Church and Leyshon 2005: 15 and 18)

Leyshon's dramaturgical exercise helped to map out the structural and dramaturgical parameters for writer and director, but she also created a narrative of the entire performance and therefore helped them to articulate its 'inner logic'.

On-the-Spot Dramaturgy

The dramaturg's documentation process presupposes that all ideas are potentially significant and could be used in new contexts. At times, the dramaturg may draw on this documentation to make direct rehearsal interventions. Canny describes how, when working on *Light*, he could be looking through documentation of previous rehearsals, suggesting text, or actions drawn from this record. Similarly, Mari uses her notes to make direct interventions during rehearsals: 'I will say, "What about that thing that Gemma did the other day? Or that Heather did the other day? That would work well here"' (2006: 29).

Mari's intervention helps to move the rehearsal on, but importantly Canny and Mari are, in their suggestions, beginning to link moments together and are thus in the process of 'writing' or, perhaps, 'wrighting' the dramaturgy inside the rehearsal process. Thus, the dramaturg is a creative collaborator within the artistic process, engaged in on-the-spot dramaturgical composition. Williams describes what he calls a 'three-part conversation' (Williams 2006a: 8) with Lone Twin Theatre directors Gregg Whelan and Gary Winters when devising *Alice Bell*. Although contributing with new ideas, Williams would primarily focus on the compositional structure. He comments that in such a process, he tries 'to consciously look at continuities or continuities that are being made' (2006a: 9).

The dramaturg, then, intervenes in the rehearsal process in order to establish connections, to examine what each element might mean in relation to the whole piece. The dramaturg can help the director to assess how emerging material or key decisions may affect the narrative or the direction of the piece. In discussing the dramaturg's interventions during rehearsal, director of the Canadian company Number Eleven, Ker Wells, suggests that in fact it would be very useful to have someone beside him who could advise and intervene as 'an immediate witness' (Barton 2005: 112). Barton's article provides a vivid discussion of the challenges and possibilities of dramaturgical presence in physical theatre and devised processes. Barton cites Wells's argument that in these kinds of processes things are moving so fast that what is really needed from a dramaturg is direct intervention as soon as he or she identifies problems or potential for development.

Certainly, this kind of 'on-the-spot' dramaturgy might not be to every director's liking. Indeed, there are clearly overlaps between the dramaturg's skills and those of the director and some directors are wary of bringing in a dramaturg. However, most dramaturgs see it as their function to support the director, rather than to impose their own vision onto a work. As Franz puts it, it's a great thing to have someone you can rely on and discuss the work with, who is not interested in 'stealing the limelight' (Franz 2005a).

Conclusion

The dramaturgs discussed here all negotiate the delicate position of being both a creative collaborator in the process and, at the same time, the person who has to be able to stand back, to view the work with some objectivity in order to identify overarching structures and possible narratives. And although all production dramaturgs are in this position, the dramaturg working in devising probably faces the greatest challenge in retaining this curious balance of intimacy and distance.

What emerges from the examples given in this chapter is that the dramaturg is often very closely involved with creating the work *in situ*, in the rehearsals, at times literally co-writing, co-editing text on the spot or intervening with suggestions from the 'memory bank'. The dramaturg offers practical and creative suggestions and at the same time, has to assess whether these will work within the larger context and structure. Both dramaturg and director have to share the skills of transforming ideas, interests and abstract questions into the tangible elements of a performance. Clearly, this is not a conceptual, theoretical task, but very much an active, practical and intimate activity. Yet, at the same time as being a creative contributor, the dramaturg is focused on facilitating the creativity of others in the company. We see in Leyshon's structuring exercise, that while she was involved in writing the structure, she was also 'firing questions' at the writer and director: she was prompting the director and writer to work out solutions.

Williams comments on the dramaturg's position:

> The most difficult thing of all, I suppose, is that sense of being kind of close up and far away [at the same time] ... having a real sense of how things are put together and how those details might relate to some broader structure that in turn will feed back into the micro-detail ... It is the sense of the relationship between the very small and the ... overview that allows you to dive into the micro-detail that somehow undoes what is being sought. (Williams 2006a: 3–4)

Williams's evocative phrase, 'the micro-detail that somehow undoes what is being sought', suggests that the dramaturg must also be ready to be challenged, to see the micro-detail that necessitates a complete reappraisal of the overview, that, like the discovery of the atom, changes its world. At the same time, the dramaturg must be prepared to challenge the company and director, not in order to dictate the direction of the work, but to push them to re-evaluate the integrity of the decisions being made, and their implications for the whole.

The dramaturg must be a diplomat, finding the right language to pose difficult, but necessary questions and sometimes to make what might seem uncomfortable observations about the decisions being made. Canny recalls the search for, 'the right language to express your considerations, thoughts or doubts about the piece, whether it's about just one elephant or the broader construction of the piece as a whole' (Canny 2006: 11). Similarly, Franz points out that as a dramaturg one must not be afraid to 'say no to some things' (Franz 2005a). This does not mean engaging in a power struggle with the director, but Franz sees it as necessary to be honest in her feedback and observations.

We might consider the dramaturg as a builder of bridges, helping the company to cohere. Mari is conscious of the fact that her documentation makes the material potentially, 'accessible to anybody' (Mari and Uprichard 2006: 35). Uprichard discusses the importance of having a mechanism in place for open discussion and evaluation of the work, in order to facilitate a sense of 'ownership' for everyone within the ensemble. Describing Mari as the ingredient that 'keeps everything together' (2006: 42), Uprichard comments that Mari facilitates a democratic process, because everybody's contribution is captured, recorded and documented from the very early stages. But she also helps performers and other collaborators to discern a shared trajectory, vital to the development of the piece. Uprichard and Mari discuss a particular moment in their devising of *Tropicana* (2002), where the process had ground to a standstill and no one was sure of the exact direction. As Mari explains, the uncertainty created momentary panic where everybody on the production started to offer up their own individual explanation of what the performance was about. Mari explains:

> Then you've suddenly got ten completely different suggestions ... and it starts becoming ten different shows. ... And then what we do is to go back and ask. Where did it start? What did we have? Let's go back to here and let's share it with everybody and then start moving forward together. (Mari and Uprichard 2006: 35)

Clearly it might be advisable that a company works with a dramaturg who has compatible aesthetic and artistic interests. Both Williams and Mari emphasize friendship as an important ingredient in their collaboration. And Canny comments: 'You have to have that relationship and that friendship and that sense of trust and that understanding of why a person might want to approach a certain type of work' (Canny 2006: 3–4). Indeed, as Canny suggests, the dramaturg needs to contribute creatively and be 'full of mischief' (Canny 2006: 32), yet at the same time hold onto the overall shape, the bigger vision and create a sense of order in the creative chaos. This might seem a paradoxical role: the dramaturg both keeps the process on track and yet (purposefully) might throw it off course. But the question the dramaturg confronts is precisely *how* to facilitate and inspire the artists, the process and the work.

Williams comments that he aims to stimulate imagination and to open up possibilities. For him, much time is spent watching, imagining what could be possible with the material and coming up with strategies to enable people to be inventive, or to find their own solutions to difficulties (Williams 2006a: 5). So perhaps, despite the need for a dramaturgical overview, the dramaturg also aims to create a space for the performers and the director to drift, wander, dream and play. At the same time the dramaturg can also provide new perspectives on the work. Canny comments:

> You need to be inquisitive, hungry and full of mischief. You need to be able to throw in something unexpected or something which appears to be unrelated or stupid and that's true of the research or the preparation of the text or moving towards the text and in the production process as well. Your desire to pursue pieces of information or bits of research makes a significant impact on the integrity of the production because you need to interrogate every possible avenue and if you don't take pleasure in doing that, it's probably not the job for you. (Canny 2006: 32)

We have suggested that, above all, the dramaturg within the devising process is faced with the necessity of identifying the shape and direction of a work, not as something that is based on an existing source (as in the Berliner Ensemble's extended processes of textual analysis), but as something that is emerging and in process. The dramaturg is therefore not an authority that has all the answers. Perhaps the dramaturg is a map-maker, but is nevertheless, like the other devisers, engaged in a journey of exploration.

Part III

8 Millennial Dramaturgies

In Part II, we described and examined some of the ways in which dramaturgs are working in the contemporary theatre. However, it is important also to look forward, to ask what challenges might be emerging for the dramaturg and what kinds of question are animating the development of contemporary dramaturgies.

Contemporary theatre is, of course, multi-faceted, and we cannot presume that it necessarily always produces work that can be considered 'new' or 'original', or has universal aspirations to do so. While we are attempting to identify some current concerns and strategies, they may be peculiar to certain aspects of Northern European and North American 'experimental' theatre and its audiences. Nor can one describe them as being entirely *new*, since individual works frequently draw on ideas that have been evident in the works of modernists such as Artaud, Beckett, Brecht and others. However, some common themes and approaches seem to emerge from an examination of recent performances.

It has often been suggested that the twentieth century saw a crisis in the dramatic form (Szondi 1987, Derrida 1978, Sarrazac 1998, Fuchs 1996, Lehmann 2006). This crisis is closely concerned with the questioning of mimetic representational strategies. However, the first seven years of the new millennium have seen some developments (it should be noted that Lehmann's book was first published in German in 1999). Though we have not seen a return to 'the drama', perhaps we are increasingly seeing ways in which theatre is finding a new relationship with representation – one in which stories can be told, while the modes of telling, the tellers and even the stories themselves may be suspect, ambiguous and multiple. One could argue that this is, in some respects, a return to Brecht's dialectical theatre, and if, in Brechtian theatre, 'the whole thing is dramaturgy' (Adler 2005: 14), we could say the same for certain contemporary practices. However, there is a shift in emphasis. Brecht's theatre was centred in the story, though it made the audience aware of the story-teller. This theatre perhaps makes the audience aware of a story, but seems centred in the telling.

The Real and the Represented

When Antonin Artaud sought to abandon mimesis in favour of the autonomous 'real' of the stage, this marked, for Derrida, 'the closure of classical representation' (Derrida 1978: 9). Yet Artaud's theatre implicitly rejects one idea of authenticity only to institute another: the unattainable purity of a non-representational present or, as Derrida puts it, 'representation ... as the autopresentation of pure visibility and even pure sensibility' (Derrida 1978: 9). Postmodernism rejects this ideal: the layered forms, deconstructed narratives, mediatized performances (one thinks of the use of microphones and TV screens) and fragmented images of postmodernist work tend to destabilize presence, just as they undermine the production of meaning through representation.

Yet as the new century begins, we seem to be seeing a strategic re-entry of narrative, textuality and even of representational strategies existing, perhaps paradoxically, alongside an increased awareness, even valorization, of theatrical presence: what, in a recent discussion between UK directors Tim Etchells and Phelim McDermott and North American writer and director Richard Maxwell, was variously termed 'the now', 'live moments', 'what is happening ... the energy in a room right now' (Rewiring/Rewriting Theatre, 2006). At the same time, the work is not naive (or if it is, this naivety is, as David Williams puts it, a quality 'to be worked and affirmed and celebrated' [Williams 2006a: 2]): as André Lepecki observes, contemporary dramaturgies interrogate 'the mechanism of representation ... putting pressure on all its buttons and pulleys' (Lepecki 2006: 40). One might also suggest that they interrogate presence, even while they heighten our awareness of its effects.

While remaining ambivalent towards representation, contemporary performance seems interested in exploring the *range* of ways in which 'reality' can be produced, explored and understood. Or, to put it another way, the ways in which 'make-believe' is made believable. Such dramaturgies continue to challenge conventional narrative structures, yet also seem to open up a space in which new stories can be told and, indeed, we *can* 'make-believe', perhaps cannot help but do so. These concerns lead us to a dramaturgy of process and production, one which does not so much plunge into relativism, dismissing the possibility of making meaning, as involve itself in an exploration of how meaning is (and has been) made.

For example, Lone Twin Theatre's *Alice Bell* (2006) gives us a strikingly simple narrative, a biographical story with a tragic, yet redemptive ending. Yet this story is not depicted in mimetic actions: in Brechtian fashion, the characters speak their words as though reporting them, and the key actions of the story are abstracted into choreographic and textual figures. To give only two instances: Nicholas's character is first presented through a monologue that mimics the generalized aggression of a guard dog; Alice Bell's transformation into Clara Day becomes a rhythmic exchange of increasingly abstracted questions and answers that act as the motor for a choreographed movement sequence in which chairs, table and characters cross from one end of the traverse stage to the other. The details of Alice's story are implicit, rather than presented; the playfulness of the telling and the use of songs and ukeleles seem an appeal to the audience to enter into the game, to fill in the gaps, to see the abstracted moment as a possible evocation of the real.

Lone Twin's performances employ complex narrative strategies and their dramaturg(s) must be able to identify and to work with such strategies, to move beyond an understanding of literary dramatic structures. Certain approaches recur in many of their works, both within and beyond the theatre. For example, they often propose a seemingly purposeless task, 'an act of folly', which gains meaning through the event and through investment in it, ultimately becoming a 'labour of love' (Williams 2006a: 1). Alternatively, as suggested above, formal elements are abstracted from simple, everyday actions and may then be referenced in other contexts. It is evident that Williams's long-standing knowledge of Lone Twin's performances was helpful in enabling him to work with them as a dramaturg, since he was aware of such 'recurrent propositions at play' in their work (Williams 2006a: 1).

This range of narrative strategies allows the company to play with levels and degrees of 'reality' and theatricality. In the discussion mentioned above, Phelim McDermott suggested that when his company, Improbable Theatre, created *Life Games* (1998) they played with 'shifts of register'. He commented that by showing the performer's shift from everyday persona into the persona of the character, the audiences paradoxically came to 'believe the story' more than they might have with a straightforward mimetic representation. Tim Etchells concurred, suggesting that such 'shifts in register' were also part of his company, Forced Entertainment's methodology. McDermott commented that it was interesting that the more a work was revealed to be a performance, the more people seemed inclined to believe in it (Rewiring/Rewriting Theatre 2006). All three companies are aware of the paradox of having it both ways, finding that by revealing the mechanisms of the performance, they invite the audience's imaginative complicity.

Another common strategy in recent work is the deliberate incorporation of documentary, testimony or other obvious 'real life' elements into the structure of a play. For instance, there has been a surge of interest in 'verbatim theatre' in the UK – theatre in which the dialogue is based on interviews or other documentary material. The Tricycle Theatre's 1999 production, *The Colour of Justice* was based on the transcripts of the Stephen Lawrence enquiry, edited by Richard Norton-Taylor, while David Hare's *The Permanent Way* (2003), created with Out of Joint Theatre Company, was based on interviews with those associated with the rail crash at Potter's Bar. These and other such works present material that can be read as 'authentic', yet which is edited and presented as a play.

'Verbatim theatre' is rarely ironic, but rather draws theatre away from its association with fictional representation, towards a notion of the stage as a public platform for debate. The editing of the material into an overall composition is clearly a dramaturgical task requiring some sensitivity and self-awareness (whether it is undertaken by writer, dramaturg or director). In acknowledging their own interventions, such works often overtly point to the relationship between the theatrical and the 'real', foregrounding their own construction and the process of negotiation with the material. For instance, in *The Permanent Way*, the characters are often heard to address the author, 'David', thus reminding us of the interviewing process. This self-reflexive quality is paralleled in other plays' examination of the acts of speaking, writing or composition.

Getting the 'now' into the Text

Sarrazac has suggested that post-1960s theatre might be thought of as 'rhapsodic', a term that suggests the fragments of epic recited by the Greek 'rhapsodes', the irregular digressions of those who 'rhapsodize' as well as the free composition of the musical 'rhapsody'. The 'rhapsodic' theatre is hybrid, shifting between the dramatic, the epic and the lyric, the high and the low, tragic and comic, theatrical and extra-theatrical in a 'dynamic montage', which is, Sarrazac suggests, an appropriate response to the fragmentation of the modern world. It is characterized by the entry of a 'voice other than that of the characters', a voice lacking the authority of Szondi's 'epic voice', which is rather 'the hesitant, veiled, stammering voice of the modern rhapsode ... a voice of questions, voice of doubts, of palinodes, voice of the multiplication of possibilities'. This is, Sarrazac suggests, 'the voice of orality, even at the moment where it exceeds dramatic writing' (Sarrazac 1998: 201–2, our translation). We might add that this uncertain voice, that of the 'author-rhapsode', presents the process of shaping and communicating these hybrid compositions as a live act, one that potentially invites author, characters, performers and audience to become aware of their own creative roles.

This happens in many different ways and goes beyond the numerous depictions of the lives of writers, a trend noted by Christopher Innes as persistent in post-1960s plays by a multitude of well-known playwrights (Innes 2003: 10–12). If, as Innes suggests, this trend originates with Samuel Beckett, it is Beckett, too, whose work anticipates recent plays that *make the act of writing present*, implicitly or explicitly. In *Krapp's Last Tape* (1958), for example, we see a man in the process of writing and erasing his own autobiography. There is surely an echo of this in David Greig's *The Cosmonaut's Last Message to the Woman He Once Loved in the Former Soviet Union* (1999), in which we see all the characters repeatedly attempting to communicate in a number of inadequate media, including faulty transmitters, unfamiliar languages, cryptic signals and the halting speech of post-stroke recovery. The 'message' of the title, first attempted in repeated sound-recordings, suggestive of Krapp himself, becomes the detonation of the cosmonaut's capsule, a last burst of light in the night sky.

Martin Crimp's *Attempts on her Life* (1997) is more explicitly self-referential: the performance involves the creation of scenarios for a performance. The violence of the creative act is highlighted in the obsessive, brutal and exuberantly wasteful imaginations of the unnamed performers, as they dream up endless ways of representing a character, whose name embraces several variants of 'Anne' and whose role shifts from victim to perpetrator, from object to agent. Similarly emphasizing the mechanisms of performance, the German writer, Roland Schimmelpfennig, 'takes Brecht's recommendations for actors literally' (Haas 2003: 156), by making them narrators of their own story in his play, *Die Arabische Nacht* (2001). But unlike Brecht's exercises for *Antigone*, for example (see Brecht 2003: 208–15), Schimmelpfennig's actors' narrative is in the first person. By this means, the audience becomes aware of the construction of stage reality through language, with the characters seeming to be both authors and prisoners of the story they are telling. Images of imprisonment, disempowerment and disorientation create a sense of helpless thraldom or enchantment, even while the 'spell' seems to be woven by the very subjects of the tale.

Without wanting to dismiss the differences between them, one could identify a similar attention to live narration in a number of other recent plays, including, in the UK, Conor McPherson's *The Weir* (1998), Michael Frayn's *Copenhagen* (1998), Caryl Churchill's *Far Away* (2000) and others. In France, one might look at the work of Michel Vinaver, in Austria, Elfriede Jelinek, in the US, Richard Foreman and Richard Maxwell.

The process of composition as both theme and formal concern is not peculiar to playwrights. Forced Entertainment's work has, since the 1990s, included a strand in which the company explores what might be termed, after Ludwig Wittgenstein (1974), 'language-games', usually placed against minimalist staging and sometimes presented as performance installation, where the audience members enter and depart as they please. *And On The Thousandth Night...* (2000) is one such performance installation based on a simple, improvisational structure and again, like Schimmelpfennig's work, referencing the *Arabian Nights* as a story-telling model. Each of the eight performers is engaged in telling stories. Each story is interrupted by a story from another performer. Each story is framed by the story-telling tradition associated with the *Arabian Nights*, yet within this, there is immense scope for variation, the performers pushing at the edges of what a story might be, racking their brains for a constant supply of new stories, new subject matter. This struggle to tell the stories is at the centre of the event. We listen to the stories emerge, written in their moment of enunciation, each impelled by the urgency of the game.

All the works discussed above concern the authorial struggle to make sense of the world and the word, implicitly inviting our participation and emphasizing this struggle as taking place in the present, rather than as something that precedes the performance.

Given their emphasis on performance as process, perhaps it is not surprising that in a number of the playscripts mentioned, certain aspects of classical Aristotelian dramaturgy (place, time, character, action) are not merely fragmented, but completely ambiguous, open to a wide range of interpretative possibilities and to be partly resolved in and through performance. Thus, for example, Crimp's play is uncertain in terms of both speakers and staging (though he explicitly discourages a minimalist approach); Schimmelpfennig's script does not identify when the narrative should be 'acted out' and when left entirely to the listener's imagination; while even Greig's play poses unusual scenographic challenges and plays with enigmatic doublings of characters/performers. Forced Entertainment's work, of course, is inherently open, as an improvisational structure.

Such dramaturgical openness has been the source of some ambivalence. We may remember that, as discussed in Chapter 1, Sarah Kane's later works, *Crave* (1998) and *4:48 Psychosis* (1999), are ambiguous in their suggestion of place, character and action. Both plays' unsettling evocation of mental breakdown has led some to suggest that her dramaturgy is not so much open or ambiguous as fragmented or insufficient. Sanja Nikcevic writes, 'The inarticulacy of the playwright's solipsistic world, even as experienced, was not expressed precisely in theatrical terms. So everything except the fact of shocking violence was left in the hands of the directors' (Nikcevic, 2005: 267). The suggestion of 'inarticulacy' is telling: is Kane's work, in fact, built around problems of articulation? Are the gaps, evasions, silences, ambiguities of the works discussed, indicative of the limits of what can be said? Patrice Pavis (2000) proposes that recent French texts make the actor into an 'actor-dramaturg', whose work is necessary to 'unfold', rather than 'interpret' the text, 'participating in dramaturgic choices and changes'. Is it therefore the role of the 'actor-dramaturg' to bring to Kane's plays the materiality of the body, the semiotic qualities of the voice, to enter into these problems of articulation without necessarily resolving them?

Production dramaturgs are implicated in Nikcevic's criticism, depicted as complicit substitutes for the writer in a director's theatre. While there is no doubt that such open dramaturgies pose exciting challenges for directors, dramaturgs and performers, it need not be assumed that the writer's creative role is thereby diminished. One might, for example, consider the important contribution made by German dramaturg Tilman Raabke towards the appreciation of Nobel-prize-winning author Jelinek's dense word play (Honegger 2005: 7–8).

If, in Phelim McDermott's words (Rewiring/Rewriting Theatre 2006), an interesting concern for contemporary performance might be ways of getting 'the now' into the written text (even if it is only 'written' in the moment of speaking), then all the works discussed above emphasize speaking, writing and composition as shared activities, taking place in the present and creatively infiltrated, at times, deconstructed, by the physical and visual presences of the performers and *mise en scène*. What all these works have in common, is a dramaturgy of process – a dramaturgy that makes us aware of the mechanisms of communication and the artificial construction of imaginary (real) worlds, even while we are moved and engaged by them.

Such tendencies are paralleled in a distinct shift towards engaging the writer in collaborative creation, as opposed to solitary composition prior to rehearsal. Ruth Little, then dramaturg at the Young Vic, now literary manager at the Royal Court clarifies this change of approach and its implications for the dramaturg:

> We are now regularly making work which takes the dramatic script as a 'theatrical score'; where the playwright participates alongside director, designer, composer, choreographer, puppeteer, performer, drawing on live resources in action to produce a text ... Writers are developing new confidence in the languages of theatre, and in the dramatic potential of their own language ... This 'convergent' theatre-making ... is shifting dramaturgical practice away from linear, strictly causal models towards a recognition of the play as a living system, subject to complex and subtle environmental forces and feedback from within the play and beyond it (in its relationship with its audiences). The implications of this for writers, dramaturgs and theatre-makers are, I think, profound. (Little 2007: 2)

Artist and Spill festival director Robert Pacitti confirms this when he suggests that, 'British theatre needs to look very hard at what it means by new writing'. Pacitti clarifies that 'My practice is very body-based and very visual, but it always starts with writing. There is a text ... In the past, it often seemed you were either for live art, or you were for theatre; we are trying to build a bridge between the two' (Pacitti, cited in Gardner 2007b). As mentioned in Chapter 5, Claire MacDonald's project, 'The Space Between Words', takes a similar view.

As Little suggests, such a recognition of a play as 'a living system' is also indicative of a shift in relationship to the audience. Malgorzata Sugiera, discussing the works of Schimmelpfennig, Loher and others, suggests that:

> Nowadays, the basic structural principle of texts written for theatre increasingly often turns out to be their immanent theatricality, which is ... a means of inducing the audience to watch themselves as subjects which perceive, acquire knowledge and partly create the objects of their cognition ... the very object of the theatrical mimesis has changed. (Sugiera 2004: 7)

If the relationship with the audience has changed, it is perhaps unsurprising that the space of performance is also subject to scrutiny. The location of performance – indeed of the theatre – has often been extended to include the audience and very frequently to range beyond the theatre building itself.

The 'spatial turn'

Edward Soja has noted the 'spatial turn' of contemporary critical studies in the humanities and social sciences, adding to the critique of historicality and sociality, 'a third critical perspective, associated with an explicitly spatial imagination', suggesting that this reflects an 'ontological shift' in which 'the inherent and encompassing spatiality of being and becoming is beginning to be more forcefully recognized than ever before' (Soja 2000: 13–14).

This 'spatial imagination' seems, perhaps unsurprisingly, to be reflected in contemporary theatre and performance, where we see a number of works in which spatial, rather than chronological principles are fundamental to the dramaturgy. The 1990s seems to have seen a rapid increase in the number of companies creating site-specific performances (or, at least, those who identified their work as such, see Wilkie 2002). However, a spatial sensibility is already evident in early modernist work, pre-empted in Gertrude Stein's 'landscape theatre' and developed not only in recent site-specific theatre, but also in visually and architecturally oriented dramaturgies, such as that of US director Robert Wilson.

In many recent works, the space of the performance is conceived as a space that is shared with the audience, rather than separated from it. Punchdrunk's performances of classic texts have effectively operated by turning a chronological narrative into a landscape to be explored. For example, in *Faust* (2006), audience members wandered freely through a building in Wapping Lane, stumbling on fragments of the play, or characters in transition from one scene to the next. Sometimes the space itself seemed to tell the story. The scenes of the play (a significantly and severely edited selection) were performed in sequence but as a performance 'loop', thus making it possible to see them out of their original order. This production undid narrative time, while allowing the audience to enter and explore a sensory play world. Punchdrunk's work allows each audience member a dramaturgical role, as they choose their route through the building. For instance, it is possible to follow the story of the performances, by following an actor through the various scenes. Alternatively, one can explore the space, experiencing the scenes as one stumbles across them. If the work discussed earlier makes the audience aware of the compositional process in various ways, this work does so by engaging the audience directly in that composition.

A similar sensory, spatial awareness can be identified in other, site-related theatre such as Shunt's *Tropicana* (2004), or in Geraldine

Pilgrim's large-scale site-specific performances in the St Pancras Chambers (2000) or Elizabeth Garrett Anderson hospital (2003). Here again, the traces of a chronological narrative are subordinate to the architectural and experiential narrative of the audience's movement through space.

Heidi Taylor has explored the implications of site-specific theatre for the dramaturg, proposing five principles for a 'deep dramaturgy' of site-specific practice:

- All signs in the performance space have meaning, independent of their usefulness to the project
- Accidents and contradictions contribute to the complexity of the work – if they are embraced rather than ignored, they may satisfy the idiosyncratic and deep-felt structures of the work
- Active choice about every element of the production, from the first audience contact to the end of the event, has the potential to increase the audience's ability and willingness to attend to and appreciate our obsession to [sic] detail
- The diversity of theatre flourishes with increased audience contact, which is not synonymous with larger audiences
- Basic ideological, political, economic and technological structures must therefore change. (Taylor 2004: 19)

Taylor's suggestions emphasize the 'unscripted *texts*' of a space, the 'rhythm' of sound, movement and architecture and the 'audience's bodily journey'. She proposes a dramaturgy that embraces the unpredictability and fluidity of these elements, rather than attempting to control them.

Taylor acknowledges that such a dramaturgy is often at odds with dramatic form, suggesting that, 'the more individuated the audience members, the harder it is to create one narrative arc' (Taylor 2004: 18). In productions by Punchdrunk, Shunt, or other such companies, any remaining elements of conventional drama – for example, elements of narrative told through dialogue between characters and suggesting a sequence of causally linked actions – tend to force a pause in the flow of audience movement and collapse the sense of simultaneity into a single moment of action. Theatre, like the lens of a camera, also has a tendency to place a focus on the performer, rather than on the space, which becomes relegated to a background or 'backdrop'. The theatrical frame can therefore be a source of tension within site-specific performance and performance installation, provoking expectations that work against the spatial structures of the event.

Alternatively, within live art we find live works (some of them borrowing from theatre practice) that, as in some of the earliest modernist works, refuse to separate the artwork from the 'real' or 'everyday' world. These works engage with the 'everyday' precisely as a way of allowing the artwork to be influenced and infiltrated by the 'real' (and vice versa), again drawing attention to the ways in which the 'real' is experienced.

For example, FrenchMottershead's early work invited audience members into a space where they were not differentiated from performers. In *My Word is My Bond* (2002), in Throgmorton's Restaurant and Bar opposite the London Stock Exchange, audience members closely scrutinized each other's behaviour, on the look-out for 'actors' staging 'micro-performances', based on the behaviours of those who habitually frequent the venue. The distinction between 'authentic' behaviours and 'performance' was thus made deliberately unclear.

Other performances have dramaturgies that might be considered as 'nomadic', in that they traverse everyday spaces, often taking the form of a journey. Site-specific company Wrights & Sites, for example, have moved away from theatre structures, to an interest in journeying through a space, in a series of 'Mis-Guides', which include guided tours, unstructured 'drifts' and books which offer suggestions for walking. In 2006, the festival Liverpool Live was titled 'A Festival of Urban Apparition' and featured 'four days of interventions, occurrences and happenings that punctuate the shifting landscape of the city centre', including 'performative walks' and 'guided tours', among other site-related practices (festival brochure). Marcus Young walked 'at a snail's pace' through the city centre; Mat Fraser and Max Zadow offered a coach tour of buildings that lacked disabled access; Gustavo Ciriaco and Andrea Sonnberger led a silent walk; Joshua Sofaer provided an audio tour of public artworks, delivered in 'fake national languages of the artists', while Chinese performance artist He Yun Chang passed through on his 3,000-mile walk around Great Britain carrying a rock.

The journey through the city proposes a structure that is deliberately open to the invasions of the everyday. Still more so than in the site-specific theatre pieces, this engagement with space seems to force open the dramaturgy of the work, making the audience aware of their own (literal) progress through the performances. Again, we see a dramaturgy of process – one that deliberately forces itself into a live engagement with space and audience, rather than attempting to predict and dominate that encounter.

Little's interesting question, 'What might happen if we begin to consider the playwright and the director as the "disturbers" of living systems?' might be applied to the exchange between performance and the everyday, inherent in these site-specific practices. The performance is in constant exchange with its surroundings, and the performance event remains to some extent uncertain. To use Little's own analogy, it is as unpredictable as the weather (indeed, sometimes dependent upon it!).

Interactivity and New Technologies

As we have seen, site-specific performance tends towards a high level of interactivity, where the spectator is expected to construct a narrative, fill in the gaps, make choices, adopt a position or even engage directly in the action. However, this tendency is found across a wide range of contemporary dramaturgies. The idea of the audience as 'witness', rather than spectator, implicates the audience member in the making of meaning (Etchells 1999: 17–18). Richard Maxwell suggests that performance is a 'shared responsibility' between performer and audience, while Etchells suggests that performance is about negotiation with the audience and 'to feel the fragility of ourselves in the room' (Rewiring/Rewriting Theatre 2006).

The interactivity of new media has played its part in encouraging the active participation of the audience member. Virtual space and interactive video games offer new dramaturgical possibilities, while also drawing on and provoking the interactivity of the theatre event.

Such media is itself influenced by older forms of performance. For instance, Boal's 'Theatre of the Oppressed' has led Gonzalo Frasca to speculate on the political potential of 'Videogames of the Oppressed' (Frasca 2001). One of these models is based on *The Sims*: 'Think of it as F[orum] T[heatre] with games instead of scenes' (Frasca 2001: 3). This model would allow users to create different versions of the characters in the game, editing the basic templates to create new characters, 'based on behavioural details that they think need improvement in order to have a higher degree of verisimilitude' (Frasca 2001: 3). In fact, this model is rather different from Forum Theatre in key respects – most crucially in that, rather than seeking solutions to identified problems, the interactivity and politics of the game would revolve around modifying the possible range of simulations, in an attempt to reflect social realities. Frasca suggests that part of the game's political potential would lie in drawing attention to the activity and attitudes of the amateur designers: 'The fact that several design strategies coexist in the game – and that the player knows that other players designed most of the behaviours – enhances the perception of the simulation as a constructed artefact' (Frasca 2001: 5). The principal aim of all Frasca's suggested 'games' would be to generate discussion, and he suggests that they might particularly prove useful tools for work with teenagers.

While Frasca makes an analogy with Boal's theatre, Kjetil Sandvik suggests that it is important to recognize the distinct and innovative dramaturgies of computer games:

> Computer games are not just digital novels, movies or theatre performances. They may bear resemblances to the old media, but when it comes to narrativity, computer games have their own characteristics which tie them both to a technological and a ludological dimension. (Sandvik 2004: 1)

Sandvik argues that these characteristics include 'intermedial' and 'interactive' elements, which make the computer games into 'complex and dynamic systems … in which stories are dynamic, dramatic processes' (Sandvik 2004: 1). While we might argue that theatre can also be interactive (Boal's theatre being one example), Sandvik makes the case for considering the particular strategies of computer games. For instance, he points out that the player invariably has a dual role, not as author, but as role-player and spectator, simultaneously. Similarly, there are always two dramaturgies at work: the dramaturgy of the overall game structure, and the evolving dramaturgy of the particular game. While the structure of the overall game is complex, organized to produce multiple possibilities, the individual game will often produce a fairly simple, recognizable narrative structure, based on models drawn from, 'fantasy, action, horror, science fiction and so on'. As Sandvik suggests, this is a way of 'making the dramaturgy visible', so that the player instantly feels familiar with the genre (Sandvik 2004: 2–3).

Sandvik gives examples of a number of dramaturgical models for computer games. The simplest is the 'linear model', which produces a fixed chain of events, with points of 'local interactivity' that do not necessarily make it possible to alter the overall story (Sandvik 2004: 4). The most complex is the 'circle model', which offers a narrative space capable of producing many different stories, often over a long period (the examples Sandvik gives are *Ultima Online*, *The Sims* and *SimCity*) (Sandvik 2004: 6).

Online communities such as *YouTube* and *Second Life* offer still more radically open spaces where people can construct or broadcast their own virtual performances of various kinds. The occupants of *Second Life* choose virtual identities and can purchase online 'real estate', while also being able to meet and converse with other people.

One aspect of *Second Life* is its offer of endless opportunities for online consumption, involving 'real' money in exchange for virtual goods – often clothes. Elinor Fuchs is interesting in her suggestion that the increasing interactivity of theatre may be merely a reflection of a consumer culture. She describes interactive spectacle as 'an instant, ever-shifting simulation in which I "try on" the physical and imaginative conditions imposed by the surrounding space'. The new spectator, 'too restless and driven to be contained in a theatre seat … prowls the total entertainment, simultaneously consuming and consumed' (Fuchs 1996: 140–1). This is a serious criticism, one that casts a shadow over the pleasure of exploring Punchdrunk's environments, or even the more sophisticated engagement required by Blast Theory's work discussed below. In relation to these works, it would seem a harsh judgement. On first glance, it might seem a good description of *Second Life*; Tim Adams writes that, 'the simple genius of Second Life is that it combines elements of Big Brother with the spirit of Ebay' (Adams 2006: 3). In some ways, this is a space that reflects predictions quoted by Fuchs and made by theatre producer Barrie Wexler: 'playing environments in which you shop, and shopping environments in which you play – the line between these two will become thinner and thinner' (Fuchs 1996: 142). Nevertheless, *Second Life* is open to other possibilities. Dave Surface, a virtual reality designer, comments that, 'There are too many efforts here that simply aim at duplicating R[eal] L[ife] … We need more innovation that leverages our own environment' (quoted in Adams 2006: 4).

As we write, performance works are already being commissioned specifically for *Second Life*. For example, Exeter Phoenix is in the process of commissioning work for this context. And indeed, commissioned or not, artists are already working in *Second Life*. For example, Dancoyote Antonelli has created a Museum of Hyperformalism and explored interactive artwork and performance: 'Many believe Antonelli has created a breakthrough that establishes *Second Life* as a new form for artists' (Rymaszewski *et al.* 2007: 252). It is entirely possible to conceive of a dramaturg who works in *Second Life*'s virtual spaces.

Interactive media in turn have their effect on live performance, providing the opportunity for new structures that combine 'real' and virtual elements (again we see work shifting between different levels of reality or 'registers'). Indeed, this is a significant part of the shift

Eckersall observes, when he points out that:

> Performance dramaturgy … has created the need for creative specialists who keep track of the complicated flow of ideas, technologies and forms associated with such work. Professional dramaturgy has therefore moved beyond literary modes of production into new fields of performance, dance and technical and production work. (Eckersall 2006: 287)

The new dramaturg may need to understand new technologies – their structures, if not their operation.

In the UK, Blast Theory have undoubtedly been at the forefront of performance that investigates the relationship between virtual media and live acts. They are currently part of IperG, a European consortium investigating 'pervasive games', which interweave the computer game with everyday life: 'The pervasive game player … is uncertain about the ontology of what they see and experience. Caught in a parallel and yet fully believable existence, they operate in dialectical tension between their lives and the game' (Giannachi, www.presence.stanford.edu). Blast Theory's own recent contribution was *The Day of the Figurines* (2006), created in collaboration with Nottingham University's Mixed Reality Lab and Sony Net Services. This game, in the version used at its launch in Berlin, unfolds over twenty-four days and operates via text messaging. While the player is occupied with their everyday life, their *alter ego*, a chosen 'figurine' moves through the model of an imaginary city. Blast Theory's Matt Adams writes:

> The player moves in space and time whilst also being presented with dilemmas, in the form of multiple choice questions and open questions, some formulated in real time by the game operators. Special events unfold: a fete, an eclipse, an explosion. (Adams 2005, quoted at www.presence.stanford.edu)

Initial evaluations suggest that the way the game is interwoven with everyday life results in a cross-contamination of the 'real' and the artwork. Gabriella Giannachi comments that the 'idea of bleeding through, producing a contamination between life and game, art and technology, fact and imagination, is at the heart of the game'. She continues, 'Unlike in a conventional theatre experience, the player of *Day of the Figurines* would not be so much inside or in front of another space (a theatre, a city) as interfered with, from within their everyday life, by the game'. She suggests that the game 'follows a viral aesthetic. This is a game of contamination and inter-penetration working at a very subtle level.' Like some of the other artworks discussed in this chapter, the pervasive game challenges us to examine the ways in which we identify, produce and respond to circumstances as 'real'. *Day of the Figurines* makes the player a collaborator in the work, which is, 'a programme *and* an event, a performance *and* a document, a game *and* a scientific experiment' (Giannachi, www.presence.stanford.edu, italics in original).

Virtual media also, potentially, extend the scope and influence of performance works, so that the dramaturgy of a project extends beyond the live event to associated new media works, thus dispersing the artwork across a much wider geographic area than would otherwise be possible. For instance, London's Moti Roti recently worked with New York's The Builder's Association on a project entitled *Alladeen* (2003), which comprised a theatre performance, a web-based project and a music video for MTV-Asia. The performance was also concerned with alter egos and alternative 'realities', in that it examined the training of staff working at call centres in Bangalore, who are taught to 'pass' as American.

These are just a few examples. One might also discuss the ways in which interactive media offer new ways of engaging with the stage scene: one might think, for example, of Forced Entertainment's experimentations with CD-Rom, *Frozen Palaces* (1999) and *Nightwalks* (1998), which allow the viewer to explore virtual environments. The significance, for theatre, of new technologies of all kinds is too vast a subject to discuss here, while the impact of interactive media on theatre performance is also immeasurable, reflected in structures and processes, even where a direct engagement with such media is not self-evident. However, this impact, while remaining unpredictable, is likely to be of increasing significance, suggesting new dramaturgies, new challenges, new 'shifts of register' for future exploration.

Conclusion

We began by suggesting that what links the works discussed in this chapter is that they present us with a dramaturgy of process and production. One could put this another way, suggesting that most of them deliberately engage with the present tense, the 'now' of live performance – less a matter of live *presence* than of live *encounter*. They each, as Matthew Goulish puts it, consider the work as,

> an object overflowing its frame, converging into a series of other objects each overflowing their frames, not becoming one another, but becoming

events, each moving in the direction of their own infinite singularity and difference. (Goulish 2000: 100)

These works, to varying degrees, make the audience aware of the unfolding process of making meaning through performance. The dramaturg might play an important role in helping to provide a vocabulary for discussing and identifying the various 'shifts of register' and in negotiating deliberately ambiguous or open structures in contemporary work. On the other hand, one could suggest that much contemporary work exposes and explores its own dramaturgical processes and thus calls on a dramaturgical sensibility from all those involved, including not only the dramaturg, writer and director, but also the 'actor-dramaturg' and the individual spectator.

While it may (possibly) inhibit the 'suspension of disbelief', this awareness of the performance process does not, as Brecht knew, lead to a lack of emotional engagement. Is it purely coincidental that three of the works cited make direct appeal to one of the oldest reference points for story-telling, the *Arabian Nights*? At its simplest, the live encounter of contemporary theatre may be represented by the relationship between the story-teller and the listener, a relationship that presupposes some level of interaction and critique, as well as a shared imaginative engagement. We may well experience ourselves becoming, like Schimmelpfennig's characters, enchanters enchanted as we realize our share in creating, imaginatively, the fictions that enthral us.

Bibliography

Adams, Tim (2006), 'Goodbye, cruel world ... ', *Guardian*, 29 October.

Adler, Henrik (2005), unpublished interview with Synne Behrndt and Cathy Turner, 17 September, Berlin.

Adolphe, Jean-Marc (1998), 'Dramaturgy of Movement: A Plea for a Dramaturgy of Perception', *Ballet International*, No. 6, pp. 27–9.

Albright, Daniel (2003), *Beckett and Aesthetics* (Cambridge: Cambridge University Press).

Allsopp, Ric (1999), 'Performance Writing', *Performing Arts Journal*, Vol. 61, No. 21, pp. 76–80.

Ansorge, Peter (1975), *Disrupting the Spectacle: Five Years of Experimental and Fringe Theatre in Britain* (London: Pitman).

Aristotle (1987), *The Poetics of Aristotle*, trans. and ed. by Stephen Halliwell (London: Duckworth).

Arntzen, Knut Ove (1994), 'A Visual Kind of Dramaturgy', *Theaterschrift*, No. 5–6, pp. 274–6.

Arts Council England (2000), 'The Next Stage' (London: ACE).

Aston, Elaine (1995), *An Introduction to Feminism and Theatre* (London: Routledge).

Aston, Elaine and Janelle Reinelt (2000) (eds), *The Cambridge Companion to Modern British Women Playwrights* (London: Cambridge University Press).

Aston, Elaine and George Savona (1991) *Theatre as a Sign-system. A Semiotics of Text and Performance* (London: Routledge).

Auslander, Philip (1992), *Presence and Resistance: Postmodernism and Cultural Politics in Contemporary Performance* (Ann Arbor: University of Michigan Press).

Barba, Eugenio (1985), 'The Nature of Dramaturgy: Describing Actions at Work', *New Theatre Quarterly*, Vol. 1, No. 1, February, pp. 75–8.

Barton, Bruce (2005), 'Navigating Turbulence: The Dramaturg in Physical Theatre', *Theatre Topics*, Vol. 15, No. 1, pp. 103–19.

Bassnett, Susan (1987a), 'Women Experiment with Theatre: Magdalena 86', *New Theatre Quarterly*, Vol. 3, No. 11, pp. 224–34.

Bassnett, Susan (1987b), *Magdalena: International Women's Experimental Theatre* (Berg: Oxford).

Beacham, Richard (1978), 'Literary Management at the National Theatre, London: An Interview with John Russell Brown', *Theater*, Vol. 10, No. 1, Autumn, pp. 38–42.

Beckley, Richard (1961–2), 'Adaptation as a Feature of Brecht's Dramatic Technique', *German Life and Letters*, 15, pp. 274–93.

Benjamin, Walter (1973), 'Conversations with Brecht', *New Left Review*, Vol. 1, No. 77, January–February, pp. 51–7.

Ben-Tovim, Ruth (2007), telephone conversation with Synne Behrndt, 3 April. Notes taken by Synne Behrndt.

Berghahn, Klaus L. (1997), 'German Literary Theory from Gottsched to Goethe', in H.B Nisbet and Claude Rawson (eds), *The Cambridge History of Literary Criticism: The Eighteenth Century*, Vol. 4 (Cambridge: Cambridge University Press), pp. 522–45.

Bergvall, Caroline (1999), keynote address, 'In the Event of Text' conference, Utrecht.

Bergvall, Caroline (1996), 'What Do We Mean by Performance Writing?', keynote address, Performance Writing Symposium, Dartington College of Arts, available online at <www.dartington.ac.uk/pw/keynote.html>, accessed 8 February 2007.

Berlau, Ruth (1949) (ed.), *Antigonemodell* (Berlin: Weiss).

Berliner Ensemble (1953), programme for Strittmatter's *Katzgraben*, (ed.) Carl Weber, Berlin.

Berliner Ensemble and Helene Weigel (eds) (1961), *Theaterarbeit: 6 Aufführungen des Berliner Ensembles*, 2nd edn (Berlin: Suhrkamp).

Bharucha, Rustom (2000), *The Politics of Cultural Practice: Thinking through Theater in an Age of Globalization* (New England: Wesleyan University Press).

Bicât, Tina and Chris Baldwin (2002), *Devised and Collaborative Theatre: A Practical Guide* (Ramsbury: Crowood Press).

Bille, Karen-Maria (2005), unpublished interview with Synne Behrndt and Cathy Turner, 13 April, Copenhagen.

Billington, Michael (2007), 'Hidden Agendas', *Guardian*, 15 January.

Billington, Michael (2006), 'It's Raining Men!', *Guardian*, 5 December.

Billington, Michael (2001), 'Tynan's gift was to make criticism glamorous and sexy', *Guardian*, 24 September.

Blast Theory (2006), 'Day of the Figurines', documented at <http://www.presence.stanford.edu:3455/Collaboratory/627>, accessed 5 January 2007.

Bleeker, Maaike (2003), 'Dramaturgy as a Mode of Looking', in André Lepecki and Cindy Brizzell (eds), *Women and Performance: A Journal of Feminist Theory*, Issue 26, Vol. 13, No. 3, pp. 163–72.

Bly, Mark (2001), *The Production Notebooks. Theatre in Process, Vol. II* (New York: Theatre Communications Group).

Bly, Mark (1996), *The Production Notebooks. Theatre in Process, Vol. I* (New York: Theatre Communications Group).

Bogart, Anne (2001), *A Director Prepares: Seven Essays on Art and Theatre* (London: Routledge).

Borecca, Art (1993), 'Political Dramaturgy. A Dramaturg's (Re)view', in *The Drama Review*, Vol. 37, pp. 56–79.

Braidotti, Rosi (1994), *Nomadic Subjects: Embodiment and Sexual Difference, in Contemporary Feminist Theory* (New York: Columbia University Press).

Brecht, Bertolt (2003), *Collected Plays: Eight*, ed. and introduced by Tom Kuhn and David Constantine (London: Methuen).

Brecht, Bertolt (1994), *Collected Plays: One*, ed. and introduced by John Willett and Ralph Manheim (London: Methuen).

Brecht, Bertolt (1993), *Journals*, 1934–55, ed. John Willett and Ralph Manheim, trans. Hugh Rorrison and John Willett (London: Methuen).

Brecht, Bertolt (1990), *Letters* 1913–1956, trans. Ralph Manheim and ed. John Willett (London: Methuen).

Brecht, Bertolt (1988), *The Tutor*, trans. Pip Broughton (London: The Old Vic Theatre Collection).

Brecht, Bertolt (1977), *The Messingkauf Dialogues*, trans. John Willett (London: Methuen).

Brecht, Bertolt (1964), *Brecht on Theatre*, ed. and trans. John Willett (London: Methuen).

Brenton, Howard (2001), unpublished interview with Cathy Turner, 17 January, London.

Brenton, Howard (1981 [1975]), 'Petrol Bombs Through the Proscenium Arch', interview with Catherine Itzin and Simon Trussler, originally for Theatre Quarterly Vol. V, No. 17, subsequently published in Simon Trussler (ed.), *New Theatre Voices of the Seventies: Sixteen Interviews from Theatre Quarterly* 1970–1980 (London: Eyre Methuen), pp.85–97.

Brewer, Daniel (1993), *The Discourse of Enlightenment in Eighteenth Century France: Diderot and the Art of Philosophizing* (Cambridge: Cambridge University Press).

Brown, Russell E. (2000), 'Bertolt Brecht as Dramaturg', in Bert Cardullo (ed.), *What is Dramaturgy?* (New York: Peter Lang), pp. 57–63.

Brizzell, Cindy and André Lepecki (2003) 'Introduction: The Labor of the question is the (feminist) question of Dramaturgy', *Women and Performance: A Journal of Feminist Theory*, Issue 26, Vol. 13, No. 2, pp.15–16.

Butler, Judith (1993), *Bodies that Matter: On the Discursive Limits of 'Sex'* (London: Routledge).

Butler, Judith (1990), *Gender Trouble: Feminism and the Subversion of Identity* (London: Routledge).

Canaris, Volker (1975), 'Style and the Director', in Ronald Hayman (ed.), *The German Theatre* (London: Oswald Wolff), pp. 247–73.

Canny, Steven (2006), unpublished interview with Synne Behrndt, May, London.

Cardullo, Bert (1995), *What is Dramaturgy?* (New York: Peter Lang).

Carlson, Marvin (1993), *Theories of the Theatre. A Historical and Critical Survey, from the Greeks to the Present* (Ithaca: Cornell University Press).

Cattaneo, Anne (2006), unpublished interview with Synne Behrndt, 29 March, New York.

Cattaneo, Anne (2002), 'Anne Cattaneo', interviewed in Judith Rudakoff and Lynn M. Thomson (eds), *Between the Lines: The Process of Dramaturgy* (Toronto: Playwrights of Canada Press), pp. 223–45.

Cattaneo, Anne (1997), 'Dramaturgy: An Overview', in Susan Jonas, Geoff Proehl and Michael Lupu (eds), *Dramaturgy in American Theater: A Source Book* (Orlando: Harcourt Brace College Publishers), pp. 3–15.

Church, Catherine and Nell Leyshon (2005), unpublished interview with Cathy Turner, 1 July, Bournemouth.

Coleman, Heidi and Tamsen Wolff (1998), '*American Silents*. A dramaturgical collaboration with Anne Bogart', *TheatreForum*, No. 12, pp. 1 –27.

Copfermann, Emile (1960), 'Qu'est-ce q'un "Dramaturge"? Entretien avec Joachim Tenschert, Dramaturge au Berliner Ensemble', *Théâtre Populaire*, No. 38, 2, pp. 41–8.

Costa, Maddy (2006), 'Shakespeare was daring – why aren't new writers?', *Guardian*, 23 February.

Costa, Maddy (2005), 'Britain's Secret Theatre', *Guardian*, 5 October.

Costa, Maddy (2004), 'Where have all the playwrights gone?', *Guardian*, 7 October.

Coult, Tony and Baz Kershaw (1983) (eds), *Engineers of the Imagination: The Welfare State Handbook* (London and New York: Methuen).

Craze, Tony (ed.) (1995), 'Going Black Under the Skin', London Arts Board: London, available from <www.writernet.co.uk/images/286.pdf>, accessed 16 April 2006.

Davies, Andrew (1987), *Other Theatres: The Development of Alternative and Experimental Theatre in Britain* (London: Macmillan).

Delahunta, Scott (2000), 'Dance Dramaturgy: Speculations and Reflections', *Dance Theatre Journal*, Vol. 16, No. 1, pp. 20–4.

De Jongh, Nicholas (1992), *Not in Front of the Audience: Homosexuality on Stage* (London and New York: Routledge).

De Marinis, Marco (1987), 'Dramaturgy of the Spectator', *The Drama Review*, Vol. 31, No. 2, pp. 100–14.

Derrida, Jacques (1978), 'The Theatre of Cruelty and the Closure of Representation', in *Writing and Difference*, trans. Alan Bass (Chicago: University of Chicago Press), pp. 232–50.

Diamond, Elin (1988), 'Brechtian Theory/Feminist Theory: Towards a Gestic Feminist Criticism', *The Drama Review*, No. 32, Spring, pp. 82–94.

Dickson, Keith (1978), *Towards Utopia: A Study of Brecht* (Oxford: Clarendon Press).

Dromgoole, Dominic (2004), 'The Fast Shows', *Guardian*, 7 October.

Eckersall, Peter (2006), 'Towards an Expanded Dramaturgical Practice: A report on the Cultural Intervention Project', in *Theatre Research International*, Vol. 31, No. 3, pp. 383–97.

Eckersall, Peter (2003), 'What is Dramaturgy? What is a Dramaturg?', keynote address, 'Dramaturgy Now: Dramaturgies II', University of Melbourne, <www.realtimearts.net/dramaturgy/dramatugy2day1.html>, accessed 10 January, 2007.

Edgar, David (2007), seminar paper, University of Exeter, Series of Playwriting and Dramaturgy Research Seminars and Symposia, 14 February.

Edgar, David (2005), 'Steady States: Theories of Contemporary New Writing', *Contemporary Theatre Review*, Vol. 15, No. 3, pp. 297–308.

Edgar, David (1999), 'Provocative Acts: British Playwriting in the Post-war Era and Beyond', in David Edgar (ed.), *State of Play: Playwrights on Playwriting* (London: Faber and Faber), pp. 3–34.

Edgar, David (1979), 'Ten Years of Political Theatre, 1968–78', *Theatre Quarterly*, Vol. 8, No. 32, pp. 25–33.

Editors of Theatre Quarterly (1995), 'The Critic Comes Full Circle: An Interview with Kenneth Tynan', in Bert Cardullo (ed.), *What is Dramaturgy?* (New York: Peter Lang), pp. 197–212.

Esslin, Martin (1990), 'Some Reflections on Brecht and Acting', in Pia Kleber and Colin Visser (eds), *ReInterpreting Brecht: His Influence on Contemporary Drama and Film* (Cambridge: Cambridge University Press), pp. 135–46.

Esslin, Martin (1978), 'The Role of the Dramaturg in European Theater', *Theater*, Vol. 10, No.1, pp. 48–50.

Etchells, Tim (1999), *Certain Fragments* (London: Routledge).

Fabião, Eleonora (2003), 'Dramaturging with Mabou Mines: Six Proposals for Ecco Porco', *Women and Performance: A Journal of Feminist Theory*, Issue 26, Vol. 13, No. 3, pp. 29–40.

Fischer-Licthe, Erika (1999), *Kurze Geschichte des Deutschen Theaters* (Tübingen: A. Francke Verlag).

Foucault, Michel (1988), 'What Is An Author?', in David Lodge (ed.), *Modern Criticism and Theory: A Reader* (London and New York: Longman).

Fox, John (2002), *Eyes on Stalks* (London: Methuen).

Frank, Thomas (2005), unpublished interview with Synne Behrndt and Cathy Turner, 3 June, Birmingham.

Frank, Thomas and Mark Waugh (2005), 'Curators on Audiences', in Thomas Frank and Mark Waugh (eds), *We Love You: On Audiences* (Frankfurt am Main: Revolver), pp. 100–23.

Franz, Frauke (2005a), conversation with Synne Behrndt and Cathy Turner, notes taken by Synne Behrndt and Cathy Turner, 19 March, London.

Franz, Frauke (2005b), 'Playgrounding: A New Writing Scheme by Polka Theatre', *Dramaturg's Network Newsletter*, Spring, pp. 6–9.

Franz, Frauke (2005c), panel presentation, 'What is Dramaturgy?', Symposium, Birmingham Repertory Theatre, 3 June.

Frasca, Gonzalo (2001), 'Chapter VII: The Videogames of the Oppressed', MA thesis, Georgia Institute of Technology, available on-line at http://www.ludology.org/articles/thesis/videogamesoftheoppressed.html, accessed 25 November 2006.

Fretton, Tony (1999), 'Dramaturgy and Architecture', in Total Theatre and CSSD, *Dramaturgy: A User's Guide* (London: Central School of Speech and Drama and Total Theatre), pp. 14–15.

Freytag, Gustav (1922 [1863]), *Die Technik des Dramas* (Leipzig: Herzel).

Friedman, Dan (2002), 'The Dramaturg: Help or Hindrance?', *Back Stage*, Vol. 43, No. 39, 27 September, pp. 1–8.

Frisch, Norman (2002), Norman Frisch interviewed in Judith Rudakoff and
    Lynn M. Thomson (eds), *Between the Lines: The Process of Dramaturgy*
    (Toronto: Playwrights of Canada Press), pp. 273–99.
Frisch, Norman (1994), 'Just deal with it! An interview with Norman Frisch',
    Theaterschrift, No. 5–6, pp.150–180.
Fry, Chris (2007), *The Way of Magdalena* (Holstebro: The Open Page).
Fuchs, Elinor (2004), 'EF's Visit to a Small Planet: Some Questions to Ask a
    Play', *Theater*, Vol. 59, No. 34, January, pp. 5–9.
Fuchs, Elinor (1996), *The Death of Character: Perspectives on Theater after
    Modernism* (Bloomington: Indiana University Press).
Fuegi, John (1974), 'Whodunit: "Brecht's" adaptations of Molière's Don Juan',
    Comparative Literature Studies, Vol. XI, No. 2, pp. 158–72.
Fuegi, John (1972), 'The Form and Pressure: Shakespeare's Haunting of
    Bertolt Brecht', *Modern Drama*, Vol. 15, pp. 291–304.
Gadberry, Glen W. (ed.) (1995), *Theatre in the Third Reich* (London:
    Greenwood Press).
Gardner, Lyn (2007a), 'This Arts Council Cut Will Devastate Theatre',
    30 March, <http://blogs.guardian.co.uk/theatre/2007/03/this_arts_council_
    cut_will_dev.html>, accessed 7 April.
Gardner, Lyn (2007b), 'Live and Kicking', *Guardian*, 3 April.
Gaston, Bruce (2003), 'Brecht's Pastiche History Play: Renaissance Drama and
    Modernist Theatre in *Leben Eduards des Zweiten von England*', *German Life
    and Letters*, Vol. 56, No. 4, October, pp. 344–62.
Gilman, Richard (1999), *The Making of Modern Drama* (Newhaven: Yale
    University Press).
Gilpin, Heidi (1997) 'Shaping Critical Spaces: Issues in the Dramaturgy of
    Movement Performance', in Susan Jonas, Geoff Proehl and Michael Lupu
    (eds), *Dramaturgy in American Theater. A Source Book* (Orlando: Harcourt
    Brace College), pp. 83–7.
Godiwala, Dimple (2006), 'Genealogies, archaeologies, histories: the revolu-
    tionary "interculturalism" of Asian theatre in Britain', *Studies in Theatre and
    Performance*, Vol. 26, No. 1, pp. 33–47.
Goebbels, Heiner (1997), 'Text as Landscape', *Performance Research*, 2(1),
    pp. 61–5.
Goffman, Erving (1959), *The Presentation of Self in Everyday Life* (New York:
    Doubleday and Anchor Books).
Gold, Penny (2005), unpublished interview with Cathy Turner, London,
    13 May.
Goulish, Matthew (2000), *39 Microlectures in Proximity of Performance*
    (London: Routledge).
Greig, David (2001), Introduction to *Complete Plays, Sarah Kane* (London:
    Methuen), pp. I–xviii.
Greig, Noël (2005a), panel presentation, 'What is Dramaturgy?', Symposium,
    Birmingham Repertory Theatre, 3 June.
Greig, Noël (2005b), *Playwriting: A Practical Guide* (London: Routledge).

Greisenegger-Georgila, Vana (2004), 'Caspar Neher's Dialektische Bühne für Brecht', in Michael Schwaiger (ed.), *Bertolt Brecht und Erwin Piscator: Experimentelles Theater im Berlin der Zwanzigerjahre* (Wien: Christian Brandstätter).

Haas, Birgit (2003), *Modern German Political Drama 1980–2000* (Rochester: Camden House).

Hanna, Gillian (1978), 'Feminism and Theatre', an interview with Peter Hulton in a dedicated issue, *Theatre Papers*, 2nd Series, No. 8.

Hansen, Pil (2005), 'Dance Dramaturgy: Possible Work Relations and Tools', in Miriam Frandsen and Jesper Schou-Knudsen (eds), *Space and Composition: A Nordic Symposium on Physical/Visual Stage Dramaturgy* (Copenhagen: NordScen and Statens Teaterskole).

Hayman, Ronald (1983), *Brecht: A Biography* (London: Wiedenfeld and Nicolson).

Heddon, Deirdre and Milling, Jane (2006), *Devising Performance: A Critical History* (Basingstoke: Palgrave Macmillan).

Herrington, Joan (2002), 'Breathing Common Air. The SITI Company Creates Cabin Pressure', *The Drama Review*, Vol. 46, No. 2, Summer, pp. 122–44.

Hewison, Robert (1986), *Too Much: Art and Society in the Sixties – 1960–75* (London: Methuen).

Higgins, Charlotte (2006), 'Less Shakespeare in RSC Renaissance', *Guardian*, 21 November.

Honegger, Gitta (2005), 'Elfriede Jelinek: How to Get the Nobel Prize without Really Trying', *Theater*, Vol. 36, No. 2, pp. 82–94.

Iden, Peter (2005), *Peter Palitzsch: Theater Muss Die Welt Verändern* (Berlin: Henschel).

Imschoot, Myriam van (2003) 'Anxious Dramaturgy', in *Women and Performance: A Journal of Feminist Theory*, Issue 26, Vol. 13, No. 3, pp. 57–68.

Innes, Christopher (2003), 'Baring the Breast – or "Author! Author!" ', *European Journal of English Studies*, Vol. 7, No. 1, pp. 9–23.

Innes, Christopher (2002), *Modern British Drama* (Cambridge: Cambridge University Press).

Itzin, Catherine (1980), *Stages in the Revolution: Political Theatre in Britain since 1968* (London: Methuen).

Jonas, Susan, Geoff Proehl and Michael Lupu (1997) (eds), *Dramaturgy in American Theater: A Source Book* (Orlando: Harcourt Brace College).

Kaye, Nick (2000), *Site-Specific Art* (London: Routledge).

Kaye, Nick (1996), *Art into Theatre: Performance Interviews and Documents* (Amsterdam: Harwood Academic Press).

Kaynar, Gad (2006), 'Pragmatic Dramaturgy: Text as Context as Text', *Theatre Research International*, Vol. 31, No. 3, pp. 245–59.

Kellaway, Kate (2003), 'Do the shake and Vic', *The Observer*, 9 March.

Kemp, Edward (2007), seminar paper, University of Exeter, Series of Playwriting and Dramaturgy Research Seminars and Symposia, 17 January.

Kemp, Edward (2005), 'Edward Kemp: The playwright and dramaturg talks to Dominic Cavendish about adapting *Nathan the Wise* (1779), now at Hampstead Theatre', interview 19 September, available on www.theatrevoice.com/the_archive, accessed 6 January 2006.

Kerkhoven, Marianne van (1994a), 'Introduction to "On Dramaturgy"', *Theaterschrift* (Brussels: Kaaitheater) No. 5–6, pp. 8–34.

Kerkhoven, Marianne van (1994b), 'Looking Without Pencil in Hand', *Theaterschrift*, No. 5–6, pp. 142–4.

Kershaw, Baz (1999), *The Radical in Performance: Between Brecht and Baudrillard* (London: Routledge).

Kershaw, Baz (1992), *The Politics of Performance: Radical Theatre as Cultural Intervention* (London: Routledge).

Kesting, Marianne (1959), *Das Epische Theater* (Stuttgart: Kohlhammer GmbH).

Korish, David (2000), 'The Mud and the Wind: An Inquiry into Dramaturgy', *New Theatre Quarterly*, Vol. 18, No. 70, pp. 284–9.

Kotte, Andreas (2005), *Theaterwissenschaft* (Köln: Bohlau).

Kugler, D. D. (2002), 'D. D. Kugler' interview in Judith Rudakoff and Lynn M. Thomson (eds), *Between the Lines. The Process of Dramaturgy* (Toronto: Playwrights of Canada Press), pp. 93–112.

Lamers, Jan Joris (1994), 'A Continuing Dialogue', *Theaterschrift*, No. 5–6, pp. 278–305.

Lamport, F. J. (1971), *A Student's Guide to Goethe* (London: Heinemann International).

Lane, David (2006a), 'Reading Between the Lines', *Writernet Bulletin*, Vol. 8, No. 8, December.

Lane, David (2006b), unpublished notes on an interview with Cathy Turner, 23 October 2006.

Lecompte, Elizabeth (1994), 'A Library of Cultural Detritus: An Interview with Elisabeth Lecompte', *Theaterschrift*, No. 5–6, pp. 192–209.

Lehmann, Hans-Thies (2006), *Postdramatic Theatre*, trans. Karen Jürs-Munby (London: Routledge).

Lehmann, Hans-Thies (1997), 'From Logos to Landscape: Text in Contemporary Dramaturgy', *Performance Research*, Vol. 2, No. 1, pp. 55–60.

Lepecki, André (2006), unpublished interview with Synne Behrndt, 28 March, New York.

Lepecki, André. (2001), 'Dance without Distance', *Ballet Tanz International*, No. 2, pp. 29–31.

Lessing, Gotthold Ephraim (1962), *Hamburg Dramaturgy*, trans. Helen Zimmern (New York: Dover Publications).

Levy, Deborah (2000), *Plays: 1* (London: Methuen).

Levy, Deborah (1993), interviewed by Ireni Charitou, *New Theatre Quarterly*, Vol. 9, No. 35, pp. 226–7.

Ley, Graham (1995), 'The Significance of Diderot', *New Theatre Quarterly*, Vol. 11, No. 44, pp. 342–54.

Little, Ruth (2007), notes in response to questions from Synne Behrndt and Cathy Turner, 2 March.

Liverpool Live (2006), 'A Festival of Urban Apparition', festival brochure.

London, John (2000), *Theatre Under the Nazis* (Manchester: Manchester University Press).

Luckhurst, Mary (2006a), *Dramaturgy: A Revolution in Theatre* (Cambridge: Cambridge University Press).

Luckhurst, Mary (2006b), 'Revolutionising Theatre: Brecht's Reinvention of the Dramaturg', in Peter Thomson and Glendyr Sacks (eds), *The Cambridge Companion to Brecht*, 2nd edn (Cambridge: Cambridge University Press), pp. 193–208.

Luckhurst, Mary (2005), panel presentation, 'What is Dramaturgy?', Birmingham Repertory Theatre, 3 June.

Luckhurst, Mary (1999), 'Mentors or Censors? Script Development Conference, 29–31 January 1999', in *NPT News*, No. 123, February, pp. 3–4.

Lynn, Kirk and Shawn Sides (2003), 'Collective Dramaturgy: A co-Consideration of the Dramaturgical Role in Collaborative Creation', *Theatre Topics*, Vol. 13, No. 1, pp. 111–15.

MacDonald, Claire (2007), 'The Space Between Words', unpublished summary of research project, February.

MacDonald, Claire (2001), unpublished interview with Cathy Turner, Dartington.

MacDonald, Claire (2000), 'Writing Outside the Mainstream', in Elaine Aston and Janelle Reinelt (eds), *The Cambridge Companion to Modern British Women Playwrights* (Cambridge: Cambridge University Press), pp. 235–52.

MacDonald, Claire (1992 [1989]), 'Storm from Paradise', in Deborah Levy (ed.), *Walks on Water* (London: Methuen), pp. 165–181.

Mari, Louise and Heather Uprichard (2006), unpublished interview with Synne Behrndt, April, London.

Marx, Karl (1845), 'Theses on Feuerbach', part XI, found at <http://marx.eserver.org/1845-feuerbach.theses.txt>, accessed 5 September 2006.

Masuch, Bettina (2006), unpublished interview with Synne Behrndt, March, Berlin.

McCabe, Terry (2001), *Mis-Directing the Play: An Argument Against Contemporary Theatre* (Chicago: I.R. Dee).

McGrath, John (1981), *A Good Night Out: Popular Theatre: Audience, Class and Form* (London: Methuen).

Meth, Jonathan (2003), 'Playwright's living dangerously: what's this got to do with the price of fish?', available online at <http://www.writernet.co.uk/php2/news.php?id=321&item=170>, accessed 9 February 2007.

Monk, Egon (2005), 'Was hatte ein Dramaturg bei Brecht zu tun?', *Theater Heute*, No. 2, February, p. 17.

Morris Hargreaves MacIntyre (2005), 'An Introduction to Audience Builder' found at <www.a-m-a.co.uk/new/images/downloads/audiencebuilder.pdf>, accessed 11 January 2005.

Müller-Schöll, Nikolaus (2004), 'Theatre of Potentiality. Communicability and the Political in Contemporary Performance Practice', *Theatre Research International*, Vol. 29, No. 1, pp. 42–56.

Neill, Heather (2004), 'NT Associates', found at <www.nationaltheatre.org.uk>, accessed 22 January 2007.

Nikcevic, Sanja (2005), 'British Brutalism, the "New European Drama" and the Role of the Director', *New Theatre Quarterly*, Vol. XXI, Part 3, August, pp. 255–72.

Oddey, Alison (1998), 'Devising (Women's) Theatre as Meeting the Needs of Changing Times', in Lizbeth Goodman (ed.) with Jane de Gay, *The Routledge Reader in Gender and Performance* (London and New York: Routledge).

Oddey, Alison (1994), *Devising Theatre: A Practical and Theoretical Handbook* (London: Routledge).

Osborne, Deirdre (2006), 'Writing Black Back: An Overview of Black Theatre and Performance in Britain', *Studies in Theatre and Performance*, Vol. 26, No. 1, pp. 13–31.

Osment, Philip (1989), *Gay Sweatshop: Four Plays and a Company* (London: Methuen).

Painter, Susan (1996), *Edgar: The Playwright* (London: Methuen).

Parker, Christian (2006), unpublished interview with Synne Behrndt, 24 March, New York.

Pavis, Patrice (2003), *Analyzing Performance: Theatre, Dance and Film*, translated by David Williams (Ann Arbor: University of Michigan Press).

Pavis, Patrice (2000), 'Premature Synthesis: temporary closure for an end-of-century inventory', *TheatreForum*, No. 17, Summer/Autumn, pp. 74 –80.

Pavis, Patrice (1998), *Dictionary of the Theatre: Terms, Concepts and Analysis* (Toronto: University of Toronto Press).

Payne, Ben (2006), unpublished interview with Cathy Turner, 9 February, Birmingham.

Payne, Ben (2000), unpublished interview with Cathy Turner, 28 November, Birmingham.

Payne, Ben and Amber Lone (2005), 'Case Study' Presentation, 'Dramatrix 05', symposium at the Oval House Theatre, London, 12 December.

Pearson, Mike and Michael Shanks (2001), *Theatre/Archaeology* (London: Routledge).

Pettengill, Richard (2006), 'Peter Sellar's Merchant of Venice: A Retrospective Critique of Process', *Theatre Research International*, Vol. 31, No. 3, pp. 298–314.

Phelan, Peggy (1993), *Unmarked: The Politics of Performance* (London: Routledge).

Piscator, Erwin (1980), *The Political Theatre*, trans. Hugh Rorrison (London: Methuen).

Powell, Lucy (2006), 'Whose lines are they anyway?', *The Times*, 13 March.

Prentki, Tim and Jan Selman (2000), *Popular Theatre in Political Culture: Britain and Canada in Focus* (Bristol: Intellect).

Price, Antony (1970), 'The Freedom of the German Repertoire', *Modern Drama*, December, pp. 237–46.

Prudhoe, John (1973), *The Theatre of Goethe and Schiller* (Oxford: Basil Blackwell).

Quigley, Austin (1985), *The Modern Stage and Other Worlds* (London: Methuen).

Quirt, Brian (2006), informal interview with Synne Behrndt, London. Notes taken by Synne Behrndt

Radosavljevic, Duska (2005), unpublished interview with Synne Behrndt and Cathy Turner, 3 June, Birmingham.

Rebellato, Dan (1999), *1956 And All That: The Making of Modern British Drama* (London: Routledge).

Red Ladder (2006), 'The Changing Shapes of Red Ladder', found at <www.redladder.co.uk/history.htm>, accessed 2 April 2007.

Reinelt, Janelle (2004), 'Politics, Playwriting, Postmodernism: An Interview with David Edgar', *Contemporary Theatre Review*, Vol. 14, No. 4, pp. 42–53.

Reinelt, Janelle (1996), 'Beyond Brecht: Britain's New Feminist Drama', in Helen Keyssar (ed.), *Feminist Theatre and Theory: Contemporary Critical Essays* (Basingstoke: Palgrave Macmillan), pp. 35–48.

Reinelt, Janelle (1994), *After Brecht: British Epic Theater* (Ann Arbor: University of Michigan Press).

Reiss, Hans (1997), 'The Rise of Aesthetics from Baumgarten to Humboldt', in H.B. Nisbet and Claude Rawson (eds), *The Cambridge History of Literary Criticism: The Eighteenth Century, Vol. 4* (Cambridge: Cambridge University Press), pp. 658–80.

Rewiring/Rewriting Theatre (2006), panel discussion chaired by Adrian Heathfield, with Tim Etchells (Forced Entertainment), Phelim McDermott (Improbable Theatre), Richard Maxwell (New York City Players), 18 November, Riverside Studios. Notes taken by Synne Behrndt.

Richardson, Esther (2005a), unpublished interview with Cathy Turner, 26 May, Nottingham.

Richardson, Esther (2005b), 'Case Study' Presentation, 'Dramatrix 05', Symposium at The Oval House, London, 12 December.

Ritchie, Rob (1987) (ed.), *The Joint Stock Book: The Making of a Theatre Collective* (London: Methuen).

Roberts, Philip (1999), *The Royal Court Theatre and the Modern Stage* (Cambridge: Cambridge University Press).

Rokem, Freddie (2006) 'Antigone Remembers: Dramaturgical Analysis and *Oedipus Tyrannos*', *Theatre Research International*, Vol. 31, No. 3, pp. 260–9.

Rosen, Carol (1978), 'Literary Management at the RSC Warehouse, London: An Interview with Walter Donohue', *Theater*, Vol. 10, No. 1, Autumn, pp. 43–6.

Rouse, John (2000), 'Frank Castorf's Deconstructive Storytelling. Sartre's Dirty Hands at the Volksbühne', *TheatreForum*, No. 17, Summer/Autumn, pp. 82–92.

Royal Shakespeare Company (2006), 'RSC Brings New Work to the Forefront with Key Projects for Writers', press release, 15 March.

Rudakoff, Judith and Thomson, Lynn M. (eds) (2002), *Between the Lines. The Process of Dramaturgy* (Toronto: Playwrights of Canada Press).

Rymaszewski, Michael, Wagner James Au, Mark Wallace, Catherine Winters, Cory Ondrejka, Benjamin Batstone-Cunningham and Second Life residents (2007), *Second Life: The Official Guide* (Indianapolis: Wiley).

Sandvik, Kjetil (2004), 'Models for Computer-Mediated Interactive Stories', unpublished paper, 2 June.

Sannicolas, Nikki (1997), 'Erving Goffman, Dramaturgy and On-line Relationships, *Cybersociology*, September, found at <www.socio.demon. co.uk/magazine/1/is1nikki.html>, accessed 27 April 2006.

Sarrazac, Jean-Pierre (1998), *L'Avenir du Drame*, 2nd edn (Belfort: Circé).

Schechter, Joel (1997), 'In the Beginning There Was Lessing ... Then Brecht Müller and Other Dramaturgs', in Susan Jonas, Geoff Proehl and Michael Lupu (eds), *Dramaturgy in American Theatre: A Source Book* (Orlando: Harcourt Brace College), pp. 16–24.

Schechter, Joel (1978), 'Brecht and Other Dramaturgs', *Theater*, Vol. 10, No. 1, Autumn, pp. 57–9.

Shellard, Dominic (2003), *Kenneth Tynan: A Life* (Newhaven: Yale University Press).

Sierz, Aleks (2006), 'Can Old Forms be Reinvigorated? Radical Populism and New Writing in British Theatre Today', *Contemporary Theatre Review*, Vol. 16, No. 3, pp. 301–11.

Sierz, Aleks (2003), 'Art Flourishes in Times of Struggle: Creativity, Funding and New Writing', *Contemporary Theatre Review*, Vol. 13, Issue 1, February, pp. 33–45.

Sierz, Aleks (2001), *In-Yer-Face Theatre: British Drama Today* (London: Faber and Faber).

Skopnik, Günter (1960), 'An Unusual Person – Der Dramaturg – Une Institution Proprement Allemagne', *World Theatre*, Vol. 9, No. 3, Autumn, pp. 233–8.

Slättne, Hanna (2005a), unpublished interview with Synne Behrndt, London.

Slättne, Hanna (2005b), panel presentation, 'What is Dramaturgy?', Birmingham Repertory Theatre, 3 June.

Smith, Phil (2005), 'O, Dramaturgy!', Dramaturg's Network Newsletter, Spring, pp. 2–4, found at <http://ee.dramaturgy.co.uk/images/uploads/ dramaturgs_newsletter_spring_2005.pdf>, accessed 7 April 2007.

Soja, Edward (2000), 'Thirdspace: expanding the scope of the geographical imagination', in Alan Read (ed.), *Architecturally Speaking: Practices of Art, Architecture and the Everyday* (London: Routledge), pp. 13–30.

Spalter, Max (1967), *Brecht's Tradition* (Baltimore: Johns Hopkins Press).

'Structures in Devising' (2003), public seminar organized by Dramaturgs' Network with Battersea Arts Centre.

Subiotto, Arrigo (1975), *Bertolt Brecht's Adaptations for the Berliner Ensemble* (London: Modern Humanities Research Association).

Sugiera, Malgorzata (2004), 'Beyond Drama: Writing for Postdramatic Theatre', *Theatre Research International*, Vol. 29, No. 1, pp. 6–28.

Sutcliffe, Tom (1998), 'Schiller and the Revolution in Opera', *Schiller: Five Plays* (London: Oberon), pp. 53–64.

Szondi, Peter (1987), *Theory of the Modern Drama*, ed. and trans. Michael Hays (Cambridge: Polity).

Taylor, Anna-Marie (1997), 'Surviving on the Edge: Patterns of Contemporary Theatre Making', in Anna-Marie Taylor (ed.), *Staging Wales* (Cardiff: University of Wales Press), pp. 33–46.

Taylor, Heidi (2004), 'Deep Dramaturgy: Excavating the Architecture of the Site-Specific Performance', *Canadian Theatre Review*, Summer, pp. 16–19.

Teare, Jeff (1999), 'Same Strokes, Different Folks', *Writernet Bulletin*, Vol. 1, No. 1, September, pp. 4–5.

Tenschert, Joachim (2004), 'The Origins, Aims and Objectives of the Berliner Ensemble', in Pia Kleber and Colin Visser (eds), *Re-Interpreting Brecht: His Influence on Contemporary Drama and Film* (Cambridge: Cambridge University Press), pp. 38–49.

Theaterhaus website, found at http://www.theaterhaus.com/tanzplattform2006/index.php?id=3,0,274, accessed 7 February 2007.

Theatre Quarterly Symposium (1976), *Theatre Quarterly*, Vol. 6, No. 24, Winter, pp. 35–72.

Theatre Worker (2005), 'Keeping the Dragon at Arm's Length: Crisis at the Arts Council in Wales', *Encore Theatre Magazine*, 25 February, downloaded from <www.theatre-wales.co.uk/critical/index.asp>, accessed 12 January 2006.

Thomson, Lynn M. (2006), unpublished interview with Synne Behrndt, 28 March, New York.

Thomson, Peter (2006), 'Brecht's Lives', in Peter Thomson and Glendyr Sacks (eds), *The Cambridge Companion to Brecht* (Cambridge: Cambridge University Press), pp. 22–39.

Total Theatre and CSSD (1999), *Dramaturgy: A User's Guide* (London: Central School of Speech and Drama and Total Theatre).

Trott, Lloyd (1999), 'Dramaturgical Dreaming', in Total Theatre and CSSD, *Dramaturgy: A User's Guide*, pp. 32–3.

Tschumi, Bernard (2000), 'Six Concepts', in *Architecturally Speaking: Practices of Art, Architecture and the Everyday*, (ed.) Alan Read (London: Routledge), pp. 155–76.

Turner, Cathy (2006), '*Life of Galileo*: Between Contemplation and the Command to Participate', in Peter Thomson and Glendyr Sacks (eds), *The*

Cambridge Companion to Brecht, 2nd edn (Cambridge: Cambridge University Press), pp. 143–59.

Tynan, Kenneth (1984), *A View of the English Stage* (London: Methuen).

Tynan, Kenneth (1971), 'The Critic Comes Full Circle', interview with the editors of Theatre Quarterly, *Theatre Quarterly*, Vol. 2, No. 1, pp. 37–48.

Ugwu, Catherine (1995), 'Keep on Running: The Politics of Black Performance' in Catherine Ugwu (ed.) *Let's Get it On: The Politics of Black Performance* (London and Seattle: ICA and Bay Press), pp. 54–83.

Veltman, Chloe (1998), 'Dramaturg. Dramawot?', in *NPT News*, No. 119, pp. 7–8.

Versényi, Adam (2003) 'Dramaturgy/Dramaturg', *The Oxford Encyclopedia of Theatre and Performance*, (ed.) Dennis Kennedy (Oxford: Oxford University Press), pp. 386–388.

Vuyst, Hildegard de (2006) 'Conversation with Hildegard de Vuyst', in Hildegard de Vuyst and Alain Platel, *Les Ballet C de la B* (Tielt: Uitgeverij Lannoo nv.), pp. 134–6.

Wagner, Kitte (2005), unpublished interview with Cathy Turner and Synne Behrndt, 13 April, Copenhagen.

Wandor, Micheline (2001), *Post-War British Drama: Looking Back in Gender* (London: Routledge).

Walsh, Paul (1990), ' "His Liberty is Full of Threats to all": Benno Besson's Helsinki Hamlet and Brecht's dialectical appropriation of classic texts', in Pia Kleber and Colin Visser (eds), *Re-Interpreting Brecht: His Influence on Contemporary Drama and Film* (Cambridge: Cambridge University Press), pp. 104–16.

Watson, Ian (1993), *Towards a Third Theatre. Eugenio Barba and the Odin Teatret* (London: Routledge).

Weber, Carl (2006), 'Brecht and the Berliner Ensemble – the Making of a Model', in Peter Thomson and Glendyr Sacks (eds), *The Cambridge Companion to Brecht*, 2nd edn (Cambridge: Cambridge University Press), pp. 175–92.

Weber, Carl (2005), private correspondence with Cathy Turner, 24 June.

Weber, Carl (1967), 'Brecht as Director', *Tulane Drama Review*, Vol. 12, No. 1, pp. 101–7.

Wekwerth, Manfred (1967), 'From "Brecht Today" ', trans. Martin Nicolaus, ed. Erica Munk, *Tulane Drama Review*, Vol. 12, No. 1, pp. 118–24.

White, R.Kerry (1995), *An Annotated Dictionary of Technical, Historical, and Stylistic Terms Relating to Theatre and Drama: A Handbook of Dramaturgy* (New York: The Edwin Mellen Press).

Wiens, Wolfgang (1986), 'L'avocat de l'auteur', in *Théâtre/Public*, No. 67, pp. 14–18.

Wilkie, Fiona (2002), 'Mapping the Terrain: a Survey of Site-Specific Performance in Britain', *New Theatre Quarterly*, Vol. XVIII, No. 70, May, pp. 140–60.

Willett, John (1984), *The Theatre of Bertolt Brecht* (London: Methuen).

Willett, John (1964) (ed), *Brecht on Theatre* (London: Methuen).

Willett, John and Ralph Manheim (1994), Introduction to Bertolt Brecht *Collected Plays: Seven*, eds John Willett and Ralph Manheim (London: Methuen), pp.Vii–xxviii.

Williams, David (2006a), unpublished interview with Synne Behrndt, June, Totnes.

Williams, David (2006b), *Alice Bell* production notes (unpublished).

Williams, David (2006c), Extracts from Rehearsal Journal, printed in theatre programme for *Alice Bell*, Lone Twin Theatre.

Williams, Raymond (1973), *Drama from Ibsen to Brecht* (London: Penguin).

Wittgenstein, Ludwig (1974), *Philosophical Investigations*, trans. G.E.M. Anscombe (Oxford: Basil Blackwell).

Woods, Sarah (2005), unpublished interview with Cathy Turner, 3 July, Leamington Spa.

Wright, Trevelyan (2001), 'The Door', *Writernet Bulletin*, Vol. 3, No. 1, February, pp. 7–9.

Young, T. R. and Garth Massey (1990), 'The Dramaturgical Society: Macro-Analysis', found online at <uwacadweb.uwyo.edu/RED_FEATHER/ dramasociallife/004dramaturgicalsociety.html>, accessed 6 February 2007.

Zade, Maja (2006), unpublished interview with Synne Behrndt, 8 March, Berlin.

Zelenak, Michael X. (2003), 'Why We Don't Need Directors: A Dramaturgical/Historical Manifesto', *Theatre Topics*, Vol. 13, No. 1, pp. 105–9.

Index